DEVELOPMENT OF SECONDARY EDUCATION IN INDIA

DEVELOPMENT OF SECONDARY EDUCATION IN INDIA

Access, Participation, Delivery Mechanism and Financing

K. Sujatha
P. Geetha Rani

NUEPA

SHIPRA

The findings, interpretations and views expressed by the contributors in this volume are entirely their and do not necessarily reflects the views of the NUEPA nor that of Editors.

(First Published in India in 2011)

Rs. 1250; US$ 42

ISBN: 978-81-7541-593-5

Development of Secondary Education in India: Access, Participation, Delivery Mechanism and Financing

Published by:
SHIPRA PUBLICATIONS
LG 18-19, Pankaj Central Market,
I.P. Ext., Patparganj, Delhi 110092, India
Ph.: +91 11 22235152/6152
Email: info@shiprapublication.com
Website: www.shiprapublication.com

Foreword

India has been the cradle of an ancient civilization as well as the host to one of the fastest growing economies of the world, currently. India is recognized as a leader in Information and Communication Technology (ICT). It is also creditable that the country has taken a big jump in universalizing elementary education by launching the Right to Education Act. While provision of primary education for all could ensure a reasonable improvement in the overall status of human development, it is unlikely that the country will significantly succeed in reducing poverty and creating a more equitable society without adequately focusing on improving secondary education. While primary education is a basic enabling factor for participation and freedom, for leading a life with dignity and overcoming basic deprivation, secondary education is the gateway for prosperity, for transforming the economy and establishing social justice in any country. It opens the world of work to the youth of the country and contributes to socio-economic development of the community. But, mere expansion of secondary schools, more of the same, is not likely to help. It has to radically transform its basic character in tune with the demands of the emerging knowledge intensive economy, and the far-reaching impact of the globalised market, and the fast changing structure of the knowledge generation establishment under the framework of the evolving intellectual property regime.

It is in this context that NUEPA has undertaken a research study on 'Secondary Education in India 'in Collaboration with International Institute for Educational Planning, Paris. The research study report is being published in two volumes covering different aspects of secondary education. The present book "Development of Secondary Education in India" deals with various issues concerning development of secondary education in India. Specifically the contents of the book focus on quantitative expansion, nature of delivery mechanisms-public private dichotomy and financing of secondary education in the country. The book highlights the widely varying conditions characterizing development of secondary education in different parts of the country. It is clear that Rashtriya Madhyamik Shiksha Abhiyan (RMSA) to be successful should be adaptive to local contexts; a pan-national model of financing and implementation is not likely to work. Also, any development programme in a large federal country such as India demands that the Central Government and State Governments work in close partnership in its design and implementation. Furthermore, it should be noted that a major proportion of secondary schools are in the private sector adding more complexity to the effort to expand secondary schools.

That the volume is being brought out when the RMSA is taking shape is a very significant. The findings of the studies reported in the book would hopefully provide direction to further progress in the implementation of RMSA. At the moment, NUEPA is actively involved in building a robust Secondary Education Management Information System (SEMIS) to support the implementation of RMSA. The present volume brought out by Professor K. Sujatha and Dr. P. Geetha Rani based on extensive empirical work should add further value to NUEPA's efforts in contributing to the development of secondary education in India. Let me congratulate them and record my deep appreciation for putting together such a comprehensive volume on secondary education in India.

March, 2011

R. Govinda
Vice-Chancellor
NUEPA

Preface

Secondary education holds indispensable link and inter connectivity with other levels of education by providing the required input. Indeed, primary and secondary schooling is considered as 'successive phases of a continuing process' and should be made available to all children. Realizing this, developed nations have made secondary education as either universal or compulsory.

After being implemented District Primary Education Programme and Sarva Shiksha Abhiyan for universalizing elementary education, recently Government of India has realized the need to achieve universal access and quality secondary education. Towards universalisation of secondary education, the *Rashtria Madhyamic Shiksha Abhiyan* has been launched during the Eleventh Five Year plan. In this context, it is pertinent to examine the development scenario of secondary education in India. Similarly, it would be interesting to look at progress of school education covering important aspects like access, participation, delivery mechanism and financing.

The present book on "Development of Secondary Education in India: Access, Participation, Delivery Mechanism and Financing" is part of a major research study funded by National University of Educational Planning and Administration. The study was undertaken as part of a comparative study initiated by International Institute for Educational Planning (IIEP), Paris in Developing Countries. Following the broad research framework developed by IIEP, the research design was modified to suit the Indian educational context.

The present book examines development of secondary education encompassing several aspects and issues. The book comprises six chapters covering access and coverage, growth and expansion, public-private dichotomy in providing secondary education, gender and equity in secondary education and financing of secondary education in a holistic perspective. The framework of analysis entails the linkage of secondary education with that of primary and upper-primary education.

One of the unique features of the book is its coverage from the all India level to that of the case study schools. Further, various aspects and process of secondary education development is examined in a comparative perspective across major states with a focus on four sample states i.e., Andhra Pradesh, Kerala, Maharashtra and Uttar Pradesh which are at varying levels of educational and economic development.

We would like to thank Mrs. Francoise Caillods, Deputy Director (Retd.), IIEP, Paris for providing the broad research design and her valuable guidance. We are highly grateful to Professor R. Govinda, Vice-Chancellor, NUEPA for his invaluable support and encouragement to publish this book. We acknowledge with thanks Professor B.P. Khandelwal, former Director, NIEPA for his cooperation and support in undertaking the research study.

We appreciate and thank the project staff, Dr. Gobind Pal, Dr. Mithilesh Kumar Singh , Dr. N.K. Mohanty and Mr. Pankaj Kumar Singh for their able assistance. I thank profusely Mr. Satish Kumar, NUEPA who without worrying about time or pain, assisted in word-processing the research study report. I appreciate Mr. Pramod Rawat and Mr. Amit Singhal of Publication Unit, NUEPA for their cooperation and patience in bringing out this publication. I also appreciate Shipra Publications for their interest and cooperation for bringing out the book in its present form.

K. Sujatha

Contents

1

Introduction

The broad perspective of education underlines its importance as an agency of social change and human development but rarely emphasis is given to the inter linkages between different stages of education. The way education is increasingly linked to knowledge, skill and employment at cac h stage has its relative value in the development of human capital. Of late, state policies have rightly prioritised elementary education as a thrust area and have demarcated higher education for research and development. But secondary education, that is the main link between elementary and higher education, has often remained neglected not only at the policy level but also in research and analysis. In fact, secondary education is an important sector of analysis as the increased enrolment and participation at elementary level is supplying a large number of students to the secondary level. The quality of secondary education also determines the progress, development and quality of higher education, as it provides inputs for higher education. It is also important, in the context of economic growth, technological development and the need for skilled manpower.

Secondary education is the terminal stage for a large number of students after which they end up in the job market. Therefore, it is important to connect secondary education with skill development. This has been echoed in the recommendations of various educational commissions. In an effort to make secondary education work oriented and practical the National Policy on Education (1986) had several suggestions. It envisaged the use of diverse curriculum content at the secondary level, so that skilled manpower can be supplied to the society. The National Policy on Education (1986) noted that the establishment of vocational courses or institutions will be the responsibility of the government as well as the employers in the public and private sectors; the government will however, take special steps to cater to the needs of women, rural and tribal students and the deprived sections of the society.

As an important point of transition secondary education offers a significant perspective for understanding and analysis of prevailing educational scenario in the country. Research evidences shows that secondary education is the fastest growing sector in most of the countries further emphasising the need of universalisation of secondary education. No country in the world could achieve sustainable development without providing opportunities for secondary education.

In the context of the critical overview of the educational policies in general and secondary education in particular it can be safely inferred that structure, context and content of secondary education has undergone systematic and significant transformation. At the same time, a lot of changes are taking place at the elementary level of education. The introduction and implementation of various policies and programmes to improve the access, participation and quality of elementary namely; Operation Blackboard, District Primary Education Programme (DPEP), Education for All (EFA), Sarva Siksha Abhiyan (SSA) etc., especially in the last decade and half have had serious implications for secondary education. The other aspect that has implications for secondary education is the market forces that have requisitioned new kinds of qualification, for skilled manpower, particularly with the onset of information technology and technological changes. The introduction of new economic policy in the early 1990s with emphasis on liberalization, privatization and globalization have not only had social and economic impact but also brought pressures on the educational system in general and secondary education in particular. For example, the economic liberalization along with bringing changes in individual income also has changed the consumption pattern of education, aspirations and expectations. All these dynamics has had an impact on education system in general and more so, on the secondary education. Consequently, these might have affected aspects viz. demand, access, expansion, quality of provisions and functioning of the school and internal efficiency on the one hand and performance of students on the other. All these aspects have affected the financing of secondary education, which used to be largely state-funded.

Secondary education has not received due attention either at the policy level or at the research front despite its size and importance. In fact, most of the research and documentation in education has been confined either to elementary or higher education. However, of the limited research in secondary education, some are on the study of Secondary Education Boards in various states and their role in improvement of quality, and others on the financing of secondary education. Similarly, the few documents available on secondary education have been invariably limited to the results of public examinations, conducted by different boards across the county. This shows that there has been a lack of research on curriculum, policy, access, demand, delivery mechanisms and internal efficiency of secondary education. In the back drop of this review the need and importance of the current study can be judged. This study intends to provide a comprehensive picture of secondary education in India with special emphasis on access, demand, efficiency, curriculum and the prevalence of supplementary tutoring–an entirely unexplored area of secondary education. The following are the research questions that the study intends to explore and analyse.

RESEARCH QUESTIONS

Some of the research questions that arise on the basis of available evidence on secondary education and analysis of recent trends are as follows:

1. Is the demand for secondary education increasing? If yes, then is there any variation in the demand pattern?
2. Who is meeting the demand for secondary education? Is there any variation in terms of meeting the demand including provision of facilities?
3. What is the level of quality and internal efficiency of secondary schools?
4. Whether financing of secondary education corresponds with the demand?
5. What is the administrative and management mechanism of secondary education?

The growing demand for secondary education and the need to contextualise it is in view of the internal and external challenges.

Thus it requires a thorough probing into the dimensions of demand, delivery mechanisms, modalities of administration, efficiency of the system, quality of the service provider and the issues of equity. However, these issues are complex, critical and diverse besides operating both at macro and micro level. There are interstate, inter-regional and inter-district variations which have further percolated to micro level. Such intricacies have necessitated the study of the phenomenon of secondary education and its dynamics. In this study an attempt has been made to look at these aspects particularly in the context of the above-mentioned research questions.

Major objectives of the study are as follows:

1. To examine the extent of access to secondary education;
2. To study the growth and expansion pattern of secondary schools;
3. To study the demands for secondary education in terms of participation and growth of enrolment;
4. To examine the role of government and other delivery mechanism in meeting the demand for secondary education;
5. to analyse the pattern of financing secondary education;
6. To examine the administration and management pattern of secondary education including curriculum management and equity programmes.

Given the research questions and objectives of the scope of study, the framework for analysis will include national, inter-state, regional, district and school level data. The study covers four selected states, their regional, inter-district and schools representing different levels of development (education, economic and industrial). Thus the present study attempts to examine the research questions and objectives from macro and the micro level.

SAMPLING DESIGN

Sampling constitutes an important aspect of research design as entire process of data analysis and interpretation depends on the method of sampling. In this study macro level analysis is based on primary and secondary data collected from various sources, while at the micro level we have used sampling techniques to select specific schools representing majority of the traits prevalent in the research universe. However, the sampling procedure was quite different as instead of taking random samples, we have selected the criteria and used them to select schools for case studies. Therefore, it is important to clarify few of the processes and procedures of sampling adopted in this study.

As the study is an integration of both macro and micro level analysis, it was necessary to select specific areas while following broad national pattern in other case. There are three level of analysis made in this study. Firstly, in order to provide a holistic dimension on secondary education its process and pattern i.e. access, enrolment, delivery mechanisms and functioning of secondary schools the study relied heavily on national data collected from divergent sources including Selected Educational Statistics and documents of Ministry of Human Resources Development, data from other government organisations and national and international reports etc. The first part of the description is based on the national level patterns, where educational trends of 17 major states have been discussed. For better representation, the rural-urban difference is also accounted for at the level of inter-state analysis.

The second level of analysis depicts the inter-state variation highlighting the patterns and processes of secondary education in selected sample states. In fact, in order to closely look at this phenomenon and focus on particular issues, it was essential to select a few states, consequently Kerala, Maharashtra, Andhra Pradesh (A.P.) and Uttar Pradesh (U.P.) were considered for the purpose of detailed analysis.

CHARACTERISTICS OF SAMPLE STATES

The basis of selection of state was indicators of development. For example, Kerala is an educationally developed state, Maharashtra is educationally and economically developed state, Andhra Pradesh is moderately developed both in terms of income and education, while Uttar Pradesh is an underdeveloped state in terms of these development indicators (see Table 1.1). Importantly, these four states constitute, nearly 40 per cent of the total population of the country and around 30 per cent of the territory as well. The table below depicts the variation among the sample states in terms of population, area, sex ratio, literacy and female literacy, per capita income and also their level of educational development in terms of schools and enrolment in secondary education

Table 1.1: Selected Indicators on Sample States and India

	Population (in millions)	*Area (sq.km)*	*Sex Ratio*	*Literacy*	*Female Literacy*	*Per capita Income (in Rs.)*	*No. of Districts*	*Secondary Schools*	*Enrolment (in millions)*
	2001		*2001*	*2001*	*2001*	*2004-05*	*2001*	*2003-04*	*2003-04*
Andhra Pradesh	76.21	275068	978	70.32	51.17	23153	23	16427	2.88
Kerala	31.84	38864	1058	90.92	87.86	27048	14	4157	1.15
Maharashtra	96.88	307713	922	77.27	67.51	29204	34	8706	4.55
Uttar Pradesh	166.20	238,566	898	57.36	42.97	11477	70	12387	5.8
India	1028.61	3287590	933	65.38	54.16	23241	516	145962	35.01

Source: Census, 2001, Selected Educational Statistics, 2003-04, National Accounts Statistics, Central Statistical Organisation.

With regard to secondary education institutions, the four sample stats cover around 30 per cent of the schools in India while their enrolment coverage is 40 per cent of the total secondary enrolment in the country.

States in India are comparatively large and varied in size, structure, political context, and socio-economic set up. The variations are not only limited to inter-state level but also at the intra-state level. In order to make an in-depth study of these sample states, we further stratified them into regions. There are different regions in the state again divided on the basis of their level of development[1] . For instance, Maharastra is evolved as a socio-cultural unit of 3 broad regions, Western Maharashtra, Marthawada and Vidharbha. However, for administrative purposes, the state is divided further into six regions. Andhra Pradesh comprises of three natural regions, based on historical, cultural and economic backgrounds, namely, Coastal region, Rayalseema, and Telangana. Kerala can be divided into three regions on the basis of its physical features, namely the forest highland region, the low land region bordering the sea and the mid land region consisting of Southern, Middle and Northern Region.

Uttar Pradesh is divided into four geographical regions Central, Bundelkhand, Eastern and Western Regions.

Taking cognisance of these regions and their development parameters, efforts were made to segregate them into smaller units. In the context of Indian state, these units are districts.
Therefore, four districts were chosen, from these four states for further study and analysis. These districts are moderately developed districts of respective states. The reason behind this sort of classification lies in the fact that these districts will help in providing the total picture that includes both developed and backward areas. These districts are Thiruvantapuram (Kerala), Pune (Maharashtra), Nalgonda (Andhra Pradesh) and Varanasi (Uttar Pradesh).

The aggregate data collected at national, state and even at the district level rarely reflect the dynamics taking place at the institutional level in terms of the role of delivery mechanisms and functioning of schools. Therefore, school level data were collected and analysed. For this purpose, 49 schools from four districts of four sample states were chosen. The basis of school selection was their level of performance in public examination at secondary level (X-XII) level in the past five years. In taking the public examination results as indicator it was emphasised that the consistency in the performance must be the criteria. Hence, 'results of schools' with different levels of performance namely the good, moderate and poor were selected as case studies. These schools for better representation of the universe cut across types of management, rural-urban and type of school in terms of their in-take (boys and girls).[2]

There are 49 schools in our case study. Each state has 12 schools, Uttar Pradesh has 13 schools. At the school level, information regarding infrastructure, performance in public examination, staffing, teaching—learning method, nature and extent of private tuition, investment in private tuition and socio-economic status was collected from a pool of informants consisting of the head teacher, teachers and students. The study covered a total number of 4,945 students, covering 20 per cent of the total number of students from lower and higher secondary classes of the 49 schools. Similarly, all the head teachers and 50 per cent of teachers were interviewed to obtain their perspective.[3] A total of 346 teachers were interviewed from these schools and their opinions were recorded. Students were interviewed to provide data on the extent of private tutoring, money paid for private tuition, socio-economic status of parents etc.[4] The school records and headmasters' opinion formed the basis of information regarding the caste categories of students, Parent Teacher Association, infrastructure, staffing and teaching—

learning method. The perspectives of teachers form an important dimension of the study as they are transacting the curriculum and engaged in the teaching—learning process. More importantly, the investigators in the process of field survey collected first hand information and recorded their observations thus, ensuring reliability and validity of data. These data were not only used to describe case studies but have also been referred in appropriate sections.

This book consists five chapters in addition to introduction. The preceding chapter deals with the supply and demand of secondary education in India covering access, expansion and growth of institutions and participation. The analysis in this chapter encompasses national, major states, four sample states, regional, and district and micro level scenario.

In the third chapter an attempt has been made to examine the role of public-private agencies in meeting the growing demand for secondary education following the previous framework. This chapter provides an analytical explanation for the phenomenon of expansion of private sector at secondary level. The fourth chapter focuses on gender and equity in terms of participation and demand for secondary education.

The fifth chapter of the study highlights the financing of secondary education. It looks into national and state policy affecting the grants to schools as well as the trends of budgetary allocation of resources for secondary education.

NOTES

1. It is not within the purview of the study to examine the dimensions and reasons of their particular status but based on common indicators these regions are divided on the basis of development indicators.
2. Secondary schools can be classified as co-education schools, exclusively for boys and exclusively for girls. In Uttar Pradesh the number of girls' schools at higher secondary level is more and is a state pattern. However, we have all types of schools in our sample.
3. In case of Andhra Pradesh all students and all teachers were interviewed as class size and numbers of teachers are less. For example, higher secondary sections are largely independent in Andhra Pradesh thus reducing the total number of students and teachers. On the contrary in other three states the number of sections and teachers are more.
4. The data regarding the economic status of their parents and amount paid for private tuition were collected from students thus, the reliability and validity of such an observation have limitations.

2

Educational Expansion and Participation: Access and Coverage in Secondary Education

Investment in education has long been accepted as an important dimension of development, particularly in democratic nation-states. In fact, the increasing emphasis on 'social capital' and 'good governance' as sine qua non of human development, has reinforced the importance of education, making educational studies both interesting and imperative. This is more so in case of secondary education, which is the main link between primary and higher education. Secondary education becomes an important instrument of analysis for a variety of reasons that include its position in the educational structure, its linkage with other sectors of education, its relevance to the educational context as well as its contribution towards supply of manpower in a growing economy.

Secondary education acts as a conveyer belt between the primary education at the one end and the higher education at the other. First, it creates opportunities for students by enabling them to accrue higher, technical and professional education and subsequently to reap the benefits of such education in their personal and professional life. Similarly, it also supplies manpower for primary education that in turn uses their expertise in elevating the standards of primary education. As an important point of transition secondary education makes a significant point for understanding and analysis of prevailing educational scenario in the country. Research evidences show that secondary education is the fastest growing sector in most of the countries, thus emphasizing the need of universalization of secondary education. No country in the world could achieve sustainable development without providing opportunities for secondary education.

Due to various reasons, primary education has remained the focus of state sponsorship. Literacy movements and opening of primary schools became a favourite state engagement. Similarly, the need for industrial development and technological requirements coupled with administrative compulsions ensured the growth and popularization of higher education. Needless to add that in our march towards high literacy and fancy for technical and professional education and regard for higher education, somewhere down the line secondary education could not get due attention. However, it would be wrong to assume that secondary education in India was entirely left to fend for itself. Efforts, though sporadic, were made to look into the problems of secondary education even if in relation to either primary or higher education.

Since education comes under the concurrent list, the responsibility of catering to the educational needs becomes the joint responsibility of the central and respective sate governments. Therefore, the term 'government' has a wider connotation here and needs further clarification. Government here includes state and local bodies and many schools in India are funded and managed by either of them. While state governments are largely responsible in providing schools, central government under the special scheme for transferable central government employees has opened and is managing a number of schools commonly known as Kendriya Vidyalaya (Central Schools). Similarly, in order to take care of rural talented students, the central government has opened pace-setting schools. There are a total of 508 such schools, known as Jawahar Navodaya Vidyalayas (JNVs) spread over 508 districts of the country.

A proper perspective on the development of secondary education can be evolved only when we critically look into the secondary education scenario in India. This chapter, therefore, examines the extent of access to and expansion of secondary education facilities on the one hand and the demand for secondary education at the other. The access part examines the spatial availability in terms of distance and the population coverage. The second part looks at the demand for secondary education in terms of enrolment besides capturing the overall national scenario. It is essential to examine the pattern of the growth of secondary education in different states to highlight the diversity vis-à-vis the respective levels of socio-economic development. In order to compare and evaluate the development of secondary education in different states based on diversity and disparities, the indicators viz. access, extent of growth and expansion of institutions, rate of participation, extent of enrolment and types of different management have been analyzed and explained. Besides these, rural-urban, gender and ethnic disparities too have been examined and described.

In the context of India, it is difficult to have a universal picture simply because there is so much diversity and disparity. National pictures do not reflect the correct situations and micro data have little relevance for macro policies. More often than not, macro data either conceal or inflate local contexts thus negating the very methodology of studies. In order to arrive at a comprehensive understanding of the system, we have tried to examine these issues at the national and state levels (sample states) and further down at the district level. The data from four sample states provide information on size, structure and particularities of the access scenario. Same is the case with our analysis of growth and demand. This helps us in seeking solutions to the queries relating to the extent and dimension of growth of secondary schools at the all India level, in the particular state as well at micro level.

The first section of the chapter presents an overview of educational scenario in the country and expansion of schools. The second section discusses the extent of access (in terms of distance and coverage of rural population) to secondary education, equity in access and number of schools per 10,000 populations. The trends and pattern of growth of schools at the national, inter-state, rural-urban areas, sample states, intra–state (regional levels) are presented in the third section. The fourth section focuses on trends of demand for secondary education measured in terms of growth of enrolment at different levels viz. increase in the number of institutions. Section V of the chapter deals with average class size rather section size in order to primarily assess and identify the extent of the demand in terms of participation in educational institutions and the supply in terms of the provision of institutions. The analysis on section size is pursued in a similar framework starting from the national to institutional level. The subsequent section examines the gross enrolment ratio in secondary education given the extent of growth of institutions and enrolment in its various dimensions and by different providers.

EDUCATIONAL SCENARIO: AN OVERVIEW

India has taken up the challenge of providing educational access and opportunities to its vast segments of population rather boldly. The post-independent India inherited a poor educational infrastructure from its colonial masters and had to begin from scratch the massive agenda of educational development. In fact, the Constitution of India guarantees education to all of its citizens. According to the Article 45 of the Constitution, the state shall provide free and compulsory education to the children below fourteen years of age. Similarly, Article 46 empowers the state to specially take care of the educational needs of the weaker sections of the country, namely the scheduled castes and scheduled tribes. In order to fulfil these Constitutional mandates and obligations the Indian state has taken several steps to step up educational provisions in general and school education in particular. Substantive efforts have been made in translating the Constitutional mandate to reality and even norms and principles have been made flexible to expand the base of education particularly for disadvantaged sections and the unserved areas. A brief glance at Table 2.1 shows the magnitude of educational system in India. The network of the educational system in the second highest populous country like India with its vast size, comprises of 1286 thousand schools having 239.2 million students with 6223 thousand teachers covering different levels of school education (see Table 2.1).

The educational facilities include 787.8 thousand primary schools 325.2 thousand upper primary schools and 113.8 thousand lower secondary schools, 59.2 thousand higher secondary schools, 14.17 thousand higher educational institutions and 294 universities including deemed universities and institutions of national importance in the country. During 2007-08, these educational intuitions enrolled 135.5 million students in primary, 57.2 million in upper primary, 28.2 million in lower secondary, 6.25 million in higher secondary and 10.01 million students in higher education. Such a network of institutions has been developed over a long period of time. India has one of the largest networks of educational institutions in the world.

Table 2.1: Education in India at a Glance: Total Number of Institutions, Size of Enrolment and Number of Teachers (2007-08)

Educational Institutions, Category	*Number of Institutes (in '000)*	*Size of Enrolment (in Millions)*	*Number of Teachers (in '000)*
Primary	787.8	135.5	2315.1
Upper Primary	325.2	57.2	1780.1
Secondary	113.8	28.21	1175.0
Higher Secondary	59. 2	16.25	952.8
Tech. /Indus./Arts & Crafts[$] Institutes	4.8	0.71	n.a.
Polytechnic Institutes[$]	1.1	0.37	n.a.
Teacher Training Institutes[$]	1.3	0.05	n.a.
Higher Education Institutions[$]	14.17	10.01	456.74
Universities[#$]	0.29	*	*

\# Includes deemed Universities and Intuitions of National Importance;
* Include in Higher Education Institutions;
** Figure does not include teachers in Technical/Industrial/Arts & Crafts Institutes, Polytechnic Institutes and Teacher Training Institutes;
$ Data refers to 2003-04.

Source: Selected Educational Statistics, 2007-2008. MHRD, GoI.

Institutional Expansion: Trends and Perspectives

At the backdrop of this huge educational network, it is important to underscore to what extent the facilities are able to provide access both in terms of distance and coverage of population. The following section examines in detail the access condition. The phenomenal growth of education in India can be gauged from the fact that in 1950-51 there were only 209 thousand primary schools, 13.6 thousand upper primary schools and 7.4 secondary and higher secondary schools. Compared to the existing situation mentioned earlier it pales into insignificance. However, it needs to be emphasized that the current educational development profile reflects the improvement of access conditions in a broader perspective. There had been phenomenal expansion of educational facilities at all levels of school education and more so in case of secondary education (see Table 2.2).

Table 2.2: Number of Institutions by Levels of School Education in India

(*Figures are in '000*)

Year	Primary	Upper Primary	Secondary	Hr. Secondary	Sec. and Hr. Secondary
1950-51	209.7	13.6	7.4*	--	7.4
1960-61	330.4	49.7	17.3*	--	17.3
1970-71	408.4	90.6	37.1*	--	37.1
1980-81	494.5	118.6	39.3	12.3	51.6
1990-91	560.9	151.5	59.5	19.2	79.8
2000-01	638.7	206.3	87.7	38.4	126.1
2001-02	664.0	219.6	91.4	42.1	133.5
2002-03	651.3	245.3	90.7	46.4	137.2
.003-04	712.2	262.3	99.1	46.8	145.9
2007-08	787.8	325.2	113.8	59.2	173.0

* Includes Secondary and Higher Secondary/Intermediate/pre-university/Jr. College/pre-degree Institutions.

Source: Selected Educational Statistics, Various issues, MHRD, GoI, New Delhi.

The expansion of secondary schools cannot be seen in isolation as it has both forward and backward linkages with other sectors of education, especially the lower levels of school education. More importantly, achievement in elementary education is a pre-requisite for the growth of secondary education besides various other factors, such as accessibility, availability, affordability and social demand etc. At primary level, expansion of educational institutions made in the last few decades is quite commendable. From the decade of 1950s to 2007-08 there has been a 3-fold increase in the number of primary schools. Similarly, at upper primary and secondary levels the schools have grown by around 19 and 13 times between the periods of 1951 to 2007-08. Though increased number of schools reflects importance attributed to education, it does not reveal the extent of facilities available in terms of distance and coverage of population. Towards this we need to examine access conditions.

Access and Coverage: Elementary Education

Access to educational facilities is an essential pre-condition for educational development although it is not the only condition. Access is usually defined as the absence of barriers (economic, physical etc.) that keeps an eligible student away from the school, the education service delivery point[1]. The factors that affect access to the education system include primarily, the distance from the school, travel cost etc. The lesser (more) the distance from the school, the easier (more difficult) is the access for children to participate in school. The indicator on access, ie, the proportion of population served with schools by distance is important in the sense that the availability of schools does not automatically improve the access. This is because the real physical distance from home to schools as well as the equity in distribution of schools spread over territories are of critical importance for ensuring access. By 2002, 53.4 per cent of rural habitations had been provided access to primary schools within the habitation, while 18.5 per cent of habitations had upper primary schools within the habitation. However, 87 per cent of rural habitations had schools within habitations. In case of upper primary stage people in 78 per cent of habitations had access to schools within a distance of three kilometres. This was possible as a result of phenomenal expansion of educational facilities during 2002. However, it is only a marginal improvement over a decade. Given the number and location of rural habitations, this significant improvement in access condition was possible due to focus and concerted effort on elementary education. Alternative schools were also made available where establishing formal schools were absolutely unviable. The extent of access in case of sample states is given in Table 2.3.

Table 2.3: Access* to Primary and Upper Primary Schools Across Sample States

(in %)

States	*Primary*				*Upper Primary*			
	1993		*2002*		*1993*		*2002*	
	Within habitations	*Up to 1 km**	*Within habitations*	*Up to 1 km**	*Within habitations*	*Up to 3 km**	*Within habitations*	*Up to 3 km**
Andhra Pradesh	69.73	88.57	78.49	93.91	13.82	65.40	24.49	74.73
Kerala	61.64	82.23	60.73	79.46	35.56	89.00	38.61	84.12
Maharashtra	64.70	84.22	67.64	91.17	25.37	78.42	28.95	78.18
Uttar Pradesh	29.34	80.45	40.56	87.96	7.25	78.36	12.35	78.43
India	49.79	83.36	53.04	86.96	13.87	76.15	18.45	78.11

* Per cent of population having access to primary and upper primary schools.

Source: Based on 7th AIES, Flash Data.

The percentage of rural population served by primary schools within the habitations is around 50 per cent and this varies from state to state, ranging from 79 per cent in Punjab to only 28 per cent in Himachal Pradesh. Ten states have higher average than the national average and some states have more than 70 per cent of rural population having access to school within the habitation. Interestingly these states are economically developed ones.

At the upper primary level, the access condition is rather poor with only 18 per cent of rural population have been provided with schools within the habitation. The access condition varies from a high of 64.39 per cent in Gujarat to 6.32 per cent in West Bengal. However, a few states have better coverage of population with upper primary schools within the habitation and above the national average. These states are of developed and backward categories.

Provision of upper primary schools within the 3 kilometres distance of habitation has meant that three-fourths of rural populations have access to schools. Only four states have lagged behind in making this access possible to their rural population. However, some states viz. Tamil Nadu and Himachal Pradesh have done well in universalising elementary education despite having a relatively poor access condition. The access condition of elementary education has since 1993 improved considerably with better coverage of population except a few states.

Among the four sample states at primary level, Andhra Pradesh has the maximum percentage of rural population having access to primary school within the habitation as well as within one kilometre from the habitation. Maharashtra has the next best access condition for its rural population, followed by Uttar Pradesh. Kerala, the state that has achieved universalization of elementary education, interestingly has only 60 per cent of population covered by a primary school within the habitation and 79 per cent of population having access within 1 kilometre.

All the states, except Kerala, have improved as far as access and coverage in upper primary school is concerned. In all the states there has been improvement in coverage of population and access to upper primary schools within the habitation compared to 1993. However, unlike primary level, Kerala already has better access condition with 38 per cent of its rural population having schools within the habitation, and 84 per cent of rural population having access to schools within 3 kilometres radius of habitations. Further, considering the low population growth and lower enrolment at primary level, Kerala's position is understandable. Backward states like Andhra Pradesh and Uttar Pradesh have made a great progress in improving the access conditions. However, more than one-fourth of population in Andhra

Pradesh and a little less than one-fourth of population in Uttar Pradesh need to travel more than 3 kilometres to access upper primary education.

Secondary Education: Access and Coverage

It is pertinent to have a look at access and coverage at elementary level before delving into secondary education. The importance of elementary education lies in its role as a feeder for secondary schools. Further, access, coverage and infrastructure have lot of implications for the secondary level. At the lower secondary level, there were 20.6 per cent secondary schools within the habitation, while 27.16 per cent of people were being served by lower secondary schools located within a radius of two kilometres (see Table 2.4). Nearly 80 per cent of rural population was having secondary schools within 5 kilometres of radius of their habitations, whereas 8 per cent of people had to travel more than 8 kilometres to access the lower secondary school in 2002. This again is only a marginal improvement over 1993.

Table 2.4: Rural Population Served with Schools by Distance Across Levels of Education in India

(in %)

Primary			*Upper Primary*		
Distance	*1993*	*2002*	*Distance*	*1993*	*2002*
Within habitation	49.8	53.4	Within habitation	13.9	18.5
Up to 1 km	83.4	87.0	Up to 3 km	76.2	78.1
	Secondary		Higher Secondary		
Distance	1993	2002	Distance	1993	2002
Within habitation	18.3	20.6	Within habitation	5.4	20.6
Up to 2 km	27.2	25.4	Up to 2 km	15.4	25.4
Up to 5 km	77.9	80.4	Up to 6 km	51.4	80.4
Up to 8 km	90.1	91.9	Up to 8 km	63.6	91.9
More than 8 km	9.9	8.1	More than 8 km	36.4	8.1

Source: Sixth and Seventh All India Educational Surveys, NCERT, New Delhi, 1993 and 2002.

On the contrary, substantial improvement can be observed at higher secondary level both within the habitation and also up to a distance of 2 kilometres. 58 per cent of the population could have an access to a higher secondary school within 6 kms and similarly

68 per cent of the population could have an access to a higher secondary school within 8 kms, which is an impressive improvement over 1993. As a consequence, a mere 8 per cent of the population were required to travel more than 8 kms to a higher secondary school. This evidently suggests the expansion and demand for secondary education in India.

By 2002, at all India level, 80.4 per cent of rural population had access to lower secondary schools within a distance of 5 kilometres of their habitations (see Annexure, Table A1). However, during the same period 92 per cent of rural population were served by lower secondary schools within a distance of 8 kilometres. Eight percent of population had to travel beyond 8 kilometres to access lower secondary school. Compared to 1993, there has been improvement in access to secondary education albeit marginal in many states. Considering the vast rural population and geographical topography and socio-economic diversity, this increase is a considerable achievement. Compared to national level, most of the states have higher percentage of population having better access to lower secondary schools. The extent of access and coverage of population at secondary level varies across the states. There are high variations among the states in terms of percentage of population having access to lower secondary schools within a 5 kilometres distance, ranging from a maximum of 97.5 per cent in the state of Haryana to 62.0 per cent in Madhya Pradesh which belong to economically developed and backward states respectively. Likewise, at elementary level, the states with higher levels of economical and educational standard, are found to have higher percentage of population having access to lower secondary schools within 5 kilometres distance. Even states with moderate economic and educational development, like West Bengal, have better access condition. This is largely due to respective state policies and geographical conditions. During the same period, 1993-2002, there has been a significant increase in the percentage of population with access to secondary schools within a radius of 8 kilometres. However, despite making fast improvement, a few educationally backward and larger states are far behind other states.

At higher secondary level, the percentage of rural population having access to schools was much less as compared to lower secondary level. In 1993, only 51 per cent of rural population had access to higher secondary schools within a distance of six kilometres and 36.4 per cent of rural population had to travel more than

8 kilometres to reach higher secondary schools. A degree of improvement can be found in access situation during 1993-2002. In 2002, the percentage of population having access to higher secondary schools within a distance of six kilometres and 8 kilometres have increased to 57.98 and 68.51 respectively. However, nearly one-third of rural population still have to travel beyond 8 kilometres to access higher secondary school. Obviously, the developed states have better access conditions in the rural areas than in the educationally and economically backward states. Since infrastructure (roads and transport) in rural areas in general and in backward states in particular, is poor, it further hinders the rural population in accessing higher secondary schools. However, there are wider variations among states in terms of providing access to higher secondary schools to rural population. The percentage of rural population to whom higher secondary schools are available within 6 kms varies from 90.35 to 22.19 per cent of among the states. In fact more than 50 per cent of the rural population in some states have to travel beyond 8 kilometres to avail the facility of higher secondary school. In the last one decade, along with developed states, some of the educationally and economically backward states have also witnessed improvement in the distance-related access conditions (see Annexure, Table A2).

Out of 17 major states, in 14 states more than three-fourths of the rural population had been provided with the lower secondary school service with a radius of five kilometres during both 2002 and 1993. All the states have shown increased coverage of population by 2002. It is an encouraging trend that many educationally backward states like Andhra Pradesh, Madhya Pradesh and Rajasthan, have improved their population coverage substantially along with the educationally advanced states of Kerala and Himachal Pradesh and the economically advanced states of Maharashtra to provide access to secondary education within a radius of 5 kms by 2002. However, the states like Punjab, Kerala, Haryana and West Bengal who had provided lower secondary schools to more than 90 per cent of their rural population within a five kilometres distance of their habitation retained their position in 2002 with marginal improvement. There was no other state that had achieved 90 per cent coverage of population in this respect by 2002.

Substantial improvement had been found at the higher secondary level in the form of coverage of population, in 12 out of 17 states. These states have provided higher secondary schools within a radius of 6 kms; there were just 9 such states in 1993. Kerala tops with 91 per cent of population having been covered in this respect (55.2% in 1993) (Table 2.5). Likewise Punjab could 90.35 per cent of its population by the same distance (68.4% in 1993). On the contrary, the worst as well as deteriorating population coverage can be observed in Bihar, both during 1993 and 2002.

Over the years, all the four sample states have improved the coverage substantially. Among these, Kerala has the distinction of highest percentage of population (92.7) covered with facility of lower and higher secondary school within 5 kilometres. Similarly, the percentage of rural population having access to secondary and higher secondary schools within a distance of 8 kilometres have reached 99 per cent and 95.27 per cent respectively. This near universalization of secondary education has been achieved because of concerted efforts of the government by investing in education over a period of time. Further, there is no watertight rural-urban divide in the state, rather there is a continuum between the two, thus bridging the educational gap.

The state of Maharashtra has also made rapid strides in the area of educational access. Access to lower and higher secondary education has significantly improved over the years. As a result 96.4 per cent of rural population are having secondary schools within 8 kilometres distance. At higher secondary level, 63.17 per cent of rural population is availing the facility of schools within a distance of 8 kilometres. However, still a large proportion of rural populations (36.83) has to travel beyond 8 kilometres to access higher secondary schools. It is interesting to note that an industrially and economically developed state which requires constant supply of skilled manpower has such a poor access condition.

Andhra Pradesh has made consistent and considerable efforts in creating better access conditions of secondary education for its rural population. Consequently 94.1 per cent of rural population have been provided with secondary schools within 8 kilometre distance. However, among the sample states, access conditions at higher secondary level is lowest in Andhra Pradesh. This evident from the fact that 41.22 per cent of rural population have to travel more than 8 kilometres for accessing higher secondary school. It seems that despite government efforts and growth of private unaided sector, the access conditions have not improved at ground level. This pattern of access to higher secondary education, for rural children has extremely constrained their participation in school, especially for girl students, where physical distances are really difficult to overcome.

Table 2.5: Percentage of Population Having Access to Secondary and Higher Secondary Schools by Distance Across Sample States

State	Secondary						Higher Secondary					
	1993			2002			1993			2002		
	Up to 5 km	*Up to 8 km*	*Above 8 km*	*Up to 5 km*	*Up to 8 km*	*Above 8 km*	*Up to 6 km*	*Up to 8 km*	*Above 8 km*	*Up to 6 km*	*Up to 8 km*	*More than 8 km*
Andhra Pradesh	78.2	91.0	9.1	85.0	94.1	5.9	35.4	45.8	54.2	46.37	58.78	41.22
Kerala	92.7	98.3	1.7	96.0	99.0	1.0	55.2	67.6	32.4	91.33	95.27	4.73
Maharashtra	83.0	93.2	6.8	88.4	96.4	3.6	45.4	56.2	43.8	52.30	63.17	36.83
Uttar Pradesh	68.8	86.5	13.5	71.1	87.8	12.2	65.5	78.5	21.5	70.95	82.33	17.67
India	77.9	90.1	9.9	80.4	91.9	8.1	51.4	63.6	36.4	57.98	68.51	31.49

Source: Sixth and Seventh All India Educational Surveys, NCERT, New Delhi, 1993 and 2002.

Uttar Pradesh has the lowest percentage of rural population with access to secondary schools within 5 or even 8 kilometres distance. By 2002, still 12.2 per cent of rural population still had to cover more than 8 kilometres to reach a secondary schools (see Table 2.5). The situation is different in respect of higher secondary schools. Barring Kerala, Uttar Pradesh had the highest percentage of rural population covered with higher secondary schools within 6 or even 8 kms radius. Yet a little less than one-fifth of its rural population had to travel more than 8 kms to access a higher secondary school.

Besides the indicator on population having access to secondary and higher secondary schools by distance, another indicator used to understand the access ability is the number of schools per 10,000 population.

Number of Schools per 10,000 Population

The expansion of schooling facilities in many states could have affected the access condition. In order to understand this phenomenon, an attempt has been made to examine access in terms of number of schools available per 10,000 population, across major states in rural and urban areas during the year 2001. This proportion depends on size of population and the number of schools. It is found that Maharashtra and Andhra Pradesh have the larger number of lower secondary schools in terms of absolute number. The discrepancy becomes clear when we look at the number of schools in bigger states with large population, viz. Uttar Pradesh, Bihar and Madhya Pradesh. The number of lower secondary schools in Uttar Pradesh is comparable to that of smaller states with lesser population.

Number of schools per 10,000 population is not only less at all India level but also varies between rural and urban areas and among different states. At all India level, there were only 0.9 lower secondary and 0.4 higher secondary schools per 10,000 population. Rural areas have comparatively less schooling facilities compared to urban areas (see Annexure, Table A3). However, in 9 of the 17 major states, there were one or more lower secondary schools per 10,000 population and in 5 of these states; the number of lower secondary schools per 10,000 population was more in rural areas than in urban areas. Among these 5 states, except Orissa, other states are economically and educationally developed states.

The educationally developed state of Himachal Pradesh has the distinction of having the highest number of lower secondary schools, both at the state level and in rural areas, per 10,000 population. Considering the geographical and topographical features (hilly and high altitude areas) of the state with low density of population, the state has been successful in extending access to lower secondary education in close proximity by providing 2.1 and 2.6 lower secondary schools per 10,000 population in rural and urban areas respectively. Educationally and economically developed states like Maharashtra, Punjab, Gujarat, Haryana, and Tamil Nadu are characterized with favourable access to schooling facilities in general and rural areas in particular, whereas the underdeveloped and poorer states like Uttar Pradesh and Bihar, the number of schools in proportion of population is comparatively less. Further rural areas in these states are at a disadvantage of having low access to secondary schools.

At higher secondary level, the number of schools per 10,000 population is not only low (0.4) but the disparity is much more in case of rural areas. Among all the major states, 7 states have a better average than the national average with Himachal Pradesh leading the list. In this context, it can be stated that in recent times, Himachal Pradesh has progressed fast in terms of educational development indicators, following Kerala (Table 2.6). Except Maharashtra and Punjab, no other state has better institutional facilities in rural areas. Comparatively, at lower secondary level the access to school is better than at the higher secondary level especially in rural areas.

Table 2.6: Number of Secondary Schools per 10,000 Population in Major States in 2001

State	Secondary			Higher Secondary		
	Rural	Urban	Total	Rural	Urban	Total
Andhra Pradesh	1.5	2.0	1.6	0.2	0.7	0.4
Kerala*	N.A	NA	0.9	0.4	0.7	0.5
Maharashtra	1.6	1.1	1.4	0.4	0.3	0.4
UP	0.2	0.5	0.3	0.3	0.9	0.4
India	0.9	1.0	0.9	0.3	0.8	0.4

Source: (i) Census of India, 2001, GOI, New Delhi.

(ii) Seventh All India Educational Survey, 2001-02, NCERT, New Delhi.

Among the four sample states, Maharashtra and Andhra Pradesh are in better position with regard to provision of secondary school facilities according to population coverage. These states show better access condition, while Uttar Pradesh characterizes backwardness by having inadequate number of secondary schools by population coverage, resulting in lesser access. In fact Uttar Pradesh with largest population in the country had less number of (3275) lower secondary schools compared even to smaller states like Kerala and Haryana. However, interestingly, at higher secondary level, all the three sample states have similar access conditions, except Kerala, which has more schools per 10,000 population (see Table 2.6).

Proportion of Schools in Rural India

The distribution of schools varies in rural-urban regions of the country. As levels of education go up, the proportion of educational institutions in rural areas declines. Majority of the schools at primary level are located in rural areas but with increased level of education, the location-wise shift is towards urban areas (see Table 2.7). In 2002, at all India level, 88 per cent of primary schools, 79 per cent of upper primary schools, 70 per cent of lower secondary and 52 per cent of higher secondary schools were located in rural areas, covering 82 per cent, 72 per cent, 57 per cent and 40 per cent of total students enrolled in respective levels.

Table 2.7: Proportion of Schools in Rural Areas among All Schools in India

(in %)

Year	*Primary*		*Upper Primary*		*Secondary*		*Higher Secondary*	
	Schools	*Enrolment*	*Schools*	*Enrolment*	*Schools*	*Enrolment*	*Schools*	*Enrolment*
1993	89.0	74.7	89.0	63.0	73.0	55.3	49.0	38.1
2002	88.0	81.8	79.0	72.3	70.01	57.5	52.2	39.6

Source: 6th AIES-1993 and 7th AIES-2002 NCERT, New Delhi.

During the period of 1993-2002, the percentage of lower secondary schools located in rural areas has slightly declined at all India level, though the share of rural enrolment has increased by about 2 per cent, whereas at higher secondary level, percentage share of both schools and enrolment in rural areas have slightly increased during the same period (see Annexure, Table A4).

The proportion of schools in rural areas varied among different states both at lower secondary and higher secondary levels. During 2002, the percentage share of lower secondary schools in rural areas ranged from 88.4 to 55.5 per cent among the 17 major states. However, during 1993-2002, the proportion of lower secondary schools in rural areas declined in 9 of the 17 major states. Similarly, at higher secondary stage, the proportion of schools in rural areas varied between 79.7 per cent as the highest and 33.1 per cent as the lowest in Himachal Pradesh and Tamil Nadu, respectively. During the last decade, the percentage share of higher secondary schools declined in six states and while it increased in the other 11 states.

Both at lower secondary and higher secondary levels, the percentage share of enrolment in rural areas has increased at the national level as well as in many states during 1993-2001 (see Annexure, Table A4). However, the percentage share of lower secondary schools in rural areas has declined both at national level and in many states. In few of the educationally backward states along with enrolment the percentage of schools also increased, though marginally. At higher secondary level, during same period the percentage share of schools in rural areas increased along with the enrolment both nationally and in states.

Among the four sample states, Kerala has the highest percentage of schools located in rural areas, both at lower secondary and higher secondary levels, covering majority of students enrolled in respective stages of education. In Kerala, about three-fourths of lower secondary schools and students, and nearly two-thirds of higher secondary schools and students are from the rural areas. Uttar Pradesh has the lowest percentage of lower secondary schools in rural areas, compared to other states At the higher secondary level, Andhra Pradesh is relegated to the last position, behind Uttar Pradesh, in terms of proportion of schools in rural areas (see Table 2.8).

During 1993-2002, there has been a decline in the percentage share of secondary schools in rural areas in Uttar Pradesh and Andhra Pradesh, whereas in Maharashtra, it has increased. At higher secondary level, the percentage share of rural school increased in Maharashtra, Andhra Pradesh and Uttar Pradesh but in Kerala it declined slightly. The states where secondary and higher secondary levels of education are integrated, viz. U.P., Kerala and Maharashtra, have an advantage of having higher percentage of schools in rural areas unlike in Andhra Pradesh where higher secondary education is separated.

Table 2.8: Share of Schools and Enrolment in Rural Areas at Secondary Level during 1993 and 2002 (in %)

State	*Secondary*				*Higher Secondary*			
	1993		*2002*		*1993*		*2002*	
	School	*Enrolment*	*School*	*Enrolment*	*School*	*Enrolment*	*School*	*Enrolment*
Andhra Pradesh	68.4	54.5	67.0	62.2	40.5	31.1	50.0	35.2
Kerala	74.2	72.2	74.2	71.2	69.5	66.0	65.2	65.8
Mahara-shtra	66.1	49.5	67.0	53.3	55.1	45.7	59.5	36.1
U.P.	67.7	53.3	63.1	61.0	53.9	38.8	55.5	50.9
India	73.0	55.3	70.1	57.5	49.0	38.1	52.2	39.6

Source: VI (1993) and VII (2002) All India Educational Surveys, NCERT, New Delhi.

The rural-urban distribution of secondary schools depicts that despite having higher number of schools located in rural areas, the balance is still tilted towards urban areas, and more so in case of higher secondary schools in backward states. This can be found from a comparative picture of the number of schools and the corresponding population in rural areas. This, in fact, has more limitations in terms of physical access to higher secondary schools in rural areas, in view of poor road and transport facilities.

Integration of Schools

One of the important dimensions of access to education is the extent of integration of different levels of schooling. Provision of schools, though essential, is not sufficient for participation and completion of a given stage of education. This is more so in the access for continuing higher levels of school education. In other words, it is generally believed that if access to different levels of school education is provided through integration of lower and higher grades, demand for higher levels of school education would increase, in addition to encouraging higher participation at lower levels.

In view of this, an attempt has been made to examine the extent of integration of schools at different levels in India and among major states. Secondary education in India is characterized by integration of schools where upper primary sections are attached to secondary and higher secondary schools. In some cases, the schools are integrated from primary to upper primary/lower secondary/up to higher secondary level (see Annexure, Table A5).

Among the sample states, the state of Uttar Pradesh has the highest percentage of integration of primary, upper primary, secondary and higher secondary sections (9.0), followed by Kerala, Maharashtra and Andhra Pradesh in that order (see Table 2.9). Uttar Pradesh also had the highest percentage of integration of upper primary, secondary and higher secondary (53.6%) while in the case of Andhra Pradesh, the highest percentage of lower secondary schools (72%) were integrated with upper primary sections. Nearly half of the lower secondary schools, both in Maharashtra and Kerala, and about one-third in Uttar Pradesh, were integrated with upper primary sections. The percentage of secondary schools with only secondary sections among the sample states is rather low.

The extent and nature of integration of secondary and higher secondary schools not only vary across the states, but also among rural and urban areas apart from different management-type schools. This is evident from the micro level data of sample schools of case studies. Two-thirds of the sample schools under government and private aided management had integrated at upper primary, secondary and higher secondary levels of education whereas only one-third of private unaided management schools were having similar integration. In other words, a large percentage of private unaided schools were having only secondary and higher secondary sections in view of managerial and cost considerations.

Table 2.9: Percentage of Schools According to Integration of Schools

States	*Total*	*P only*	*UP only*	*S only*	*HS only*	*P, UP*	*UP, S*	*P,UP, S*	*S, HS*	*UP,S, HS*	*P,UP, H,HS*
AP	63773	77.06	0.03	0.11	1.56	9.98	8.19	2.62	0.12	0.23	0.12
Kerala	12104	48.90	5.68	3.67	0.02	24.93	9.30	5.09	0.37	1.34	0.70
Maharashtra	72374	55.20	0.06	4.39	0.06	27.87	8.41	0.79	0.16	2.96	0.10
UP	112497	76.93	15.95	0.10	0.00	1.04	1.94	0.21	0.02	3.26	0.55
All India	822486	69.36	5.76	2.52	0.24	14.04	3.61	1.84	0.58	1.48	0.58

Note: P-Primary; UP-Upper Primary; S-Secondary, H.S. = Higher Secondary.
Source: Sixth All India Educational Survey, NCERT, New Delhi, 1993.

Growth and Expansion of Educational Institutions

The access to education undoubtedly is an important indicator of educational development, but more than that it is the growth of educational institution that needs to be seriously addressed to draw a complete picture of educational development. The previous sections centered on overall expansion of the educational system, the issue of access to education primarily in rural areas, equity issues, and number of schools per 10,000 population etc. Access aspects, to a large extent, indicate supply side but they do not provide the holistic understanding of varied trends and patterns of educational development, especially demand and supply aspect, hence, the necessity to examine the trends of growth of educational institutions and enrolment.

Elementary Scenario

The growth of educational institutions is the result of decades of planning, implementation of programmes, policy initiative as well as willingness and commitment on the part of states, both to create equal opportunities and respond to the demands. Examining the trends of growth of educational institutions helps in capturing the broad themes as well as important policy issues at the national as well as regional levels. Towards this, compound annual growth rate (CAGR), based on number of schools at different points of time, is used. The compound annual growth rate of schools of different levels shows important trends for further analysis and calculation (see Table 2.10).

Table 2.10: Growth Rates of Institutions and Enrolment at Elementary Levels of Education in India

Year	Institutions		Enrolment	
	Primary	Upper Primary	Primary	Upper Primary
1950-51 to 1960-61	4.7	13.8	6.2	7.9
1960-61 to 1970-71	2.1	6.2	5.0	7.1
1970-71 to 1980-81	1.9	2.7	2.6	4.5
1980-81 to 1990-91	1.3	2.5	2.8	5.1
1990-91 to 2000-01	1.3	3.1	1.6	2.3
1950-51 to 2000-01	2.3	5.6	3.6	5.4

Formula for Calculating Compound Annual Growth Rate (CAGR) is (((LY/BY) ^ (1/N) – 1) × 100)

Source: Selected Educational Statistic, Various issues, MHRD, GOI, New Delhi.

During 1990-91 to 2000-01, the growth of enrolment at national level for primary and upper primary levels was 1.6 and

2.3 respectively, which varied widely among the states (see Annexure, Table A6). The enrolment ranged from 5.3 to –2.8 at primary level and 8.6 to –0.4 per cent at upper primary level. The highest growth rate for both the primary and upper primary levels was observed in one of the most backward states of India i.e. Rajasthan. Tamil Nadu and Kerala, however, showed negative growth rate at primary and upper primary level respectively. It may be noted that, except in a few states, the growth rate has declined across the states at both the levels, particularly when compared to the last decade. While the demand for primary education continues, it has shown increasing trend in backward states, which are still in the process of catching up with other advanced states, with regard to universalisation of primary education. Similarly, at upper primary level, both developed and backward states showed higher growth rate, in view of its bearing on demand for secondary level of education in future. However, not all the educationally underdeveloped states have a uniform pattern in growth of enrolment, either at primary or upper primary levels.

Growth of Secondary Schools

The growth rate of lower secondary schools in the country has been rather steady. Similarly, an increase in the growth rate of secondary education institutions can be seen since 1980s. The period of 1980-81–2000-01 had proved to be more favourable for expansion of lower secondary schools. At the lower secondary level, the growth rate is higher than at the primary and upper primary levels but a marginal decline can be observed from 4.2 per cent in 1991 to 4.0 in 2001 (Table 2.11). The Compound Annual Growth Rate (CAGR) for higher secondary level has increased at much better rate in comparison to other levels between the periods under study (from 4.6% in 1991 to 7.2% in 2001). Though the growth rate at primary level is apparently lower, it may not be so due to the huge base of primary education that effectively absorbs the growth rate in comparison to other levels of schools. On the other hand, with the increase in level of education, the number of schools being lesser, the expansion displays higher growth rate.

Table 2.11: Growth Rates of Institutions at Secondary and Higher Secondary Schools in India

Year	*Secondary*	*Hr. Secondary*	*Sec and Hr. Sec combined*
1950-51 to 1960-61	8.9*	--	8.9
1960-61 to 1970-71	7.9*	--	7.9
1970-71 to 1980-81	0.6	12.3	3.4
1980-81 to 1990-91	4.2	4.6	4.5
1990-91 to 2000-01	4.0	7.2	4.7
1950-51 to 2000-01	4.1**	5.9**	4.1

Formula for Calculating Compound Annual Growth Rate (CAGR) is (((LY/BY) ^ (1/N) – 1) × 100)

* Includes Secondary and Higher Secondary/Intermediate/pre-university/Jr. college/pre-degree Institutions.

** Growth Rates from 1970-71 onwards.

Source: Selected Educational Statistic, Various issues, MHRD, GOI, New Delhi.

Inter-State Variations in Institutional Growth Rate at Secondary Level

The national scenario may not necessarily reflect the state level reality since the growth of educational institutions at different levels varies from state to state. The national data, which is an aggregate picture, rather hides variations and differences in the trends of growth of educational institutions among different states, as there are significant inter-state variations based on economic, geographical, social and political contexts and educational policy of each state (see Annexure, Table A7).

Even though negative growth rates of educational institutions have been registered in a few of the states at the primary and upper primary levels, in the context of secondary education the scenario is much different and requires wider attention. The analysis of CAGR of secondary schools depicts that, except one state (Punjab), all other states have positive growth rate at lower and higher secondary levels and so is the national scenario (see Annexure, Table A7).

During the last decade the growth rate of lower secondary schools ranges between 10.42 and 1.01 per cent among the states. Interestingly, both the states with the highest and lowest percentages belong to category of economically and educationally backward areas. Some of the states, however, have shown not only a low growth rate but also a steeply declining trend in comparison to the earlier decade. For educationally developed states, like Kerala, it may not be a case for concern. Rather it can be a case of reaching at the limits of threshold. But for states which are yet to achieve universal literacy, it requires a look at the state policy.

When we compare the growth rate of lower secondary schools, some startling figures come into picture. Except Bihar all other economically and educationally backward states, known as 'BiMARU', have shown an impressive growth during the last decade along with Andhra Pradesh, which too is an educationally backward state. However, in many states the growth rate declined cutting across levels of socio-economic development.

The growth rate of higher secondary schools ranges from 25.36 to 4.85 per cent the highest being in the state of Kerala. While some of the educationally and advanced and smaller states (Haryana and Himachal Pradesh) have 13-15 per cent of growth rate, which, by any standard, is noteworthy.

A comparison of growth rate of higher secondary education during 1981-1991 and 1991-2001 shows that many states have achieved an increasing growth rate except, six states. In fact, some states with declining growth rate at lower secondary level, have also shown rather impressive growth rate at the higher secondary level. A few educationally and economically developed states have seen a higher growth rate at higher secondary level than at lower secondary level, thus reflecting an automatic threshold increase at lower secondary level. Haryana, on the contrary, is an economically and industrially developed state with large agrarian population; it is fast picking up in secondary education, especially in the private sector. One reason could be the difference in priorities of these two sectors of education, namely the linkage of higher secondary education to higher education.

Among the four sample states, during the 1980s, Andhra Pradesh and Maharashtra were having similar pattern of growth, while Uttar Pradesh had a dismal rate of growth in contrast to other sample states. During the 1990s, while Andhra Pradesh had increased the pace of growth rate to a higher level like many other backward states, the industrially progressive state of Maharashtra could not maintain the pace; it rather showed a marginal decline in the same period. Contrary to this, Uttar Pradesh, the most populous state of India, which was having a poor growth rate till 1980s, showed considerable improvement in its growth pattern in the 1990s (see Table 2.12).

Table 2.12: Growth Rates* of Educational Institutions at Secondary and Higher Secondary Levels in Sample States

States	*1980-81 to 1990-91*		*1990-91 to 2000-01*	
	Sec	*Hr. Sec*	*Sec*	*Hr. Sec*
Andhra Pradesh	4.2	6.4	5.3	9.5
Kerala	2.0	15.5	1.1	25.4
Maharashtra	4.0	6.1	3.3	4.9
Uttar Pradesh	0.4	2.0	4.2	5.0
All India	4.2	4.6	4.0	7.2

* Indicates Compounded Annual Growth Rate. Formula for calculating Compound Annual Growth Rate (CAGR) is (((LY/BY) ^ (1/N) – 1) × 100).

Source: Based on Selected Educational Statistics, 1980-81; 1990-91 and 2000-01, MHRD, Government of India, New Delhi.

In a socially progressive state like Kerala, the growth of educational institutions was negative up to primary level, very low at upper primary level, moderate at lower secondary level, and extremely high at higher secondary level. The trend of institutional growth in Kerala needs to be seen in an altogether different perspective. The state has achieved universalisation of basic education and is ahead of other states in terms of provision of facilities at lower secondary level, as higher secondary level has been de-linked from higher education to provide more access, leading to unprecedented growth rate.

Thus the growth of lower and higher secondary schools not only varies across the states but shows higher and increased growth rates in most of the backward states. The growth pattern of schools among economically and educationally developed states too shows variation. The mixed trend can be rightly comprehended after examining the demand pattern and the nature of different management types, which are discussed in the next two chapters.

Feeder Schools

It indicates a step-wise growth of educational institutions as a result of expansion of primary and upper primary at earlier periods and subsequently necessitating expansion of lower secondary and higher secondary schools at a later period of time. However, expansion of lower secondary schools could not keep pace with the growth of upper primary and primary schools, in the earlier decades of 1950-70s, leading to increased ratio between upper primary and lower secondary schools. After 1980s, however, the proportion of lower and higher secondary schools has declined. The ratio between lower and higher secondary schools shows the cascading effect of growth of schools at different levels. This also explains the extent of meeting the demand for the secondary schools.

During 1950-51, there was one upper primary school for every 15.4 primary schools; however, this ratio has favourably changed by the year 2001 where there was one upper primary school to nearly three primary schools (see Table 2.13).

Table 2.13: Proportions of Feeder Schools at Various Levels, 1950-51 to 2000-2001

Years	*No. of Primary Schools Per Upper Primary School*	*No. of Upper Primary Schools Per Secondary School*	*No. of Secondary Schools Per Higher Secondary School*
1950-51	15.4	1.8**	–
1960-61	6.7	2.9**	–
1970-71	4.5	2.4**	–
1980-81	4.2	3.0	3.2
1990-91	3.7	2.5	3.1
2000-01	3.1	2.4	2.2
2003-04*	3.0	2.4	2.2

*Provisional, ** Includes secondary and higher secondary.

Source: Based on Selected Educational Statistics, Various Issues, MHRD, GOI, and New Delhi.

But in the case of ratio of upper primary to lower secondary schools, the ratio has increased from 1.8 upper primary schools to one secondary school in 1950-51 to 2.4 lower secondary schools in 2000-01. Although there has been considerable growth of lower secondary schools, it did not match the growth rate of primary-upper primary schools for obvious reasons. This in turn enhanced the average size of the lower secondary school leading to overcrowding of classes, poor physical infrastructure and subsequent anomalies. However, in case of higher secondary schools, there has been a declining trend in the ratio i.e. the number of lower secondary schools per higher secondary schools declined from 3.2 in 1980-81 to 2.2 in 2000-01.

This shows that the number of upper primary schools have grown significantly along with the primary schools simply because a lot of primary schools have been upgraded to upper primary schools in the last 15 years as a strategy for universalization of elementary education. It is believed that the increased access to upper primary schools will act as a catalyst for increasing enrolment and decreasing dropout rate at primary level. However, such arguments seem to be not considered for lower secondary schools.

Feeder Schools at Inter-State Level

There is an inter-relationship between the lower and higher levels of education. The forward-backward relationship between the two levels of education expresses the dependency of one on the other. Though the growth rate depicts the progress of levels of education, ultimately it is the catchment area and interlinking growth between levels of these education, that exactly denotes the demand and growth of educational institutions in an area. Therefore, the logical development of different levels of education could be seen through the ratio of schools at the higher and lower levels or in other words, through the number of feeder schools. Based on the growth rate of schools at different levels, the ratio among feeder schools also varies across the states.

At all India level, the ratio of primary schools to upper primary school was 1:3.8 during 1990-91; it declined to 1:3 during the year 2001-02, indicating increased number of upper primary schools (see Annexure, Table A8). However, the proportion of upper primary schools to secondary schools has remained more or less the same (1:25-1:2.4), despite the lower secondary level registering higher growth rate than that of upper primary contrast the ratio between higher secondary and the lower secondary level has declined from 1:3.1 to 1:2.2. With the increased level of school education, the ratio of feeder schools (lower level schools) to higher levels of schools had become more viable in the last few decades.

The ratio in terms of feeder schools indicates the access and the growth of institutions as well as the degree of demand. The ratio of upper primary schools to lower secondary school varied from 1:6.2 to 1:0.4 among the major states, whereas it was higher in seven states than the national average of 1:2.4. Despite the higher growth rate of lower secondary schools in some of the backward states, the proportion of feeder schools with respect to a lower secondary school is still unfavourably placed when compared with developed states. However, even a few of the educationally and economically developed states were at a disadvantage as far as the proportion of feeder schools to a lower secondary school was concerned.

The average ratio between lower and higher secondary schools is relatively less and varied across the states. Seven of the major states had higher ratio of lower to higher secondary schools compared to all India average. Interestingly, among major states, Uttar Pradesh has the lowest ratio between lower and higher secondary schools, conforming to the effect of higher growth rate of institutions at higher secondary level and large number of higher secondary schools that have been integrated with lower secondary sections in the state. The varied pattern of ratio of schools of different levels evidently shows differential policies and priorities of states in providing lower and higher secondary schools in addition to the integration of lower and higher secondary levels. The uneven expansion of schools at different levels evidently proves the high ratio and large number of feeder schools.

In all the four sample states, there has been a favourable ratio of lower secondary to higher secondary, more so in case of Kerala. However, it must be taken into account that this ratio has decreased in all four sample states in the last one decade, except the ratio of upper primary to lower secondary in Uttar Pradesh (see Table 2.14).

Table 2.14: Proportion of Feeder Schools in the Major States of India in 1990-91 and 2001-02

States	*1990-91*		*2001-02*	
	Upper Primary to Secondary	*Secondary to Hr. Secondary*	*Upper Primary to Secondary*	*Secondary to Hr. Secondary*
Andhra Pradesh	1.1	6.4	1.3	4.1
Kerala	1.2	21.0	1.1	1.9
Maharashtra	2.3	3.8	2.1	3.0
Uttar Pradesh	6.0	0.7	6.2	0.6
India	2.5	3.1	2.4	2.2

Note: P= Primary Schools, UP = Upper Primary Schools, S = Secondary Schools, HS = Higher Secondary Schools

Source: Based on the Institutional Data in Selected Educational Statistics, 1990-91 and 2001-02, MHRD, GOI.

At the backdrop of expansion and growth of educational institutions at different levels in India and in major states, nevertheless it is important to examine the extent of demand for secondary education in terms of participation, to look at whether the increase of facilities and demand for schooling are in consonance with each other.

DEMAND FOR SECONDARY EDUCATION: GROWTH OF ENROLMENT

India has witnessed an exponential increase in the number of students enrolled at all levels of school education in the last five decade, as discussed earlier. The magnitude of students enrolled at secondary level of education has been as a result of growth of enrolment and expansion of institutions over the years. The growth rate of enrolment varied at different levels and also at different periods of time (see Table 2.15).

Table 2.15: Growth of Enrolment at Secondary Levels in India

Year	*Secondary*	*Hr. Secondary*	*Secondary and Hr. Secondary Together*
1950-51	1.5*	–	1.5
1960-61	3.4 (8.5)*	–	3.4 (8.5)
1970-71	7.6 (8.4)*	–	7.6 (8.4)
1980-81	7.1	4.1	11.2 (4.1)
1990-91	14.5 (7.4)	6.4 (4.6)	20.9 (6.4)
2000-01	19.0 (2.7)	9.9 (4.5)	28.9 (3.3)
1950-2000	40.6 (5.0)**	2.04 (4.5)**	73.6 (6.1)

Note: Figures in parentheses indicate the Compound Annual Growth Rate (CAGR) over decades

* Includes Secondary and Higher Secondary, Intermediate/pre-university/Jr. college/pre-degree Institutions.

** From 1980-81 to 2000-01

Source: Selected Educational Statistic, Various Issues, MHRD, GOI, New Delhi.

The total enrolment during 1950-51 to 2000-01 had increased at the primary, upper primary and secondary stages by 6, 14 and 20 times respectively. A look at the enrolment and decadal growth rate suggests that during 1950-70, there has been more than five-time increase in the growth of enrolment at secondary level. This figure, of course, includes intermediate/pre-university/junior colleges/pre-degree institutions-the names by which higher secondary sections have been known. The trend of enrolment also points that 1970s can be truly called as the 'golden period' of enrolment as more students joined the schools during this period. However, it may be noted that though the enrolment for primary education has shown an increase in terms of absolute numbers, its growth rate has actually declined, when compared to that of 1950-60s. At the all India level, one can discern the cumulative growth of CAGR with increase in the level of school education till secondary stage during the period 1980-81 to 1990-91, while in the decade of 1991-2001 there has been continuous increase of growth rate for enrolment at all levels, including the higher secondary stage.

There was a sudden decline in the growth rate of enrolment at secondary level during the 1970s as after 70s the enrolment started stabilizing. The shift to 10+2+3[2] pattern after educational restructuring led to the enrolment in Grade VIII being clubbed with upper primary stage for the national level accounting of educational statistics. However, during 1980s, the enrolment for lower secondary education had more than doubled from 7.1 millions to 14.5 millions. This substantial rise was not an overnight phenomenon, rather it was because of the factors like increase at the lower level. This growth was not independent rather influenced by efforts to increase the enrolment at the base. In the 70s, enrolment at upper primary level rose significantly, the result of which could be found in the subsequent increase in enrolment at lower secondary level during the 1980s. Many other factors, viz. growth of institutions, fee concessions, free lower secondary education in some states, etc. were responsible for this increase. The compound annual growth rate remained at about the same level in the last decade for higher secondary level.

Pattern of Demand: Across the States

In order to have a clear understanding of correspondence between demand and supply mechanism in school education, the inter-state growth pattern of enrolment needs to be examined.

The demand for secondary education is not independent of other levels of education, especially lower levels. In other words, growth of enrolment at secondary level has both backward and forward linkages with the enrolment at different levels of education. To have holistic view, demand for education at lower levels and secondary level had been examined. The growth rate of enrolment at primary level not only varies among different states but also has declined in the last decade in most of the states compared to earlier decade, except in one state. These states cut across different levels of socio-economic development (see Annexure, Table A9).

Demand at Lower Secondary Level

From an impressive growth rate of 7.4 per cent in 1980-91 at lower secondary level, the growth of enrolment got reduced to mere 2.7 per cent in 1991-2001 at the national level. In fact, during 1990-2001, all the states, except one, had shown a positive growth rate in terms of enrolment. The disparities among the states is quite apparent from the index of the growth rate of enrolment at lower secondary levels which ranged between 6.6 per cent as the highest and –1.6 as the lowest. Interestingly, both the highest and lowest rates were found in economically and educationally backward states. The higher growth rate was found in a few backward states along with some developed states who had continued to maintain a higher growth rate, which was better than the national average. The growth rate not only declined steeply to 2.7 per cent during 1990-91 to 2000-01 at all India level but in most states also along with decrease in the disparities.

Even most of the large and developed states which showed higher growth rate during 1980-1990, tended to depict reduced growth rate which was same for smaller and backward states. However, a few educationally and economically backward states which had shown lower growth rate during the previous decade, could achieve increased rate during 1991-2001. Similarly, in some of the states, the demand for lower secondary education has continued to increase for the last two decades.

The demand for higher secondary education at national level remained at the same level unlike the lower secondary for the last two decades showing a sign of stabilization. During 1990-91 to 2001, there had been change in the demand pattern at higher secondary level attributed to three different pattern—(i) few economically developed states (Haryana and Karnataka) either continued to have higher or increased demand during 1990s; (ii) some of the poor and educationally backward states (Madhya Pradesh, Orissa and

Rajasthan) showed increased demand, but (iii) there had been considerable decline in the growth of enrolment, including a negative growth rate in the educationally backward state like Bihar. However, the occurrence of either increase or decline in enrolment between two decades cuts across both the developed and the underdeveloped states. More interestingly, it witnessed in most states a step-wise increase in enrolment or demand from one level to another at different points of time.

Among the four sample states, the growth rates for enrolment at different levels during 1980-81 to 1990-91 varied too widely. However, Maharashtra and Andhra Pradesh showed similar patterns of demand at lower secondary levels. Kerala. which has attained higher levels of educational development understandably had lower growth rate of enrolment till lower secondary levels. But educationally backward state of Uttar Pradesh had shown low growth rate at lower and higher secondary levels despite having a better growth rate during the earlier decade (see Table 2.16).

Table 2.16: Growth Rates* of Enrolment Across Sample States at Secondary and Higher Secondary Levels

	1980-81 to 1990-91		*1990-91 to 2000-01*	
	Sec	*Hr.Sec*	*Sec*	*Hr.Sec*
Andhra Pradesh	6.1	2.8	2.3	6.0
Kerala	1.1	4.3	1.1	3.8
Maharashtra	6.9	12.5	3.5	0.8
Uttar Pradesh	4.5	3.5	1.5	0.8
All India	7.4	4.6	2.7	4.5

* Indicates Compounded Annual Growth Rate. Formula for calculating Compound Annual Growth Rate (CAGR) is (((LY/BY) ^ (1/N) – 1) × 100)

Source: Based on Selected Educational Statistics, 1980-81; 1990-91 and 2000-2001, Statistics Division, Dept. of Sec. and Hr. Sec Education, MHRD, Government of India.

At higher secondary level of education also, there was a downward trend in growth of enrolment among the sample states, except in Andhra Pradesh. In case of demand for secondary education, like the general trend, the sample states did not show any particular pattern.

Demand for Secondary Education in Rural India

The growth of enrolment and educational facilities not only varies across the states, but also within a state, the disparities among rural and urban areas are more significant. An attempt has been made to examine the extent of growth of schools and enrolment across rural-urban areas, both at national level and among different states (See Annexure, Table A10).

The growth rate of enrolment ranges from as high as 10.3 per cent to as low as 1 per cent at lower secondary level among the states. Both at the lower and the higher secondary levels. The growth rate was not only higher at all India level but was also in most of the states (except in two where the difference was marginal) while the growth rate of schools was higher in urban areas except in two states. In other words, rural areas have shown more demand in the form of higher growth of enrolment both at lower and higher secondary levels but this has not been matched by institutional growth, especially at lower secondary level. This evidently proves that there is a mismatch between demand and supply of lower secondary education in rural localities, irrespective of the levels of development of states. This kind of imbalances could be the result of differential roles played by different management types, in meeting the educational demand in rural and urban areas, particularly by private sector. This issue has been separately addressed to in the chapter on public-private dichotomy.

At the higher secondary level, the growth rate of schools in both rural and urban areas was much higher than that of lower secondary schools, with a significant number of states showing double digit growth. Both the developed and backward states have shown higher growth rate of higher secondary schools in rural area, except five states. Higher growth rate of institutions in rural areas did not mean lower growth rate in urban areas as both sets of states have shown considerable growth rate of higher secondary schools in urban areas as well.

Similar to the higher growth rate of institutions in rural areas, the demand was also higher in rural areas than their urban counterparts; this was the national trend in case of higher secondary schools. However, the enrolment growth rate varied from state to state and it ranged from a highest of 38.1 to a lowest of –0.5 for rural schools, and similarly, the maximum growth rate was 38.2 per cent and the minimum was 2.0 per cent for urban schools. Only three states have shown a trend contradictory to the national trend as far as the demand is concerned and two of them belong to the category of economically and educationally backward states. Although the growth rate of institutions was higher in rural areas than the urban areas, but when we compare the growth of institutions vis-à-vis demand, there is a huge gap both in rural and urban areas. This means that the higher demand for higher secondary schools despite the efforts of the state has remained largely unmet, leading to low gross enrolment ratio on the one hand, and providing scope for the private sector participation on the other, which will be discussed later. This kind of mismatch between the demand and supply is spread across the states, irrespective of their economic and educational levels of development.

Among sample states, except Kerala, the growth rate of enrolment was higher in rural areas both at the lower secondary classes. However, the growth of schools has been higher in urban areas. The state of Uttar Pradesh had the highest growth rate of enrolment at lower secondary level both in rural and urban areas, followed by Andhra Pradesh. While there was a difference in the growth rate of schools between rural and urban areas in three of the four sample states, the degree of difference was higher in the case of Uttar Pradesh in favour of rural areas; for others it was marginal. Interestingly, highest growth rate in the educationally and economically backward state of Uttar Pradesh, considering the size and population of the state, is certainly significant and shows a kind of fast changing educational scenario in the state. Like many other states, in Uttar Pradesh and Andhra Pradesh also, the growth of rate of lower secondary schools was much higher than the growth of enrolment (Table 2.17).

Table 2.17: Growth of Schools and Enrolment in Rural and Urban Areas Between 1993 and 2002 in Sample States and in India

State	*Secondary*				*Higher Secondary*			
	Schools		*Enrolment*		*Schools*		*Enrolment*	
	Rural	*Urban*	*Rural*	*Urban*	*Rural*	*Urban*	*Rural*	*Urban*
AP	7.2	8.1	7.8	3.6	12.7	7.4	13.5	10.9
Kerala	-5.2	-5.3	0.7	1.4	22.5	25.5	38.1	38.2
Maharashtra	3.9	3.4	5.7	3.7	5.9	3.6	10.5	16.1
UP	9.8	12.6	10.3	6.0	9.2	8.3	13.6	6.8
INDIA	3.2	4.8	5.1	3.9	8.2	6.7	10.2	9.3

Note: Data of Bihar, M.P. and U.P. in 2002 include Jharkhand, Chhattisgarh and Uttaranchal respectively.

Formula for calculating Compound Annual Growth Rate (CAGR) is (((LY/BY) ^ (1/N) – 1) × 100)

Source: Based on (i) Sixth All India Educational Survey, NCERT, New Delhi.
(ii) Selected Educational Statistics, MHRD, GOI, New Delhi, 2002-03.

At higher secondary level in all the states, except Maharashtra, the growth rate of enrolment in rural areas is higher than in the urban areas. Similarly, in all the states, except Kerala, the growth rate of higher secondary schools was higher in rural areas than in the urban areas. In all the sample states, except Uttar Pradesh (Urban), the growth of enrolment was in double digit showing the increasing demand for higher secondary education in both rural and urban areas. However, the educationally and economically developed Maharashtra showed higher demand in urban areas, which is understandable considering the importance and need for higher secondary education in an industrially developed state. In Maharashtra a mere 3.6 per cent growth rate of higher secondary schools in urban areas is meeting 16.1 per cent growth rate in enrolment. In contrast to this, Uttar Pradesh had 8.3 per cent institutional growth in urban areas to comply with an enrolment growth of only 6.8 per cent. However, it is important to note that at higher secondary level, there is a restriction on admission and usually is based on selected number of seats and subjects, thus often rendering a good number of candidates outside the school. This trend needs to be understood in the context of fast growing private unaided sector and this aspect has been exclusively dealt with in the next chapter.

Growth rate of institutions and enrolment provides a broader outlook to the dynamics of demand and supply but to have a closer picture of the scenario, another indicator examined here is average school size[3]. This indicator informs about the impact of increased enrolment on institutional level dynamics affecting the school size.

Changing Dynamics of Secondary Education

As it has been mentioned earlier, the Indian education scenario has since 1990s changed rather drastically. As a result, various aspects of secondary education too have changed and it is important to address such variations in order to understand the true picture of secondary education scenario. As latest state level data was not available to provide all India picture, we have confined our analysis to sample states by using the latest available data (2002-2005). However, reference year of the data differs from state to state, depending on their availability. This variation of course has little consequence considering that it is used for noting the latest development of secondary education within the sample states (see Table 2.18).

Table 2.18: Trends and Development in Lower Secondary Education

State	*Institution*			*Enrolment*		
	2000-01	*2004-05*	*% Change*	*2000-01*	*2004-05*	*% Change*
Andhra Pradesh	10277	14372	39%	1252696	1768327	41.2%
Kerala	2776	*2002-03* 2608	–6.1%	1049430	*2002-03* 1022022	–2.6%
Maharashtra	11687	*2002-03* 13181	12.8%	2608027	*2002-03* 2815398	8.0%
Uttar Pradesh	3837	*2003-04* 11758	206.4%	2400805	*2003-04* 4334964	80.6%

Source: Directorate of School Education, Govt of Andhra Pradesh; Directorate of School Education, Govt of Maharashtra, Selected Educational Statistics, MHRD, GOI; Education Since Independence, Directorate of Education, Govt of Kerala; 2004, Board of Secondary and Higher Secondary Education, Uttar Pradesh.

As discussed earlier, in the educationally and economically backward states of Uttar Pradesh and Andhra Pradesh, the context and dimensions of secondary education have undergone a sea change. For example, there has been more than 200 per cent growth in institutions and 80 per cent growth in enrolment at the lower secondary level in Uttar Pradesh in a span of barely four years (2001-2004), while in Andhra Pradesh the respective percentages were 39 and 41 around the same period (2001-2005). On the contrary, in economically and educationally developed Maharashtra, there has been 12.8 per cent increase in the institutions and just 8 per cent increase in the enrolment in two year period from 2001-03. On the hand, Kerala had shown a negative growth in both institutions and enrolment during these two years. This enormous disparity between the states and the exponential demand for secondary education in a very short span time, especially in Uttar Pradesh, necessitates an examination. Though there had been a consistent increase in demand for secondary education in the state, but the sudden and rapid demand is beyond normal explanation. It could be the culmination of various interconnected reasons viz. state policy, rise of private entrepreneurship, globalization, demand for English medium schools, urbanization, agricultural prosperity, conspicuous consumption, etc. which only manifested in the aftermath of the year 2000. Needless to add that the inadequacy of government schools in meeting these demands has helped to fuel a rapid transformation of secondary schooling (Jeffery 2005:47).

The above framework of the analysis, based on national, inter-state and sample states, denotes a kind of pattern though there are differences and similarities. In this context, if sample states are considered as representative macro units or aggregate units, then they may be seen to exhibit conformities and differences in secondary education at state levels.

Regional Diversity in Demand

States in India show large degree of difference and diversity from each other. Not only they differ from each other in size, structure, political context, they also differ in socio-economic set-ups. This is not merely an inter-state phenomenon but also an intra-state reality. Thus any state-centric observation has the potential to mislead when viewed from micro level conditions. It is, therefore, more meaningful to take into account regional level distribution of educational management types at lower secondary and higher secondary levels.

Since states in India were constituted on linguistic parameters, the socio-economic and geographical dissimilarities in a particular state are often glossed over, which has been a major cause of resentment among people over the years. For example, there are historical (tribal heartlands in general, and Kerala's northern regions in particular), political (Bihar and Uttar Pradesh), geographical (northeast region), economic (Telangana in Andhra Pradesh) and cultural (Vidarbha in Maharashtra) reasons which differentiate not only a state from the other, but even one region from the other within a state. In fact, the recent bifurcation of the states of Bihar, Uttar Pradesh and Madhya Pradesh to carve out Jharkhand, Uttaranchal and Chhattishgarh, is a result of popular resentment brewing out of uneven development and differential treatment meted out to certain regions. The recent clamouring for a separate statehood for Telangana and Vidhrabha attests to this fact. Of course, there is a political aspect to the story, but nonetheless it points out to the importance of representing regions and capturing regional realities for any substantial research. This has also been an important dimension in determining the growth of educational institutions and coverage. Based on these understandings, we assume that there would be significant variation in the growth and expansion of secondary schools as well the demand for secondary education. In order to grasp this variation an intra-state analysis of regional diversity has been used in this section.

All the four sample states viz. Kerala, Maharashtra, Andhra Pradesh and Uttar Pradesh, not only have inter-state variations but there are considerable regional and district level variations within the states, that depict wider disparity among them. Regional variations bring out interesting trends. (for the regions and districts that fall under various regions (see Appendix p. 58).

In Andhra Pradesh, during the 1980s, the growth rates at lower secondary level across the three regions were uniform though they had different economic and educational levels of development (see Annexure, Table A11). However, similar growth rate among the three regions does not imply equal growth and development, these rather show an unequal distribution of resources. By 1990s, however, the regions have shown more distributive growth even in lower secondary schools, with the underdeveloped regions having picked up the pace even beating the more developed areas. The backward Telangana and Raylaseema had shown higher demand expressed in terms of institutional and enrolment growth rate at lower secondary level, compared to the developed regions.

In Maharashtra the lower secondary schools grew faster in backward and moderately developed regions during 1980s. But in 1990s, higher growth rate was observed both in developed along and backward regions. Interestingly, the trend has been similar in the growth rate of enrolment as well. Despite the historical and socio-economic backwardness, Aurangabad region achieved higher percentage of institutional and enrolment growth. Irrespective of lower growth rate during 1990s, a few developed and one backward region have been able to retain higher growth rate.

In Kerala, the growth of lower secondary schools during the 1980s was uniform across the regions. However, during the 1990s north Kerala, a backward region, registered a higher institutional and enrolment growth rate compared to the other developed regions of the state. Unprecedented growth rate of higher secondary schools in all regions has been because of recent de-linking of higher secondary schools from higher education.

Contrary to other three sample states, Uttar Pradesh shows typical backward characteristics where the developed central and western regions registered better growth rates at secondary level during 1990s. It shows that the backward regions in underdeveloped states did not pick up the trend of improved educational access and remained chained to their backwardness. It is pertinent to mention that this trend was prevalent during early 1990s. But there has been tremendous change in the educational scenario in the state since the year 2000. Therefore, it is safe to assume that the backward regions too would have transformed. The above region-wise picture on growth of institutions suggests that the educationally and economically backward regions have registered the highest growth during the last two decades both at the lower and senior secondary levels. This clearly indicates that the demand for secondary education has been expanding in the state in these regions and areas, which were deprived of economic, social and historical affluence.

Across the sample states, the trend emerging at the micro level suggests that more expansion took place rather in backward regions of the states. Interestingly, in Uttar Pradesh, there was a mixed trend. While the backward regions showed both positive and negative growth rate of enrolment, the advanced regions had positive enrolment growth.

The above discussion leads to the understanding that backward regions in the sample states have shown higher growth rate of institutions and enrolment, particularly in backward states. There could be many reasons behind this phenomenon which could be categorized in three broad types, namely the filter down effect, low base of education, and impact of pro-active government policies. These reasons are separately discussed later in this chapter.

In consonance with the pattern of growth of institutions, the growth of enrolment across regions of sample states at secondary education level too differs widely.

Participation Rates

Unlike in the developed countries in India the relevant age groups do not strictly correspond to their likely grade due to a various influencing factors, viz. over and under age, failure, repetition etc. In the Indian context, the growth of enrolment provides a general idea about the progress of education, but it does not really indicate the level of educational development. Therefore, it is essential to take into account the participation of relevant age group in the appropriate grade. This can be measured through the gross enrolment ratio (GER) of specific age group in any given level of education.

The GER in the secondary education for the age group of 14-18 years shows that only 33 per cent of relevant age group population was enrolled during 2001-02. However, the gross enrolment ratio of this age group population has been very slow in rising to 33 per cent in 2001-02 from 11 per cent in 1960-61. Compared to the boys, the girls' participation rate is much lower, i.e., only 27.7 per cent against 38 per cent for the boys (see Annexure, Table A12).

The gross enrolment ratio that reflects the level of educational development also denotes the increasing variations and inequities among states. In 2002-03, the GER was 37.52 per cent at all India level while as many as 9 states had a better GER than the national average. Further, the inter-state variation is rather sharp with the highest being 68 per cent in the state of Himachal Pradesh and the lowest 17.39 per cent in Bihar. In fact, in case of Bihar, the GER has fluctuated from 15-17.39 in the last two decades. Similarly, a close analysis of the GER shows that in the economically and educationally advanced states like Maharashtra and Tamil Nadu, the GER is more than 50 per cent as these states ordinarily require a larger pool of skilled labour. The GER also depicts the level of gender disparity, both at the national as well as at the state level. This GER is very low in case of educationally and economically backward states like Bihar, Madhya Pradesh, Rajasthan, Uttar Pradesh and Orissa, being as low as 11.39 per cent. The states that have higher GER than the national average in general and especially the developed states, also have higher GER in rural areas.

Therefore, it is difficult to find a definite pattern or trend to describe the growth rate of lower secondary schools in the country and link it with social and economic indicators. However, based on the careful analysis of data, an attempt can be made to explain these phenomena by dividing it into a few sets of propositions:

1. A majority of backward states have shown an increased and higher rate of growth in both lower and higher secondary levels of institutions and enrolment, while some of them have shown tremendous improvement only during the last decade. This may be attributed to three reasons: (a) that the increasing demand for secondary education in these states possibly because of 'filter down' effects of the benefits of education, especially as a vehicle for economic and occupational mobility; (b) the educationally underdeveloped states are focusing more on expansion and growth of institutions and

enrolment at secondary level as a state policy; (c) this type of growth can be attributed to progress made by universalization of elementary education, particularly through programmes like DPEP, equity programmes and other policy initiatives in expanding the lower base of secondary education in the country in general and in backward states in particular.

2. A few backward states have depicted declining trend in both lower and higher secondary education during the same period though they had a better growth rate in the previous decade. This may be attributed to withdrawal of government funding private management types or failure of policy mechanism.
3. Another set of states, which are educationally and economically developed, had shown a declining growth rate at the lower secondary level but had higher growth rate at higher secondary level, thus highlighting the shift of focus from lower secondary education to higher secondary education. It is believed that these states have achieved minimum threshold level at secondary level and are now having higher demand for higher secondary level.

Looking at these propositions, it can be added that in many states, the slow and declining rate of growth has a lot to do with financial constraints than with being able to meet the demands or having lack of demand for such facility.

In the context of the above discussion, it may be said that there has been a growing demand for secondary education not only at the state levels but also among various social groups despite obvious disparities. The demand has particularly increased in the last two decades in both developed and backward states though its extent differs from state to state. Backward states like Assam, Jammu and Kashmir, Madhya Pradesh and Rajasthan, joined the developed states like Haryana, Himachal Pradesh and Maharashtra in their demand for secondary education, thereby pushing the national average. However, the question is how this growing demand has been catered to especially in terms of the response of management types. This question has been addressed to in the next part of the chapter where the focus is on management types.

Annexure

Table A1: Access* to Primary and Upper Primary Schools Across Major States

(*in %*)

State	Primary				Upper Primary			
	1993		2002		1993		2002	
	Within habitations	*Up to 1 km**	*Within habitations*	*Up to 1 km**	*Within habitations*	*Up to 3 km**	*Within habitations*	*Up to 3 km**
Andhra Pradesh	69.73	88.57	78.49	93.91	13.82	65.40	24.49	74.73
Kerala	61.64	82.23	60.73	79.43	35.56	89.00	38.61	84.12
Maharashtra	64.70	84.22	67.64	91.17	25.37	78.42	28.95	78.18
Uttar Pradesh	29.34	80.45	40.56	87.96	7.25	78.36	12.35	78.43
Assam	54.51	85.72	44.56	84.34	15.15	85.54	13.51	82.04
Bihar	58.20	92.33	56.71	88.92	13.48	87.04	13.15	81.10
Gujarat	90.43	95.76	77.92	93.62	49.35	88.31	64.39	95.52
Haryana	82.47	93.03	78.24	91.90	35.51	86.14	43.03	89.11
Himachal Pradesh	20.99	59.44	28.82	74.98	5.69	64.75	9.40	77.60
Jammu & Kashmir	59.78	80.48	50.61	78.60	16.53	75.77	16.14	75.91
Karnataka	60.36	83.75	67.44	88.41	24.71	85.32	30.66	88.26
Madhya Pradesh	58.35	81.13	69.03	89.20	11.37	61.69	22.52	79.56
Orissa	48.96	82.42	51.54	82.93	13.41	77.24	19.77	73.55
Punjab	80.82	95.72	79.25	93.46	22.21	83.69	34.79	90.50
Rajasthan	51.11	74.58	53.41	79.84	14.59	64.43	21.07	78.26
Tamil Nadu	53.46	98.62	53.93	88.48	14.73	80.79	15.89	74.31
West Bengal	38.35	87.70	35.34	92.28	5.84	84.78	6.32	79.44
India	49.79	83.36	53.04	86.96	13.87	76.15	18.45	78.11

* Percent population having access to primary and upper primary schools.

Source: Based on 7th AIES, Flash Data.

Table A2: Access to Secondary and Higher Secondary Schools by Distance*

State	Secondary						Higher Secondary					
	1993			2002			1993			2002		
	Up to 5 km	*Up to 8 km*	*Above 8 km*	*Up to 6 km*	*Up to 8 km*	*Above 8 km*	*Up to 6 km*	*Up to 8 km*	*Above 8 km*	*Upto 6.0*	*Up to 8.0*	*More than 8.0*
Andhra Pradesh	78.2	91.0	9.1	85.0	94.1	5.9	35.4	45.8	54.2	46.37	58.78	41.22
Kerala	92.7	98.3	1.7	96.0	99.0	1.0	55.2	67.6	32.4	91.33	95.27	4.73
Maharashtra	83.0	93.2	6.8	88.4	96.4	3.6	45.4	56.2	43.8	52.30	63.17	36.83
Uttar Pradesh	68.8	86.5	13.5	71.1	87.8	12.2	65.5	78.5	21.5	70.95	82.33	17.67
Assam	87.4	94.7	5.3	89.2	96.6	3.4	63.6	75.2	24.8	68.00	79.93	20.07
Bihar	79.3	91.5	8.5	80.5	93.9	6.1	36.4	50.7	49.3	22.19	30.67	69.33
Gujarat	80.4	99.3	9.3	81.0	91.1	8.9	50.9	61.6	38.4	49.24	58.52	41.48
Harayana	94.2	98.7	1.3	97.5	99.6	0.4	59.9	74	26	86.42	93.85	6.15
H. P.	78.7	91.2	8.8	87.2	95.7	4.3	39.1	49.7	50.3	70.45	78.96	21.04
J & K	82.6	93.1	6.9	83.7	93.8	6.2	52.9	66.1	33.9	55.77	69.01	30.99
Karnataka	81.1	92.6	7.4	83.6	94.2	5.8	48.4	60.3	39.7	49.59	61.61	38.39
Madhya Pradesh	55.4	74.4	25.6	62.0	81.5	18.5	44.7	56.6	43.4	48.38	62.05	37.95
Orissa	86.3	93.6	6.4	89.3	95.8	4.2	40.7	61.3	38.7	50.98	66.15	33.85
Punjab	93.2	98.7	1.3	96.3	99.5	0.5	68.4	82.5	17.5	90.35	96.25	3.75
Rajasthan	64.2	81.1	18.9	72.9	87.0	13.0	30.8	40.5	59.5	51.89	63.07	36.93
Tamil Nadu	85.0	95.2	4.8	85.6	96.1	3.9	71.6	81.9	18.1	74.82	86.03	13.97
West Bengal	91.7	97.5	2.5	94.0	98.7	1.3	66.7	76.8	23.2	80.15	89.07	10.93
India	77.9	90.1	9.9	80.4	91.9	8.1	51.4	63.6	36.4	57.98	68.51	31.49

* Percent share of population having access to secondary and higher secondary schools.

Source: Sixth and Seventh All India Educational Survey, NCERT, New Delhi, 1993 and 2002.

Table A3: Number of Secondary Schools per 10,000 Population in Major States in 2001

State	*Secondary*			*Higher Secondary*		
	Rural	*Urban*	*Total*	*Rural*	*Urban*	*Total*
Andhra Pradesh	1.5	2.0	1.6	0.2	0.7	0.4
Kerala*	N.A	NA	0.9	0.4	0.7	0.5
Maharashtra	1.6	1.1	1.4	0.4	0.3	0.4
UP	0.2	0.5	0.3	0.3	0.9	0.4
Assam	1.4	1.4	1.4	0.3	0.9	0.4
Bihar	0.3	0.6	0.4	0.0	0.5	0.1
Gujarat	1.0	0.7	0.9	0.3	0.7	0.5
Haryana	1.7	1.5	1.6	0.6	1.2	0.8
HP	2.1	2.6	2.2	1.2	2.8	1.3
J&K	1.4	1.8	1.5	0.3	0.7	0.4
Karnataka	1.3	1.7	1.5	0.3	0.5	0.3
MP	0.6	1.0	0.7	0.4	1.4	0.7
Orissa	1.8	1.3	1.7	0.2	0.5	0.3
Punjab	1.1	0.6	0.9	0.7	0.7	0.7
Rajasthan	0.9	1.3	1.0	0.4	1	0.5
Tamil Nadir	0.7	0.7	0.7	0.4	1	0.7
West Bengal	0.6	0.6	0.6	0.3	0.6	0.4
India	0.9	1.0	0.9	0.3	0.8	0.4

Source: (i) Census of India, 2001, GOI, New Delhi.
(ii) Seventh All India Educational Survey, 2001-02, NCERT, New Delhi.

Table A4: Share of Schools and Enrolment in Rural Areas at Secondary Level During 1993 & 2002 (in %)

States	*Secondary*				*Higher Secondary*			
	1993		*2002*		*1993*		*2002*	
	School	*Enrolment*	*School*	*Enrolment*	*School*	*Enrolment*	*School*	*Enrolment*
A.P.	68.4	54.5	67.0	62.2	40.5	31.1	50.0	35.2
Kerala	74.2	72.2	74.2	71.2	69.5	66.0	65.2	65.8
Maharashtra	66.1	49.5	67.0	53.3	55.1	45.7	59.5	36.1
U.P.	67.7	53.3	63.1	61.0	53.9	38.8	55.5	50.9
Assam	86.0	80.6	87.6	79.8	73.0	73.2	69.3	54.5
Bihar	82.5	66.3	83.1	64.8	55.3	59.8	46.5	30.5
Gujarat	78.0	46.1	70.5	48.8	41.9	28.1	45.2	35.6
Haryana	76.6	61.7	74.1	60.3	47.0	36.1	54.7	43.9
H.P.	89.4	83.3	88.4	83.7	69.3	54.0	79.7	69.7
J & K	78.8	65.3	70.2	64.4	47.5	26.8	53.0	31.8
Karnataka	64.6	48.7	59.9	53.4	54.6	33.9	49.6	27.6
M.P.	58.7	46.6	61.4	50.4	41.9	34.6	42.9	35.9
Orissa	88.1	77.0	89.0	80.9	78.9	81.4	73.9	61.4
Punjab	79.7	57.0	78.8	61.5	49.2	31.4	67.3	40.6
Rajasthan	79.4	53.0	68.7	56.7	38.3	25.2	56.4	34.4
Tamil Nadu	69.3	51.2	55.5	38.5	44.8	39.8	33.1	25.9
West Bengal	69.4	58.6	74.0	63.7	48.1	46.1	53.0	48.4
India	73.0	55.3	70.1	57.5	49.0	38.1	52.2	39.6

Source: Sixth (1993) and Seventh (2002) All India Educational Survey, NCERT, New Delhi.

Table A5: Percentage of Schools According to Integration of Schools

States	Total	P only	UP only	S only	HS only	P,UP	UP,S	P,UP,S	S,HS	UP,S,HS	P,UP,H,HS
Andhra Pradesh	63773	77.06	0.03	0.11	1.56	9.98	8.19	2.62	0.12	0.23	0.12
Kerala	12104	48.90	5.68	3.67	0.02	24.93	9.30	5.09	0.37	1.34	0.70
Maharashtra	72374	55.20	0.06	4.39	0.06	27.87	8.41	0.79	0.16	2.96	0.10
Uttar Pradesh	112497	76.93	15.95	0.10	0.00	1.04	1.94	0.21	0.02	3.26	0.55
Assam	39342	73.43	15.45	5.87	0.16	2.20	1.42	0.11	0.25	1.08	0.02
Bihar	71068	74.33	0.49	0.08	0.35	18.79	5.22	0.38	0.01	0.25	0.10
Gujarat	37800	35.93	1.90	9.75	0.01	47.34	0.07	0.14	4.53	0.17	0.14
Haryana	9396	55.41	0.13	0.01	0.24	15.61	1.28	21.86	0.00	2.51	2.95
HP	10095	76.48	10.54	0.69	0.32	0.44	8.74	0.72	0.06	1.70	0.31
J & K	12566	69.58	0.09	0.01	0.02	20.14	1.11	7.16	1.42	0.14	0.33
Karnataka	46495	47.22	0.86	9.88	0.38	38.47	0.22	0.61	2.11	0.15	0.10
MP	93910	76.91	12.25	1.58	0.00	4.90	0.63	0.63	1.37	1.19	0.54
Orissa	52258	69.47	10.93	8.23	0.65	8.70	1.46	0.47	0.00	0.03	0.05
Punjab	48059	26.51	2.51	0.00	0.00	0.34	3.78	0.70	0.37	1.67	0.46
Rajasthan	48059	69.39	0.11	0.01	0.00	21.07	5.56	1.36	0.37	1.67	0.46
Tamil Nadu	41429	72.62	0.36	0.05	0.00	13.42	6.71	1.42	0.03	4.41	0.99
West Bengal	57272	84.78	0.04	0.00	0.01	4.96	0.04	7.97	0.00	0.03	2.17
All India	822486	69.36	5.76	2.52	0.24	14.04	3.61	1.84	0.58	1.48	0.58

Note: P = Primary; UP = Upper Primary; S = Secondary, H.S. = Higher Secondary.
Source: Sixth All India Educational Survey, NCERT, New Delhi, 1993.

Table A6: Growth Rates* of Institutions and Enrolment Across Major States at Primary and Upper Primary Levels

State	*1980-81 to 1990-91*		*1990-91 to 2000-01*	
	Enrolment		*Enrolment*	
	Pry	*Up Pry*	*Pry*	*Up Pry*
Andhra Pradesh	3.1	5.4	1.5	2.6
Kerala	-3.5	1.5	1.7	-0.4
Maharashtra	1.9	5.1	1.4	3.4
Uttar Pradesh	3.6	4.1	0.1	1.0
Assam	5.5	5.8	1.2	3.1
Bihar	2.5	5.2	1.9	1.7
Gujarat	2.6	4.7	1.6	1.5
Haryana	2.8	3.4	1.6	2.8
Himachal	2.2	5.0	0.1	1.9
Jammu & Kashmir	2.9	5.2	3.4	3.5
Karnataka	2.6	4.6	1.5	4.4
Madhya Pradesh	4.5	7.1	3.0	2.5
Orissa	2.5	4.8	2.4	3.8
Punjab	0.0	1.8	0.3	1.4
Rajasthan	4.3	5.1	5.3	8.6
Tamil Nadu	1.9	5.0	-2.8	1.1
West Bengal	3.7	6.3	0.7	1.0
All India	2.8	5.1	1.6	2.3

* Indicates Compounded Annual Growth Rate. Formula for calculating Compound Annual Growth Rate (CAGR) is $(((LY/BY)^{(1/N)} - 1) \times 100)$.

Source: Based on Selected Educational Statistics, 1980-81; 1990-91 and 2000-2001, Statistics Division, Dept. of Sec. and Hr. Sec Education, MHRD, Government of India.

Table A7: Growth Rates* of Educational Institutions Across 17 Major States at Secondary and Higher Secondary Levels

States	*1980-81 to 1990-91*		*1990-91 to 2000-01*	
	Sec	*Hr. Sec*	*Sec*	*Hr. Sec*
Andhra Pradesh	4.2	6.4	5.3	9.5
Kerala	2.0	15.5	1.1	25.4
Maharashtra	4.0	6.1	3.3	4.9
Uttar Pradesh	0.4	2.0	4.2	5.0
Assam	4.8	8.0	2.6	5.5
Bihar	1.6	21.1	1.0	8.7
Gujarat	4.8	4.6	1.6	3.1
Haryana	3.6	8.0	3.7	15.5
Himachal	3.8	6.3	2.8	13.5

Contd.

States	1980-81 to 1990-91		1990-91 to 2000-01	
	Sec	Hr. Sec	Sec	Hr. Sec
Jammu & Kashmir	2.1	6.5	3.0	2.8
Karnataka	4.9	11.6	7.0	4.5
Madhya Pradesh	1.9	0.3	10.4	7.7
Orissa	5.9	17.0	3.0	7.8
Punjab	1.5	6.2	-0.2	8.3
Rajasthan	3.2	5.9	4.6	7.8
Tamil Nadir	3.9	4.1	3.3	5.0
West Bengal	3.1	1.0	1.8	7.4
All India	4.2	4.6	4.0	7.2

* Indicates Compounded Annual Growth Rate. Formula for calculating Compound Annual Growth Rate (CAGR) is (((LY/BY) ^ (1/N) – 1)×100).

Source: Based on Selected Educational Statistics, 1980-81; 1990-91 and 2000-01, MHRD, Government of India, New Delhi.

Table A8: Proportion of Feeder Schools in the Major States of India in 1990-91 and 2001-02

States	1990-91		2001-02	
	Upper Primary to Secondary	Secondary to Hr. Secondary	Upper Primary to Secondary	Secondary To Hr. Secondary
Andhra Pradesh	1.1	6.4	1.3	4.1
Kerala	1.2	21.0	1.1	1.9
Maharashtra	2.3	3.8	2.1	3.0
Uttar Pradesh	6.0	0.7	6.2	0.6
Assam	1.9	8.1	1.9	5.9
Bihar	3.5	12.2	3.3	4.3
Gujarat	4.7	2.5	4.6	2.2
Haryana	0.7	8.2	0.6	2.2
Himachal Pradesh	1.3	5.4	1.4	1.8
Jammu & Kashmir	2.6	4.4	3.0	4.5
Karnataka	4.1	3.5	3.2	3.9
Madhya Pradesh	8.3	0.7	5.8	1.0
Orissa	2.1	9.9	1.8	6.1
Punjab	0.6	4.5	1.1	1.3
Rajasthan	3.1	2.9	3.3	2.2
Tamil Nadu	1.8	1.6	1.2	1.4
West Bengal	0.7	4.9	0.4	2.9
India	2.5	3.1	2.4	2.2

Note: P = Primary Schools, UP = Upper Primary Schools, S = Secondary Schools, HS = Higher Secondary Schools.

Source: Based on the Institutional Data in Selected Educational Statistics, 1990-91 and 2001-02, MHRD, GOI.

Table A9: Growth Rates* of Enrolment Across Major States at Secondary and Higher Secondary Levels

	1980-81 to 1990-91		*1990-91 to 2000-01*	
	L. Sec	*Hr.Sec*	*Sec*	*Hr.Sec*
Andhra Pradesh	6.1	2.8	2.3	6.0
Kerala	1.1	4.3	1.1	3.8
Maharashtra	6.9	12.5	3.5	0.8
Uttar Pradesh	4.5	3.5	1.5	0.8
Assam	5.7	6.5	3.4	6.0
Bihar	6.4	5.1	3.3	-0.3
Gujarat	4.8	5.2	2.3	4.3
Haryana	5.1	11.7	5.0	9.5
Himachal	13.9	12.7	1.0	2.8
Jammu & Kashmir	4.8	13.3	6.6	1.5
Karnataka	5.7	8.9	3.9	11.2
Madhya Pradesh	2.0	Na^	5.3	7.9
Orissa	9.0	9.0	-1.6	11.3
Punjab	2.7	Na^	2.2	4.6
Rajasthan	2.8	Na^	4.1	5.6
Tamil Nadu	5.1	5.5	2.7	4.8
West Bengal	6.8	4.0	0.5	2.7
All India	7.4	4.6	2.7	4.5

* Indicates Compounded Annual Growth Rate. Formula for calculating Compound Annual Growth Rate (CAGR) is (((LY/BY) ^ (1/N)-1)*100)

Source: Based on Selected Educational Statistics, 1980-81; 1990-91 and 2000-2001, Statistics Division, Dept. of Sec. and Hr. Sec Education, MHRD, Government of India

Table A10: Growth of Schools and Enrolment in Rural and Urban Areas Between 1993 and 2002 in Major States in India

State	*Secondary*				*Higher Secondary*			
	Schools		*Enrolment*		*Schools*		*Enrolment*	
	Rural	*Urban*	*Rural*	*Urban*	*Rural*	*Urban*	*Rural*	*Urban*
A.P.	7.2	8.1	7.8	3.6	12.7	7.4	13.5	10.9
Kerala	-5.2	-5.3	0.7	1.4	22.5	25.5	38.1	38.2
Maharashtra	3.9	3.4	5.7	3.7	5.9	3.6	10.5	16.1
U.P.	9.8	12.6	10.3	6.0	9.2	8.3	13.6	6.8
Assam	3.0	1.4	1.0	1.6	5.5	7.7	2.4	13.5
Bihar	0.2	-0.4	1.7	2.6	6.9	11.2	9.6	27.7
Gujarat	1.3	6.4	3.5	2.1	4.7	2.9	7.2	2.7
Haryana	5.5	7.3	6.9	7.7	17.1	12.7	13.1	8.6
H.P	3.1	4.3	4.0	3.7	18.4	10.5	11.0	2.0
J & K	3.0	8.2	6.7	7.2	6.6	4.0	12.7	9.3

Contd.

State	Secondary				Higher Secondary			
	Scnools		Enrolment		Schools		Enrolment	
	Rural	Urban	Rural	Urban	Rural	Urban	Rural	Urban
Karnataka	4.7	7.3	6.0	3.5	3.0	5.5	5.8	9.8
M.P.	9.3	7.8	4.7	2.8	8.2	7.7	4.0	3.2
Orissa	2.2	1.3	4.0	0.9	10.4	13.8	11.6	26.6
Punjab	0.3	1.0	3.0	0.6	15.7	5.3	16.0	10.3
Rajasthan	4.8	12.5	5.6	3.7	17.2	7.0	10.4	4.4
Tamil Nadu	0.4	8.1	0.0	6.6	3.7	10.3	-0.5	7.8
W. Bengal	1.3	-1.5	6.4	3.6	12.2	9.5	11.2	9.9
INDIA	3.2	4.8	5.1	3.9	8.2	6.7	10.2	9.3

Note: Data of Bihar, M.P. and U.P. in 2002 include Jharkhand, Chhattisgarh and Uttaranchal respectively.
Formula for calculating Compound Annual Growth Rate (CAGR) is [((LY/BY) ^ (1/N) – 1) × 100)]

Source: Based on (i) Sixth All India Educational Survey, NCERT, New Delhi.
(ii) Selected Educational Statistics, MHRD, GOI, New Delhi, 2002-03.

Table A11: Growth (CGAR) of Secondary Educational Institutions by Regions in Sample States

Region	Lower Secondary		Higher Secondary
Andhra Pradesh	*1980-81 to 1990-91*	*1990-91 to 2002-03*	
Coastal	3.13	5.53	NA
Rayalaseema	3.89	6.66	NA
Telangana	3.86	9.18	NA
Total (A.P.)	3.81	7.47	NA
Kerala	1980-81 to 1990-91	1990-91 to 2000-01	1990-91 to 2000-01
South	1.34	0.31	41.81
Middle	1.49	0.48	38.47
North	1.75	1.15	41.77
Total (Kerala)	1.52	0.65	40.54
Maharashtra	1980-81 to 1990-91	1990-91 to 2000-01	1990-91 to 2000-01
Mumbai	2.85	1.74	2.92
Nasik	3.77	5.05	5.78
Pune	3.56	4.92	4.77
Kolhapur	3.93	3.13	5.82
Aurangabad	4.40	4.01	9.01
Amravati	4.06	2.63	5.87

Contd.

Region	Lower Secondary		Higher Secondary
Andhra Pradesh	1980-81 to 1990-91	1990-91 to 2002-03	
Nagpur	5.02	2.38	6.17
Total (Mah.)	3.95	3.60	5.90
Uttar Pradesh*	1980-81 to 1990-91	1990-91 to 2000-01	
Central	1.58	6.97	NA
Bundelkhand	0.56	4.22	NA
Eastern	1.09	5.49	NA
Western	0.02	5.51	NA
Total (U.P)	0.68	5.68	NA

*Includes both Lower and Higher Secondary

Formula for Calculating Compound Annual Growth Rate (CAGR) is (((LY/BY) ^ (1/N) – 1) × 100)

Source: (i) A.P. Statistical Abstracts, 1988, and Educational Statistics, Government of A.P., Hyderabad.
(ii) Directorate of Secondary and Higher Secondary, Pune, Maharashtra.
(iii) Statistics for planning, Directorate of Economics and Statistics, Govt. of Kerala.
(iv) Siksha Ki Pragati (1980-2002), Uttar Pradesh. ^Here there is only a single category as Secondary.

Table A12: Gross Enrolment Ratio for Children in the Age Group of 14-18 Years at Secondary Level (Combined) in Major States of India

States	1985-86		1995-96		2001-02		2002-03 (All Areas)		2002-03 (rural)	
	Girls	Total	Girls	Total	Girls	Total	Girls	Total	Girls	Total
Andhra Pradesh	14	22	24	31	29	34	35	40	32	23
Kerala	44	44	43	42	60	57	64	62	55	57
Maharashtra	21	31	36	41	48	53	50	53	45	37
Uttar Pradesh	9	23	15	25	12	21	29	36	32	20
Assam	22	30	29	35	31	36	28	29	24	23
Bihar	6	17	9	15	10	15	11	17	14	7
Gujarat	18	25	30	35	34	39	34	40	32	22
Haryana	12	19	22	27	41	46	43	47	38	29
Himachal Pradesh	18	29	41	48	57	62	65	68	61	55
Jammu & Kashmir	15	22	23	30	36	42	28	33	26	18
Karnataka	18	28	28	34	36	39	35	37	27	23
Madhya Pradesh	7	16	22	34	20	28	23	30	22	11
Orissa	13	22	15	24	26	36	26	31	31	22
Punjab	20	24	31	34	41	42	40	39	31	30
Rajasthan	6	16	14	26	16	27	18	29	26	9
Tamil Nadu	22	29	36	43	45	48	55	55	34	29
West Bengal	20	27	18	25	22	27	26	30	26	20
All India	15	24	24	31	28	33	33	37	30	21

Source: Education in India, 1985-86 and 1995-96, MHRD, GOI, 2002 and Selected Educational Statistics, 2001-02, MHRD, GOI, New Delhi.

ANNEXURE

I. Regions and Districts in Andhra Pradesh

The state comprises three natural regions, which can be distinguished from one another by their historical, cultural and economic backgrounds.

1. The *Coastal Andhra Region* consists of nine districts of Srikakulam, Vizianagaram, Visakhapatnam, East Godavari, West Gadavari, Krishna, Guntur, Prakasam and Nellore. This region represents a reasonably well-developed part of the state, as major part of the region is covered by the Krishna and Godavari delta. These two rivers irrigate the land in this region.
2. The *Rayalaseema Region* consists of four districts: Chittoor, Cuddapah, Ananthapur and Kurnool. These districts are under developed, as the region is dry and often subject to droughts.
3. The *Telengana Region* consists of the ten districts, that is, Mehabubnagar, Ranga Reddy, Hyderabad, Medak, Adilabad, Nizamabad, Karimnagar, Warangal, Kammam, and Nelgonda. These districts are, more or less, underdeveloped except Hyderabad district (being the State Capital) and parts of Ranga Reddy district.

Andhra Pradesh became a State in 1956 on linguistic basis by bringing together the eleven Telugu speaking districts of erstwhile Andhra State and the nine Telugu speaking districts of erstwhile Hyderabad State. While the former was under British rule, the latter was under Nizam's rule. At the time of formation, there were 20 districts. Later three more districts were formed by bifurcating some of the existing ones.

II. Regions and Districts in Kerala

The state can be divided into three regions on the basis of its physical features, namely the forest highland region, the lowland region bordering the sea, and the mid-land region consisting of valleys broken here and there by isolated hills. It has more than 40 rivers and streams with their sources of origin in the Western Ghats. These flow into the Arabian Sea, and provide an extensive system of inland waterways, important for commercial purpose.

Kerala, in the present study, has been divided into three regions simply as South, North and Middle.

The *Southern Region* consists of Trivandrum, Quilon, Allapulaza, and Pattanamthita.

The *Middle Region* consists of Ernakulam, Trissur, Idduki, and Kottayam.

The *Northern Region* consists of Mallapuram, Wayanad, Kozhikode, Kannur, Kasargode and Palakad.

III. Regions and Districts in Maharashtra

Maharashtra is classified into five broad regional groups historically evolved as socio-cultural and agro-climatic units: Greater Mumbai, Western Maharashtra (the rain shadow zone), Marathwada (the dry and rocky central zone), Konkan (coast), and Vidarbha (central plateau having deep black soil). These regions are divided into six revenue divisions for administrative purposes.

Konkan Division consists of Brihan Mumbai, Thane, Raigad, Ratnagiri and Sindhudurg districts on the western coast. Landholdings are small but more or less evenly distributed with no irrigation facilities worth mentioning. Relatively, this Division is affluent due to industrialaization but the vast hinterland is agrarian. It is one of the fastest growing industrial regions in the country.

Nashik Division comprises the districts of Nasik, Dhule, Jalgaon, and Ahmednagar. These districts have a large tribal population with large landholdings, and high levels of landlessness, forests. A few fertile tracts and good rainfall comprise the Mashik Division.

Pune Division consists of Pune, Satara, Sangli, Solapur and Kolhapur districts and have relatively lower rainfall, being located in the narrow rain shadow area. The Nashik and Pune Divisions together are popularly known as Western Maharashtra.

Aurangabad Division consists of districts of Aurangabad, Jalna, Parbhani, Beed, Nanded, Osmanabad, and Latur. These are culturally well tied, all of them being from the erstwhile state of Hyderabd. The region is rocky and dry with low and uncertain rainfall, large landholdings and landlessness. This region is also widely known as the Marathwada region.

Amravati Division consists of Buldhana, Akola, Amravati and Yavatmal. *Nagpur Division* comprises districts of Wardha, Nagpur, Bhandara, Chandrapur and Gadchiroli. These two divisions of Amaravati and Nagpur form the Vidharbha regions and cover part of a plateau with deep black soils, assured rainfall and medium to large landholdings and high levels of landlessness. Bhandara, Gonidiya, Chandrapur and Gadchiroli districts have a large tribal population and forest cover.

IV. Regions and Districts in Uttar Pradesh

The Gangetic Plain and the Bundelkhand and Baghelkhand Plateau of Uttar Pradesh is divided into four geographical regions (excluding the Hill Region, which has now become a separate state of Uttaranchal).

1. *The Upper Ganga-Yamuna Doab and the Rohilkhand Plain:* This is the northwestern part of the Ganga-Yamuna plain where the rainfall is the lowest. It is mainly a wheat growing area. The region is rich as regard to irrigation facilities. It has 5 divisions–Moradabad, Meerut, Saharanpur, Agra and Barielly.
2. *The Lower Doab and the Gomti Plain (the West Avadh Plains).* Here the rainfall high in comparison with the west. Wheat, rice and sugarcane are the important crops of this region. The percentage of rural population was very high (in 1970's). Because of the deep alluvial strata, this whole plain has practically no minerals. This region has two divisions–Lucknow and Kanpur.
3. *The Eastern Avadh Plain or the Purbia Plain:* This region gets the highest rainfall. Rice takes place of wheat in this region. A rich alluvial soil is an important wealth of this region. This region has got the highest numbers of divisions, that is, eight–Allahaabad, Faizabad, Gorakhpur, Kushinagar, Azamgarh, Varanasi, Mirzapur, and Davipathan Dham.
4. *The Bundelkhand and Baghelkhand Plateau:* It is the southern part of the state, which lies south of the Yamuna. The western part of this region is known as the Bundelkhand and the eastern part is known as Baghelkhand. The whole

region is made of granitic-gneiss sandstone and serrated ridges of quartz reefs. This is somewhat a dry region of the state and has little scope for agriculture. The land productivity is low, rainfall is precarious and irrigation facilities are poor. However the region is suitable for growing cotton. This region consists of two divisions–Jhansi and Chitrakut Dham.

NOTES

1. The levels of access are defined here in terms of availability of schools and educational services which deliver education free of charge to the eligible group of children.
2. This pattern (ten years of schooling) comprises of 5 years of primary, three years of upper primary and two years of lower secondary, followed by two years of higher secondary and three years of first university degree. This means ten years of schooling before higher secondary education.
3. Average school size here denotes the number of students enrolled in Grades IX and X for lower secondary and Grades XI and XII for higher secondary.

3

Role of Government and Private Sector in Secondary Education: Extent of Privatisation

In India provision of education has essentially been community—oriented since beginning. However, over the years, schools established by philanthropic individuals and institutions have continued to thrive with state recognition through grant-in-aid policy even after independence. In some states, these private initiatives have taken deep roots, leading to a virtual monopoly of a few individuals and groups, e.g., in Maharashtra, Kerala and Uttar Pradesh. In India, the practice of grant-in-aid system to private agencies has been a long-established tradition. Besides, government has also been directly operating educational institutions. The long and varied forms of educational development have led to the creation of different types of educational institutions in the country. There are at least four forms of educational provisions in India: (a) publicly managed and funded (e.g. government primary schools); (b) publicly managed, but publicly and (relatively less) privately funded (e.g. government secondary schools, colleges and universities); (c) privately managed but largely publicly funded (e.g. aided schools and colleges); and (d) privately managed and funded (e.g. unaided schools and colleges) (Tilak: 1993). Most of the schools in India belong to category (a) and to a lesser extent to category (b). Large numbers of private schools in India, as in many countries, belong to category (c); they are privately managed but receive as much as 97 per cent or higher proportion of their expenses from the state exchequer.

The first section in this chapter deals with development of schools and expansion of enrolment under different types of management at elementary levels at the national plane. Subsequently a quick review of developments across states with a focus on sample states has been attempted. A detailed analysis on the development of secondary education has been discussed for the period 1986 to 1993 (pre-liberalisation phase), and after 1993 (liberalisation phase) focusing at the national and state levels. Given the national and state variations as a prelude, the analysis relates to sample states, to regions, to districts, to institutions, and eventually captures the impact of these macro changes at the micro level, viz. schools and students through specifically designed case studies. The final part attempts to explain the phenomenon of growing private unaided sector and brings out the implications of these changes.

SCHOOLS BY TYPE OF MANAGEMENT

The beginning of the new millennium has very critical significance in the context of Indian education in general and secondary education in particular. Though the liberalization process was a decade old, the real effects of liberalization began to take shape during this period and the second phase of liberalization only hastened the pace of change. Consequently, a perceptible difference could be found in the nature and functioning of secondary education in India in terms of access, participation and the types of supply mechanisms. A glance at the number of secondary schools, their coverage and the managements that operate these institutions will facilitate to take note of these transformations at the macro level. Secondly, it would be difficult to examine changes in the secondary education without taking into account changes in primary and upper primary education. In fact there is not only forward—backward linkage between the two but also in the Indian context, it is difficult to completely separate the two levels as most often they are integrated. Therefore, this section takes a cursory glance at the changes taking place at primary and upper primary levels.

Role of Different Managements at Elementary Level

Government of India has been the major provider of schools, more so, in primary education. A simple look at the educational scenario in India shows that the government including local bodies[1], is involved in governing and financing almost all the schools at primary level.

By the beginning of the new millennium (2001-02), though there was no change in the share of government schools, the share of private aided schools continued to decline. There has been more than five times increase in the share of private unaided schools at primary level.

During the same period at upper primary level, the percentage of private unaided schools has risen from a mere 4.67 per cent in 1978-79 to a galloping 15.77 per cent in 2001-02.

Although the percentage of private unaided schools at primary level is negligible, but viewed from the large base of primary education and in absolute terms, their rate of growth and proportion is substantial. In addition to this, a large proportion of unrecognized private unaided schools at primary and upper primary levels also exist across the country since there are no regulatory measures for recognition similar to that at higher levels. These schools exist both in urban and rural areas, though more so in rural areas.

During 1993-94, though government continued to be the major provider, the proportion of government and private aided schools had declined steadily but marginally, both at primary and upper primary levels. Correspondingly, the share of private unaided sector had increased during this period (see Figure 3.1).

During 1986, 93 per cent of primary and 91 per cent of upper primary schools were under the direct control of government[2], while private aided schools and private unaided schools were negligible though their percentage shares varied at these two levels. The percentage of private aided schools at upper primary level during this period was more than three times in primary level. In fact, during late 1970s, private aided sector was the second largest provider of upper primary schools.

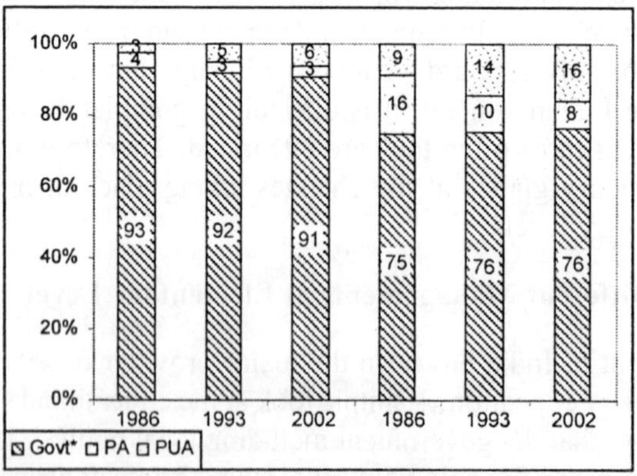

Figure 3.1: Schools by Different Management—Types at Different Levels of Education

Note: Government schools include schools run by local bodies.
Source: Selected Educational Statistics 2001-2002, MHRD, GOI, India, 2003; p. 14-15

Enrolment in different management type schools at lower primary level reveals that till seventies, the students enrolled in government schools were nearly 85 per cent; a little more than 10 per cent of children were enrolled by private aided schools and only 3 per cent of the students were studying in private unaided schools in 1978. There had been steady decline in the proportion of students in government and private aided schools though it was marginal. However, the percentage share of students covered by private unaided schools had increased five-fold, from 3 per cent in 1978 to 15 per cent in 2002 of total enrolment at the primary level itself (see Figure 3.2 and Annexure, Table A1).

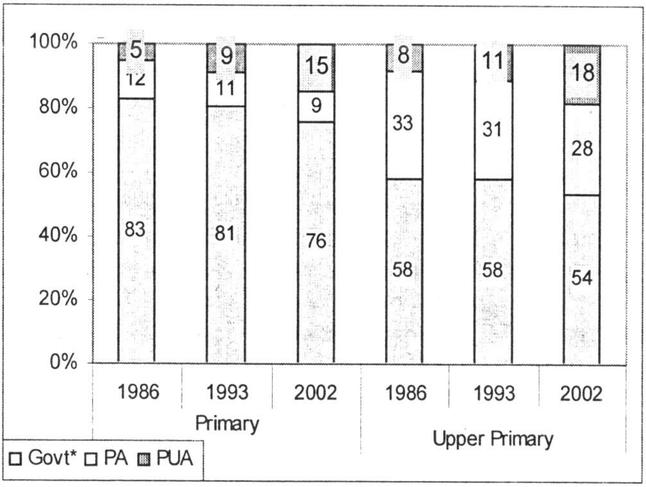

Figure 3.2: Enrolment by Type of Management at Elementary Levels of Education in India

Source: 4th, 5th, 6th All India Education Surveys, NCERT, New Delhi (1982, 1992, 1999).

Unlike at primary stage, at upper primary stage the private aided sector along with government schools was playing an important role to meet the demand for schooling. At this level, a little more than half of the students were covered by government schools, and coverage of private aided schools was 41 per cent during late seventies. While the coverage of government schools increased, the proportion of students enrolled in private aided school had declined by more than ten percentage points from 1978 to 2002. During the same period, the percentage of students seeking admission in private unaided schools had increased more than three times, amounting to one-fifth of total enrolment at upper primary level. From the extent of private unaided schools and their coverage at lower and upper primary levels indicates that private unaided sector was replacing private aided schools while government schools continued to hold their importance at lower levels of education.

Inter-state Variations

The national level aggregate picture does not decipher the pattern that exists in different states as the states in India exhibit great diversity and variation. This diversity is also characterized in terms of provision of schools by different agencies. However, it is important to note that these variations are often rooted in the state policies, social demands, political and economic conditions of the concerned states.

During 2001-02, the percentage share of government schools at primary level ranged from 100 per cent in Bihar and West Bengal to 38 per cent in Kerala, and from 99 per cent in Bihar to no schools under the management of government in West Bengal at upper primary level (see Annexure, Table A2). The role of private unaided sector also varied among the major states from 26 per cent in industrially developed Gujarat to nil in West Bengal at primary level. In comparison to primary level, more number of states had higher percentage of private unaided schools at upper primary level. Interestingly, along with the phenomenal expansion of lower and upper primary schools by different state governments, a significant increase in the percentage of unaided schools at these levels has taken place in many states, particularly during 2001-02 in comparison with 1993. Along with the increased provision of educational facilities by the government, the private unaided schools have also augmented their contribution at the lower levels. This can discerned from the percentage share of enrolment in private unaided schools at all India level which was higher than the other management schools. At upper primary level, the share of institutions and their share of enrolment were almost equal for private unaided schools in 1993. (see Annexure, Table A3).

The four sample states vary in terms of provision of lower and upper primary schools by different managements. One of the sample states, Kerala is unique with majority of lower and upper primary schools under private aided management (see Table 3.1).

Table 3.1: Proportion of Schools at Primary and Upper Primary Levels by Type of Management in Sample States at Selected Points of Time

States	Primary Level						Upper Primary					
	1993			2001-02			1993			2001-02		
	Govt	PA	PUA	Govt	PA	PUA	Govt	PA	PUA	Govt	PA	PUA
A.P.	92.9	4.1	3.0	94.5	3.4	2.2	79.9	6.9	13.2	72.7	3.5	23.8
Kerala	39.7	58.4	2.0	38.0	59.7	2.3	33.5	64.5	2.0	32.2	62.8	5.0
Maharashtra	91.5	4.5	4.0	90.4	5.1	4.5	91.4	5.9	2.7	87.7	7.9	4.5
U.P.	87.1	1.5	11.4	91.9	1.0	7.2	57.1	9.5	33.4	58.4	9.0	32.6
India	92.1	3.8	4.1	90.9	3.1	6.0	79.5	9.5	11.0	76.4	7.8	15.8

Source: All India Educational Survey, 1993, NCERT, New Delhi;
Selected Educational Statistics, 2001-02, MHRD, Govt of India.

In Kerala, nearly 60 per cent of lower primary and 63 per cent of upper primary schools were under private aided management, whereas the government schools constituted 38 per cent at lower and 32 per cent at upper primary levels. The private unaided schools in the state constituted barely 2 per cent and 5 per cent at lower and upper primary schools respectively. Compared to the earlier decade, there had been slight change in the proportion of different management type schools. Although at upper primary level, the proportion of private unaided schools had more than doubled, still they constituted a very small segment. Thus, Kerala has a combination of three different management type schools even at elementary level. However, this kind of choice between private aided and government schools was not available in other states. This choice to parents at primary level is often cited as one of the important reasons for universalization of elementary education (Shah, 1998) in Kerala. This can also be one of the reasons for low proportion of private unaided school in the state.

In an economically developed state like Maharashtra, government (including local bodies) provides about 90 per cent of schools both at lower and upper primary levels, whereas a very small section (5%) of schools are provided under private aided and unaided sectors. At primary level, the proportion of schools under different managements was more or less the same during the last decade, although there had been a very small increase in the share of private unaided schools at upper primary level and an insignificant decline in the share of government and private aided schools.

In Andhra Pradesh, both at lower and upper primary levels, government (including local bodies) provides majority of the schools. Private aided schools are negligible in numbers at both the levels. Although private unaided schools are very insignificant at lower primary levels, at upper primary level, they constitute nearly one-fourth of the total schools. In this state, interestingly, the proportion of government schools at lower primary had increased since early nineties, while at upper primary level, both government and private aided schools showed a declining trend, and the proportion of unaided schools increased significantly.

Educationally and economically, the most backward state of Uttar Pradesh presents a different scenario both at primary and upper primary levels. During 2001-02, 92 per cent of primary schools were under government management, private unaided schools constituted 7 per cent of total schools. The private aided schools were just one percent. Interestingly in the last decade, there was a decline in the percentage share of unaided schools while the share of government schools had shown marginal increase. Contrary to lower primary level, at upper primary stage one-third of schools were under private unaided management while 58 per cent of schools were being managed by government. Private aided sector covered less than one-tenth of upper primary schools in Uttar Pradesh without much change compared to the earlier decade.

The four sample states show different educational scenarios at lower and upper primary levels despite having some common features. During 1993, all the four states were having low proportion of unaided schools at lower primary level and the differences among the states were marginal. Among the four sample states, except Kerala, majority of lower and upper primary schools were operated by government. However, as an exception to this general trend, Kerala had the largest number of private aided schools both at lower and upper primary levels. While unaided schools were fewer at lower primary level in all the four states, the educationally and economically most backward state of Uttar Pradesh and educationally backward state of Andhra Pradesh had shown more propensity towards unaided schools at upper primary level. On the other hand, educationally developed state of Kerala and economically progressive state of Maharashtra showed very low preference for private unaided schools even at upper primary level. Interestingly, Uttar Pradesh has shown consistently higher proportion of private unaided schools for the last two decades at upper primary level. Similarly, the state of Andhra Pradesh has also shown more inclination towards the private unaided schools at upper primary level though not to the same extent as Uttar Pradesh. However, in Andhra Pradesh, the percentage of private unaided upper primary schools had nearly doubled during the last decade. Thus, at lower level of schooling, the four sample states showed variation in terms of provision of access to education by different managements. All the four sample states slightly differ from the national trend, especially in the extent of private aided and unaided schools.

It may be noted that the official statistics in India do not take into account the number of private unrecognized schools at primary level, which is quite sizeable. Mushrooming growth of unrecognized lower primary schools has been a common phenomenon in all the four sample states, both in urban and rural areas. This trend may be attributable to the increasing demand and especially for the preference towards English as medium of instruction. In one of the sample states, i.e., Andhra Pradesh, it is found that a large number of private unaided and un-recognized schools exist catering to the primary education even in poorer areas like slums (Tooley and Dixson, 2003). This is evident from the increased number of private unaided schools at upper primary level. To encounter this problem, many states including Maharashtra, Kerala and Andhra Pradesh, have introduced English language teaching in lower grades in government and private aided lower primary level schools. Government of Kerala has adopted a policy of having an English medium section, where the school has more than one section for a particular grade.

ROLE OF DIFFERENT AGENCIES AT SECONDARY LEVEL

The role and share of different education providers is much different in case of secondary education. Private participation in providing secondary education has a long tradition in India, dating back to pre-independence period. Secondary education was largely managed by the private agencies but was being funded by the government under grant-in-aid system. The basic philosophy behind the grant-in-aid system was to motivate the local effort and cooperation in managing secondary education. Over the years, state governments had increased the size of grants and financed almost all the expenditures of the private aided schools. Consequently, private managements have come to establish large number of institutions with corresponding number of teachers and students.

Table 3.2: Growth of Secondary Education Institutions by Type of Management in India

(in per cent)

Year	*Govt**	*Pvt Aided*	*PUA*	*Total (in Nos.)*
1973-74	37.4	57.0	5.6	
1980-81*	48.59	51.42	---	47972
1985-86	45.94	43.98	10.08	61638
1990-91	44.05	43.63	12.33	78678
1991-92	43.51	43.37	13.13	81470
1992-93	43.82	41.77	14.42	83490
1993-94	47.03	37.80	15.17	89226
1994-95	45.32	37.84	16.85	92774
1995-96	45.02	36.62	18.36	96952
1996-97	45.70	36.19	18.10	100205
2001-02**	42.45	33.99	23.56	133492
Growth Rates^ (1984-85 to 1996-97)	3.85	2.49	10.62	1.79

^ Growth Rate is calculated by fitting a semi-log linear regression equation of the form Y = a + bt.

* No separate information is available on private aided and unaided schools from 1980-81 to 84-85.

** Selected Educational Statistics

Note: Government* includes local body schools as Local Body schools are fully managed and funded by the state governments.

Source: Education in India Vol. 1 (S).

At the all India level, during 1973-74, the private aided secondary schools were the majority, the government was running a little more than one-third of secondary schools and the proportion of private unaided schools was trivial (see Table 3.2). During the last three decades, the percentage share of private aided schools declined sharply from 57 to 34 per cent, while the share of private unaided sector increased significantly, more than four times, the proportion of government schools registered a very marginal improvement. There has been a consistency in the substantial rise in the proportion of unaided schools, especially since mid-80s. These schools effectively filled the gap created by the decline in number of private aided schools. Thus by 2001-02, the private unaided sector had grown to cover nearly one-fourth of secondary schools. However, government with

42 per cent schools has replaced the private aided sector as the major player in delivering secondary education, followed by private aided sector with about one-third of total schools. This clearly reflects the dwindling state of private aided sector and to some extent government schools, as they had a growth rate of 2.5 and 3.85 per cent respectively. In contrast, private unaided schools grew at a rate of 10 per cent. It evidences the higher pace of growth of private unaided schools, particularly since late 80s. In other words, this changing trend suggests the inadequate investment of the government on secondary education, on the one hand, and the increasing participation of private sector on the other.

Along with changes in the proportions of schools under different managements, coverage of students in different managements had also changed significantly over the decades (see Figure 3.3).

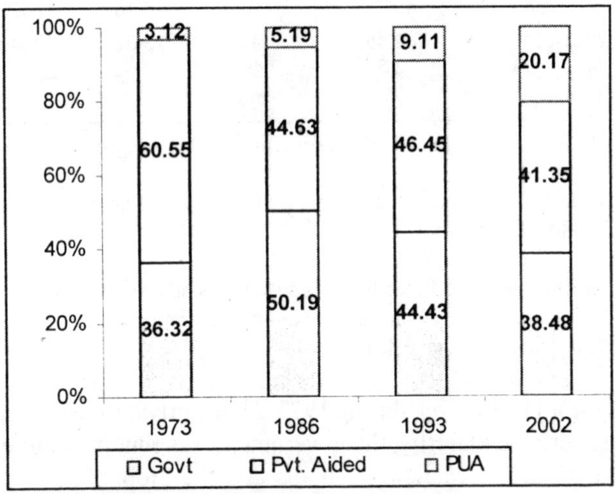

Figure 3.3: Growth of Enrolment at Secondary (Combined) Level by Types of Management in India

Source: AIESs, NCERT (1982; 1992; 1998, 2002), New Delhi

1. From early 70s to early 80s private aided schools dominated the enrolment scenario at secondary level with higher number of students.
2. From the mid-80s, government schools enrolled more students than any other management.
3. In the third phase, government and private aided schools

enjoyed equal share of enrolment and private unaided schools started gradually but significantly entering into the secondary education system.

4. From the past decade onwards, the share of enrolment has declined in the case of the government and private aided schools, while the enrolment in private unaided schools have increased and is growing rapidly.
5. However, compared to the share of private unaided schools (25%), their share enrolment (20%) is less.

Secondary Education Pre-Liberalization Phase

Provision of schools in general and secondary schools in particular, has undergone significant changes after 1990s. This can be due to *no grant-in aid* policy adopted by many states resulting in discontinuation of the practice of grant-in-aid to new schools. It could also be the consequence of liberalization and globalization that has resulted in larger private participation in the provision of education. In order to capture these policy dynamics, development in secondary education can be examined during the period 1986 and 1993, which may be referred as *pre-liberalisation phase,* and after 1993 which may be referred as *liberalisation phase.*

In this section, the interstate pattern in relation to the role of different managements in providing secondary education in pre-liberalization and post-liberalization periods has been analyzed. In federal structure states in India adopt different policies and programmes resulting in variations in providing secondary schools by different agencies.

During the period of 1986-93, the growth rate of lower secondary schools and enrolment under different managements varied widely among the major states. At the national level as well as among 17 major states of India, the growth rates of institutions and enrolment have followed an almost similar pattern, with private unaided schools showing higher growth rate. At all India level, the private aided schools had very insignificant growth rate (0.1%), private unaided school had the highest growth rate at 6.9 per cent, followed by government schools with 5 per cent. However, the growth rate of enrolment was higher in private aided sector compared to growth rate of institutions under this category. Interestingly, 11 states out of the 17 major states have witnessed a negative growth rate of private aided schools, even in these states that had a tradition of having large proportion of private aided schools (West Bengal, Gujarat, Tamil Nadu and Maharashtra). In contrast, most of these states have shown a positive growth rate of enrolment in private aided schools. The states where even the proportion of private aided schools was low have also experienced negative growth rate. However, in a few states where the growth rate was positive it was very marginal. This trend clearly indicates the effect of no grant-in-aid policy adopted by different states and also the less investment on secondary education by the states despite continued demand for government funded private schools.

Government schools though have a growth rate of 5 per cent at national level, it is quite uneven among the states. Except Orissa and Himachal Pradesh, all other states have shown positive growth rates. The states where the government is the major provider of lower secondary schools have slightly better than national growth rate. However, in economically and educationally backward states of Madhya Pradesh and Andhra Pradesh, the growth rate of government schools was more than double of national average. Similarly, the growth rate of enrolment among the government schools in these two states ranges between 0.32-7.8 per cent. Interestingly, in the states where the institutional growth rate has been higher have shown a lower enrolment growth rate and vice-versa.

This period has witnessed higher growth rate of private unaided school in some of the states. All major states except three, had shown a positive growth rate of private unaided schools. The growth rate ranged from 28.6 per cent to 1.7 per cent. The states where the base of private unaided schools was low, the high growth rate may be counted as superficial. But in states with sizeable percentage of private unaided schools, the higher growth rate depicts the increased role of private sector in secondary education.

In all the states, except two, there had been a positive growth rate of enrolment ranging from 27.42-1.42 per cent. Economically developed and educationally moderate states and also economically and educationally backward states have shown a higher demand for private unaided schools despite higher growth rate of government schools in these states. This may be attributed either to a growing disenchantment with the government schools and new found faith in private institutions. On the other hand, in some of the states (Punjab, Uttar Pradesh and Assam) the higher institutional growth has not been matched by the low demand, thus, depicting a trend of mushrooming growth of institutions and low base of private schools. But there are states (Tamil Nadu, Karnataka and Kerala), which are educationally developed states, have shown a consistency and compatibility in demand and supply of secondary education by private managements with a moderate improvement.

Scenario in Sample States

The four sample states with diverse patterns in terms of growth rate of institutions as well as enrolment, fall into different categories explained above. In Andhra Pradesh where the government is the major provider of schools is also the state that has witnessed the highest growth rate of government schools (10.9%). However, the growth rate of enrolment in these schools was quite low (3.31%) in comparison to institutional growth rate. Interestingly the state witnessed a marginal negative growth rate of private unaided schools (–1.7%) while the enrolment increased at the rate of 12.26 per cent which incidentally was highest among the sample states. This depicts the higher demand for private unaided schools and drifting of demand of government schools despite their increase. On the other hand, private aided schools showed a negative growth rate (–5.1 %) though the enrolment increased at the rate of 3.48 per cent. In Andhra Pradesh, though private aided schools were fewer and declining, the demand rather increased. However, the private aided schools in this state are much less in number. In Andhra Pradesh the growth of enrolment is very high, but on the supply side, there is a negative growth though it is very marginal.

In Kerala, the numbers of government schools and private unaided schools have increased with a growth rate of 7.6 per cent and 4.8 respectively, while private aided schools have declined with a negative growth rate of –7.9 per cent. In this context, it is interesting to note that in Kerala where government policy has been supportive of private aided sector, yet the schools in this sector have declined. Contrarily the enrolment in private aided sector has increased. At the same time, despite an increase in the government and private unaided schools, the enrolment has not risen correspondingly. The scenario indicates that during this phase the demand was largely met by the government and private aided sector and government was willing to invest in establishment of schools. This state falls in the category of that group of states where the private unaided schools are expanding as commercial ventures and increasing the internal competition to meet the limited demand.

Government schools at lower secondary level have witnessed a positive growth rate as well as enrolment in both Uttar Pradesh and Maharashtra. However, despite government school sector being small in these two states, the institutional and enrolment growth means realization of goals of equity by way establishing schools for girls and in backward areas. Unlike in other sample states, in Uttar Pradesh private aided schools have shown a marginal but positive growth rate in institutions and in enrolment. Though, economically and educationally backward state, Uttar Pradesh has experienced a very high growth rate of 20.8 per cent private unaided schools, and a growth rate of 8.1 per cent in enrolment.

Maharashtra, like other sample states, has the higher growth rate of government schools but low growth rate of enrolment. This can be attributed to the efforts of the government in increasing access to the children living in remote and backward areas. The state has witnessed a negative growth rate in private aided sector like Kerala while the enrolment has increased. It indicates the demand for the private aided schools and the subsequent pressure on existing schools in accommodating the higher demand. This could be attributed to the impact of no grant-in-aid policy of the government.

However, the growth rate of private unaided schools in the state has been most impressive with 8.1 per cent, while the enrolment was pegged at an increase of 4 per cent. In fact, both institutions and enrolment in this sector have grown faster than in the other two sectors. However, the higher growth rate of institutions suggests a kind of market driven growth of private unaided schools where the supply is higher than the demand. This higher supply meant fast growth of private unaided schools leading to increased competitiveness in this sector to meet demand even granting the benefit of restriction in admission to these schools.

The preceding discussion clearly indicates that despite the sample states belonging to different geographical, economic, social and political settings these display a similar pattern in terms of growth rate of institutions and enrolment at secondary level. All the states have shown a decline in the growth rate or very insignificant increase of private aided schools as well as increase in the enrolment. However, the degree of decline of institutions or increase of enrolment varies from state to state for different reasons.

In case of Uttar Pradesh and Maharashtra, this phenomenon could be attributed to the impact of no grant-in-aid policy of the respective governments. Similarly, the higher enrolment in these schools is related to the growing demand for and subsequent pressure on existing schools accommodating this higher demand. However, the increased enrolment in private aided schools could also have been influenced by the dynamics of the management of these schools in administrating enrolment in order to get sanction for more teachers' posts and other related benefits. In three of the sample states, private aided secondary schools are integrated with lower grades thus facilitating higher enrolment at higher grades.

Government schools have shown positive growth rate in all the sample states while the enrolment has not increased correspondingly. The reasons and the percentage of increase differs from one state to another behind such an increase. However, the differences in institutional growth and enrolment pattern in government schools need to be explained in view of equity measures undertaken by the government, particularly in improving the access to children living in backward and interior locations. However, in case of Kerala the changing demographic pattern is also responsible for lower growth rate of enrolment in government schools. In case of Andhra Pradesh, the mismatch between the institutions and enrolment depicts the drifting of students from government schools.

The private unaided schools in all the sample states, except Andhra Pradesh, have witnessed a positive yet differential growth rate. Enrolment in these schools has increased in all the states though it was not correspond with the growth rate of institutions. This shows that there has been mismatch between demand and supply of private unaided schools in all states. In fact, both institutions and enrolment in this sector have grown faster than the other two sectors. There are various reasons behind this trend which though differ from state to state. Both Kerala and Maharashtra have witnessed a higher institutional growth rate while the demand level had remained conspicuously low. These belong to a category of states where the private unaided schools are expanding as commercial ventures thereby increasing internal competition to meet the limited demand. This higher supply meant fast growth of private unaided schools leading to increased competitiveness among private unaided schools to meet demand even granting the benefit of restriction in admission to these schools.

In fact, the higher growth rate of institutions suggests a kind of market driven growth of private unaided schools where the supply is higher than the demand. In contrast to this trend Andhra Pradesh witnessed a marginal negative growth rate of private unaided schools while the enrolment increased phenomenally at 12.26 per cent which incidentally is highest among the sample states.

The trends of growth rate of institutions and enrolment between 1986 and 1993 have bought a corresponding change in the proportion of schools and enrolment under different managements. In other words, it indicates a change in the mechanism of demand and supply of educational provisions (see Annexure, Tables A4 and A5). The proportion of government schools in lower secondary level varied from 94.6 to 9.1 per cent covering an enrolment of 89.2 to 3.4 per cent across the major states. But the number of government schools was highest in 10 of the larger states, including one of the sample states. The private aided schools ranged among major states, from 88 to 3.4 per cent covering similar range of enrolment. However, the proportion of private aided schools and their coverage of enrolment were higher in some of the larger states, including three of the sample states. During this phase, the proportion of private unaided schools at lower secondary level was 16 per cent, covering an enrolment share of only 8 per cent at national level, though it varied extensively ranging from 37.9 to 0.8 per cent among larger states The considerable presence of private unaided schools, however, cuts across the levels of economic and educational development of states though these are in higher proportion in some of the larger and socio-economically less developed states, including some of the sample states.

This pattern shows the participation of different sectors in providing secondary education. While the proportion of government schools corresponded to the coverage of enrolment with the exception of a few states, the private aided schools had more percentage share of students than the share of these schools as a consequence of the negative growth rate. Nevertheless, private unaided schools had covered less proportion of students compared to their percentage share of schools. Thus, while government and government aided schools covered larger segment of the students the private unaided schools in pre-liberalization period were obviously serving a small section of students providing differential education (Varghese, 1993).

Expansion and Participation at Higher Secondary Level

At the higher secondary level the growth rate of institutions and enrolment among all the three managements was higher than at the lower secondary level at the national scale (see Annexure, Tables A6 to A9). The difference between private unaided, government and private aided has been much higher than that of lower secondary level. Except one state all other states have shown a positive growth rate of private aided schools ranging from 29.2 to 1.3. The growth of enrolment is less than the institutional growth rate on the other hand. It has been in fact negative in five states, quite unlike at the lower secondary level. In most of the states where private aided schools are predominant, the demand in terms of enrolment is showing a declining trend irrespective of higher institutional growth which is quite different from lower secondary level.

As far as government schools are concerned, all the states have shown positive growth rate ranging from 50.0 per cent to 1.6 per cent. Some of the states where government has dominated in provisioning of secondary schools have shown a stabilized growth rate. The growth rate of enrolment was nearly double the institutional growth rate at the national level which is also the case in some of the states.

The growth rate of private unaided schools at higher secondary level has not only been exceedingly higher than the lower secondary level but also was three times more than the growth rate of government schools. The growth rate ranged between 50.5 and 1.5 with most states showing positive growth rate, except one. The interesting point is that most of the educationally and economically backward states have shown an unusually high growth rate. Correspondingly, the enrolment growth rate has been lower than the institutional growth rate though there is a marginal difference. There are some states where the institutional and enrolment growth rates matched with each other showing a degree of compatibility between demand and supply. Interestingly, these are economically and educationally backward states. The second category of states have lower institutional growth rate and higher enrolment growth rate. This trend can be found in some of the industrially developed states. The third category includes a set of states which have higher institutional growth rate and lower enrolment growth rate.

There are some states where high enrolment growth has been high in all types of management schools showing increasing participation. However, institutional growth does not correspond to the demand. In some other states a different trend is found. In these states, enrolment is higher in private unaided sector also higher institutional growth rate, thus showing that the demand corresponded with the supply. The third category is of these states where there has been low institutional growth rate but higher enrolment growth rate.

Among the four sample states, the growth of higher secondary schools and enrolment shows interesting trend. Institutions under different managements showed increased growth rate in all the four states, though it varied among the states and the managements. Enrolment in the government schools has a positive growth rate among all states though with varying degree. Kerala has the highest growth rate while Andhra Pradesh showed the lowest growth rate. In all the states except Andhra Pradesh, private aided schools have depicted a negative growth rate of enrolment. Contrary to this except Maharashtra, other three states showed increased growth rate of enrolment in private unaided schools. There is mixed trend as far as the growth rate of higher secondary schools is concerned. Uttar Pradesh and Andhra Pradesh displayed higher propensity towards private unaided schools while Kerala showed an insignificant growth rate in this regard. However, in case of Kerala it was time for de-linking higher secondary grades from the higher education and in this process government took a larger responsibility. Further, science stream was available in government schools thus ensuring a higher growth rate of enrolment.

However, among major states, during 1993, the proportion of government schools ranged between 98.5 and 8.2 per cent with enrolment coverage between 97.6 per cent and 9.4 per cent as the highest and lowest. The proportion of private aided schools varied from 88 per cent to 3.8 per cent, covering similar percentage of students. In some of the larger states there was a higher demand for private aided schools irrespective of their proportion both at lower and higher secondary levels. It is interesting to note that despite this kind of demand, the proportion of private aided schools showed a declining trend in some of the states. The situation is starkly different when we examine private unaided schools at the higher secondary level; they constituted 12.6 per cent of schools with coverage of 10.2 per cent in enrolment. In almost all the major states, the proportion of enrolment in private unaided schools was lower than their percentage share in the number of schools (see Annexure, Table A4 and A5).

Table 3.3: Percentage of Schools and Enrolment by Types of Management in Sample States in 1986 and 1993

States	Lower Secondary Schools						Higher Secondary Schools					
	Schools (%)			Enrolment (%)			Schools (%)			Enrolment (%)		
	Govt.	PA	PUA	Govt.	PA	PUA	Govt.	PA	PUA	Govt.	PA	PUA
1986												
A.P.	54.89	22.66	22.45	76.49	16.39	7.12	65.94	25.46	8.60	78.00	5.84	16.16
Kerala	38.89	57.09	4.02	39.80	57.36	2.85	65.48	17.86	16.67	45.25	46.87	7.87
Maharashtra	11.08	60.15	28.77	14.47	73.72	11.81	10.64	82.92	6.44	5.45	87.39	7.16
Uttar Pradesh	19.80	65.07	15.13	11.50	82.25	6.25	16.57	82.12	1.30	13.51	85.62	0.86
India	43.48	43.86	12.66	43.30	50.19	6.51	41.69	52.36	5.96	33.38	61.30	5.31
1993												
A.P.	76.05	10.56	13.39	72.3	15.7	12.0	37.46	16.33	46.21	46.0	23.2	30.8
Kerala	36.14	58.60	5.26	41.7	55.9	2.4	74.58	18.31	7.12	73.4	21.3	5.4
Maharashtra	10.64	56.76	32.60	10.9	77.7	11.4	10.20	84.15	5.65	8.4	87.7	4.0
Uttar Pradesh	29.37	47.49	23.13	13.6	77.2	9.2	18.88	75.23	5.89	15.6	79.2	5.3
India	48.75	35.17	16.08	45.2	46.0	8.7	42.37	44.99	12.64	42.2	47.6	10.2

Source: Fifth and Sixth All India Educational Survey, 1986; 1993, NCERT, New Delhi.

The four sample states showed varied picture in terms of proportion of schools and enrolment under different managements (see Table 3.3). In the educationally progressive state of Kerala, different agencies played equally important role in providing lower secondary schools. Unlike either national figures or other states, the state of Kerala had the distinction of majority of schools under private aided management, yet more than one-third of schools were being operated by government directly and a small per cent of private unaided schools coexisted. However, in terms of coverage of students, government schools were preferred more with proportionately higher share of enrolments, it was contrary in private aided schools. Nonetheless, private unaided schools had much lesser percentage share of students compared to their share of schools. This pattern was almost similar during 1986 as well, except a marginal decline in terms of share of government schools and a marginal increase in the share of enrolment in these schools.

Unlike at the lower secondary level, the higher secondary education presented a different scenario. Three-fourths of schools were under government management; these covered equal proportion of students; a little less than one-fifth of schools were under private aided sector; these covered more than 21 per cent of students and a mere 7 per cent private unaided management schools covered 5 per cent student enrolment. This was a substantial improvement from the 1986 share in case of government schools and enrolment therein, and a drastic decline in the share of private unaided schools. This is mainly due to the process of de-linking of higher secondary education during nineties from higher education, as the state government undertook major responsibility to provide schooling until the de-linking process got consolidated. The percentage coverage of students more or less corresponded with the extent of schools under different managements though there was a slight variation in case of private aided and unaided schools.

Industrially and economically advanced state of Maharashtra displayed a different scenario. While at lower secondary level, the private aided schools constituted more than half of the total schools, and they covered more than three-fourth of students at this level, which is a much better enrolment in private aided schools compared to 1986. Although about one-third of lower secondary schools in the state were managed by private unaided sector, they enrolled only a little more than one-tenth of students, thereby indicating that private unaided schools were largely serving the selected few and especially covering urban localities; the picture was almost similar during 1986. The state had a very small proportion (one-tenth) of lower secondary schools and an equal proportion of students under the direct government management, which was a little higher during 1986. These schools are either under municipalities or local bodies. At higher secondary level not only a high majority of schools were provided by the private aided system but also most of the students were covered by it, which was an improvement over 1986. Government schools constituted one-tenth at higher secondary level with student coverage of less than the proportion of schools during 1986 as well as 1993. Private unaided schools were a little above 5 per cent but covered 4 per cent of students at this level. This share of private unaided schools was 6 per cent in 1986 and the enrolled 7 per cent students. The picture of secondary education in Maharashtra displays a few unique features in that the secondary education was by and large funded by government, where private bodies played a vital role in meeting the demand by owning responsibility of managing most of these schools. Private unaided sector played very negligible role with limited enrolment.

The state of Uttar Pradesh presented an interesting and different picture in the provision of secondary schools and coverage of students under different management types during nineties. At lower secondary level, while government directly managed about 29 per cent of schools but covered only 13.6 per cent of students. These figures were 19.8 per cent and 15.13 per cent respectively in 1986. The private-aided schools constituted 47.5 per cent, but they covered a large majority, i.e., 77 per cent of students. This proportion of private aided schools drastically declined from 1986, and constituted 65 per cent schools and above 80 per cent enrolment. The private unaided sector had a share of 23.13 per cent of schools, enrolling a little less than one-tenth of students at lower secondary level. This was a substantial improvement over 1986. Even then, private aided schools were highly crowded, while government schools had very less coverage of students when compared to their percentage share. Private unaided schools were not only fewer, but also their coverage of students was very small. At higher secondary level, the situation was quite different from that of lower secondary. A high majority of schools were under the private aided sector serving a corresponding high percentage of students. The government schools constituted less than one-fifth of the total schools and covered a small segment of enrolment. Compared to lower secondary level, unaided schools at higher secondary were a few in numbers, covering a small percentage of enrolment; which was still less during 1986.

In Andhra Pradesh, unlike the other three sample states, the state government (including local bodies) was the major provider of lower secondary education by directly managing more than three-fourths of lower secondary schools and covering nearly a similar proportion of students. The state had only 10 per cent of private aided schools, enrolling 15 per cent of students. Similarly, private unaided schools constituted 13 per cent with 12 per cent of enrolment at lower secondary level. The share of private unaided schools had declines from 22.45 per cent in 1986 to 13.4 per cent in 1993. But in higher secondary, the private unaided sector increased five-times during the same period. And hence, private unaided sector had higher proportion of schools than government schools, but covered large percentage of students than private unaided schools. Though private aided schools were 16 per cent, they covered a little less than one-fourth of students at higher secondary level in the state.

The national trend observed from Table 3.2 and Figure 3.3 almost holds good for all the four sample states. Though the provision of secondary schools by different agencies and their coverage of students had some common pattern, yet they differed among four sample states. The general characteristics among all the four sample states were that the private unaided schools constituted small proportion covering a minute segment of enrolment. However, their extent varied among the four states. While educationally developed state Kerala had the lowest percentage of private unaided schools and enrolment, the economically developed Maharashtra had higher percentage of unaided lower secondary schools, closely followed by the most underdeveloped Uttar Pradesh. In both these states, large percentage of schools and students at secondary level was under private aided sector. However, while in Maharashtra the proportion of private aided schools and their enrolment corresponded, in case of Uttar Pradesh the proportion of enrolment was much higher than the proportion of private aided schools, indicating crowded and large size of schools. In Uttar Pradesh, the enrolment in government schools was much less compared to the proportion of schools. This might be either due to more accessibility to private aided schools or limited access and restricted admissions to government schools in the state.

At higher secondary level, Maharashtra and Uttar Pradesh had majority of schools and enrolment under private aided management, whereas in Kerala and Andhra Pradesh, government schools and enrolment in them constituted larger percentage. However, except Andhra Pradesh, in all the three sample states private unaided schools and their enrolment coverage was very small and less than the national average at higher secondary level. Interestingly, educationally developed Kerala had different pattern compared to the other three sample states. In Kerala, government and private aided sectors played important role at lower secondary level, the government was major provider at higher secondary level. And at both the levels, private unaided schools and their enrolment was very insignificant. It was the policy of the state government (KER Act-1956) that ensured a larger role for the government, reflected in its proportion of schools and their enrolment at higher secondary during nineties. Contrary to the other states, in Andhra Pradesh the government was the major provider of lower secondary education with a small proportion of private aided and unaided schools. But at higher secondary level, the state had more inclination towards private unaided schools, followed by government schools.

Secondary Education Scenario: Liberalization Phase

The above discussion presented a scenario that made a break with the past and displayed a changed vision for the future. It did highlight the efforts on educational expansion and new directions in educational development by different types of management..This situation was the result of the various policies and programmes of state governments and also the National Policy on Education, 1986. It was important to underline this aspect because it provided a background to capture the entirety of educational development in the light of events that unfolded in the 1990s.

Following the introduction of macro economic policies that included stabilization and structural adjustment policies, a fiscal squeeze was experienced in all social sector investments in many developing countries, including India in the beginning of 1990s. As a follow-up of the economic reform packages, expenditure compression trickled down to public expenditure on education. As a result, many state governments not only refrained from opening new schools but also discouraged the practice of grant-in-aid. New economic policy consisting of Structural Adjustment Programme (SAP), liberalization, globalization of economy and opening of markets not only affected the economy but also the society in general and education in particular. These new policies brought with them improved access and choices for consumers, a higher level of income that resulted in burgeoning of middle class with enhanced purchasing power. The consumer choice and enhanced income level coupled with state polices on 'no-grant-in-aid' and declined investment on secondary education led to the growth of private unaided sector of education. This expansion was not limited only to urban areas but spread into rural areas as well (see Table 3.4).

Table 3.4: Per cent of Enrolment in Different Management Types Secondary and Higher Secondary Schools by Rural and Urban Regions in India in 1993 and 2002

	1993			*2002*		
	Rural	*Urban*	*Total*	*Rural*	*Urban*	*Total*
			Secondary			
Govt.	47.74	37.63	43.30	45.93	31.19	39.68
Private Aided	48.18	52.76	50.19	38.11	42.49	39.97
Private Unaided	4.09	9.61	6.51	15.95	26.32	20.35
			Higher Secondary			
Govt.	29.54	35.72	33.38	38.19	34.85	36.18
Private Aided	68.45	56.95	61.30	45.15	43.22	43.99
Private Unaided	2.01	7.33	5.31	16.66	21.93	19.83

Source: 6th and 7th AIES, NCERT, 1993 and 2002.

There has been a marginal decline in the proportion of enrolment in government secondary schools both in rural and urban areas and more so in case of urban areas during the period of 1993-2002. However, the decline has been more noticeable in case of private aided schools both in rural and urban area (10%) and interestingly the rate of decline has been the same for both these locations. In contrast to this, the proportion of enrolment in private unaided schools has increased almost 4 times in rural areas and 3 times in urban areas during the same period. In other words, the gap created by the declining enrolment rate of government and private aided schools has been effectively bridged by the increase in the proportion of enrolment in private unaided schools both in rural and urban areas. This clearly indicates that though there has been an overall increase in the demand for secondary education, the demand has been more conspicuous in case of private unaided sector. The demand for private unaided sector has increased both in rural and urban areas but the rate has been faster in rural areas though in absolute terms there is a substantial difference between the two localities so far as their demand levels are concerned. In the context of higher secondary education, there has been an increase in the proportion of enrolment of government schools in rural areas while this has declined marginally in urban areas. However, there has been a significant decrease in the proportion of enrolment of private aided schools both in rural and urban areas and especially in rural areas. This decline in the enrolment proportion of government and private aided schools have been adequately filled by the sharp rise in the percentage share of enrolment in private unaided schools during this decade. In fact, there has been a huge 8 times increase in the percentage share of enrolment in private unaided schools in rural areas and three times in case of urban areas. In other words there has been a heavy demand for private unaided schools both in rural and urban areas and especially in rural areas during this period which can be attributed to low enrolment base of private unaided schools in rural areas. This highlights the universal demand for private unaided schools and the fast changing scenario of demand for secondary education.

Gender and Social Equity: Perspective in Demand

In the event of such significant and rapid changes in the demand for secondary education and the role played by different managements, it is pertinent to examine the impact of this change on gender and social equity. In other words the pertinent question would be: Does the changing scenario of provision of schools by different managements effect at gender and social group level. An attempt is made to examine the extent of enrolment of boys and girls (rural-urban) among different management schools.

From the Table 3.5, we find that the proportion of enrolment of girls and boys in 2002 was at the same level among different management schools both in rural and urban areas. Interestingly, similar trend exists at lower and higher secondary levels.

Table 3.5: Enrolment of Boys and Girls among Different Management Schools in India in 2002

Type of Management	*Rural*			*Urban*			*Total*		
	Boys	*Girls*	*Total*	*Boys*	*Girls*	*Total*	*Boys*	*Girls*	*Total*
				Secondary					
Government	45.6	46.5	45.9	29.4	33.3	31.2	39.1	40.5	39.7
Private Aided	37.4	39.2	38.1	42.4	42.6	42.5	39.4	40.7	40.0
Private Unaided	17.0	14.3	16.0	28.1	24.1	26.3	21.4	18.8	20.3
Total	100	100	100	100	100	100	100	100	100
				Higher Secondary					
Government	39.3	36.5	38.2	34.9	34.8	34.8	36.7	35.4	36.2
Private Aided	44.0	46.9	45.1	42.7	44.0	43.2	43.2	45.1	44.0
Private Unaided	16.7	16.6	16.7	22.4	21.2	21.9	20.1	19.5	19.8
Total	100	100	100	100	100	100	100	100	100

Source: 7th Survey.

It has been observed that there has been a decline in the enrolment percentage of boys in government secondary schools in rural areas and a marginal increase in the enrolment of girls. This means that there has been a demand for government schools in rural areas at least among girls. The enrolment in private aided schools has seen negative growth rate equally among both boys and girls in rural areas (see Table 3.6).

Table 3.6: Per cent Increase/Decrease (1993–2002) of Enrolment

Management Type	*Rural*			*Urban*			*Total*		
	Boys	*Girls*	*Total*	*Boys*	*Girls*	*Total*	*Boys*	*Girls*	*Total*
				Secondary					
Government	-2.7	0.3	-1.8	-7.8	-4.9	-6.4	-4.7	-1.7	-3.6
Private Aided	-10.4	-9.9	-10.1	-10.6	-9.8	-10.3	-10.5	-10.0	-10.2
Private Unaided	13.1	9.6	11.9	18.4	14.7	16.7	15.2	11.7	13.8
				Higher Secondary					
Government	9.8	6.8	8.6	-1.1	-0.3	-0.9	3.4	1.9	2.8
Private Aided	-24.5	-21.1	-23.3	-14.5	-12.5	-13.7	-18.7	-14.9	-17.3
Private Unaided	14.8	14.3	14.7	15.7	12.9	14.6	15.3	13.0	14.5

Source: 6th and 7th AIES, NCERT, 1993 and 2002.

On the other hand, the enrolment proportion of both boys and girls has increased rather significantly in private unaided school though rate was slightly higher for boys In urban areas, both government and private aided schools have shown a decline in the proportion of enrolment of both boys and girls in comparison to the previous decade. This decline in enrolment is more in case of boys than of girls. Similar to rural areas, the urban areas have also noticed the improvement of enrolment share of both boys and girls in private unaided schools. In fact, both these areas show a degree of similarity in the context of declining enrolment of boys and girls in private aided schools and increased enrolment growth rate in private unaided schools. The trend shows that there has been a demand for private unaided schools in both rural and urban areas though demand is more among the boys. In rural areas government schools have some demand among girls while in urban areas and among boys, government schools have lost their appeal. Universally private aided schools are losing their ground i.e. both in terms of location and gender. Unlike at the lower secondary level, there is some variation at the higher secondary level as far as enrolment in concerned. For example, the government schools have a positive growth rate of enrolment of boys and girls in rural areas when compared to the last decade. However, the private aided schools have witnessed a higher negative growth rate in the enrolment of both boys and girls which is though slightly higher for boys than girls. The private unaided schools have been in demand for both the genders with almost identical margin, thereby showing a rare match in demand levels by opposite sexes. In urban areas however, the government schools have witnessed a decline in enrolment growth rate of both boys and girls and marginally more in case of boys. The decline in growth rate of enrolment has been quite high in case of private aided schools with more boys preferring to join elsewhere. The losses of government and private aided schools have been translated into gain for private unaided schools. These schools have shown significant increase in the overall percentage share of enrolment and slightly higher percentage share in case of boys. This trend highlights the demand of government schools in rural areas both among boys and girls. It also states the growing demand of private unaided school in both locations and its popularity among boys and girls.

The difference in the demand for government schools in lower and higher secondary levels need explanation. The performance of government schools at higher secondary level has been better in comparison to lower secondary schools. More importantly at higher secondary level, there are some streams which are available only in government schools. The students seeking admission in higher secondary schools are often guided by the condition of availability of subjects and marks secured by them at lower secondary level and this in turns acts as an advantage for government schools.

In a stratified society like India, it is common assumption that social hierarchy exists in accessing education and especially to different type of schools. We have examined the extent of participation of scheduled castes and scheduled tribes in different management schools and the changes in their participation during last decade. Majority of scheduled caste students at secondary and higher secondary levels are enrolled in government and private aided schools more so in rural areas. Their percentage of enrolment in private unaided schools is lower in rural areas compared to urban areas. However, the difference between scheduled castes, schedule tribes and others is very low in rural areas. During 2001-02 in the urban areas, more than one-fourth of scheduled castes and one-third of the scheduled tribe students were enrolled in private unaided schools at lower secondary level as against 41 per cent of all communities. At higher secondary level the percentage share of enrolment of scheduled castes and scheduled tribes is much lower than other communities especially low in rural areas (Tables 3.7 and 3.8).

Table 3.7: Share of Enrolment by Social Groups and by Type of Management in Secondary and Higher Secondary Schools by Rural and Urban Regions in India in 2002

Region	*Type of Management*	*Secondary*			*Higher Secondary*		
		All	*SC*	*ST*	*All*	*SC*	*ST*
Rural	Government	50.36	53.54	58.26	37.53	41.45	55.02
	Private Aided	34.57	35.14	29.32	48.84	47.85	38.99
	Private Unaided	15.07	11.32	12.42	13.64	10.70	5.99
	Total	100	100	100	100	100	100
Urban	Government	23.74	32.85	30.62	29.31	41.19	46.94
	Private Aided	35.30	40.18	34.98	41.67	44.35	32.00
	Private Unaided	40.96	26.97	34.40	29.01	14.46	21.06
	Total	100	100	100	100	100	100
Total	Government	40.55	47.26	52.20	33.13	41.33	52.20
	Private Aided	34.84	36.67	30.56	45.00	46.28	36.55
	Private Unaided	24.60	16.07	17.24	21.87	12.40	11.25
	Total	100	100	100	100	100	100

Source: 7th Survey.

Table 3.8: Increase/Decrease in Percentage Points from 2002 over 1993 of Enrolment by Social Groups and by Type of Management in Secondary and Higher Secondary Schools by Rural and Urban Regions in India

Regions	*Type of Mgt*	*Secondary*			*Higher Secondary*		
		All	*SC*	*ST*	*All*	*SC*	*ST*
Rural	Government	-0.50	1.11	1.55	-6.29	-5.24	5.55
	Private Aided	-8.35	-6.12	-7.85	1.97	3.67	-5.20
	Private Unaided	8.85	5.00	6.30	4.32	1.56	-0.35
Urban	Government	-14.54	-11.81	-19.50	-11.90	-6.16	-7.48
	Private Aided	-14.60	-7.68	-3.93	-6.34	-1.43	-5.34
	Private Unaided	29.14	19.49	23.44	18.24	7.59	12.82
Total	Government	-4.68	-2.04	0.77	-9.08	-5.73	0.77
	Private Aided	-11.20	-7.24	-10.91	-2.57	1.20	-4.93
	Private Unaided	15.88	9.28	10.15	11.65	4.53	4.16

Source: 6th and 7th AIES, NCERT, 1993 and 2002.

Compared to earlier decades, during 1993-2002 the enrolment of both scheduled castes and scheduled tribes at secondary level in government schools has declined like that in case of general castes. However, this decline is limited to only urban areas and in rural areas the proportion of enrolment has rather increased though marginal. In case of private unaided schools, the proportion of enrolment of scheduled castes and scheduled tribe communities has increased. This shows that demand for different types of schools among disadvantaged communities follows the same trend as for general community both in rural and urban areas though at a lower level. However, the similarity is more in case of urban localities than rural habitations. This is probably due to the ability to pay, increased access, awareness and more importantly they belong to a category of second generation learners.

Inter-state Level

The process of liberalization has influenced the socio-economic development of states. Since states in India differ from each other on various accounts, it is important to examine the fast changing role of different managements in the era of educational changes of such magnitude at state level. An attempt has been made in this section to map this interstate dynamics on the basis of demand and supply as well the role of agencies responsible for educational provisioning.

Compared to the previous decade, the growth rate of government schools at lower secondary level has declined. Both government and private aided schools have shown similar growth rate between 1993 and 2002 (Table 3.9). However, in case of government schools, the growth rate has declined to half while for the private aided sector, there was a marginal improvement. Private unaided schools have grown by 9.2 per cent. The growth rate was not only higher than that of previous decade but also it was nearly four times of the growth rate of government schools (2.5%) and private aided schools (2.3%) (see Annexure, Table A10). This period is marked by unprecedented growth rate of private unaided schools in most of the states. This growth rate was not only higher than the previous decade at national level but same trend is found in many states as well. Some states have shown sudden rise of private unaided schools while others have maintained a steady trend. However, the state of Bihar, which had a significant share of private unaided sector, has shown a remarkable decrease (–14.9) which can be attributed to the nationalisation of schools by the government.

At the higher secondary level, the growth rate of private unaided sector was double than the growth rate of other two categories of schools at all India level. However it witnessed a decline in the growth rate during 1993-2001 compared to the earlier decade. On the other hand, the growth rate of private aided schools has increased marginally during the same period with interstate variations ranging between 4.6 per cent in Uttar Pradesh and 1.1 per cent in Kerala.

Table 3.9: Growth Rate of Institutions at Secondary Level Between 1993 and 2001-02 in Sample States in India

	Lower Secondary				*Higher Secondary*			
States	*Govt.*	*PA*	*PUA*	*Total*	*Govt.*	*PA*	*PUA*	*Total*
Andhra Pradesh	3.9	2.2	14.4	5.7	4.3	4.0	12.9	8.9
Kerala	2.5	1.1	15.0	2.8	13.7	31.5	24.9	19.7
Maharashtra	-0.5	4.0	-0.5	2.2	-38.4	6.6	8.8	-16.7
Uttar Pradesh	-10.0	4.6	8.2	2.9	-9.3	4.4	11.5	3.3
India	2.5	2.3	9.2	3.8	5.9	5.4	11.7	6.6

Source: (i) All India Educational Survey, 1993, NCERT, New Delhi.

(ii) Selected Educational Statistics, 2001-02, MHRD, Govt of India.

At higher secondary level, the four states present different growth rates of institutions under different managements. Kerala has the highest growth rate of higher secondary schools in all the management categories. In this state, private aided schools continued to grow as in the previous decade (31.5%) while private unaided schools grew at the rate of 25 per cent which was four times higher than the previous decade (see Annexure, Table A11). However, the government schools also expanded and showed increased growth rate during the same period. The state of Maharashtra showed a steep decline in the growth rate of government schools but increased growth rate in case of private aided schools while maintaining the same rate of growth (8%) in case of private unaided school. Like Maharashtra, Uttar Pradesh also showed a declining rate of government schools but an increased rate of 4 per cent in private aided schools. In the same state private unaided schools grew at a rate of 11.5 per cent, which is considerably lower than that in the past decade. The state of Andhra Pradesh, while showing significant increase in the private unaided schools (12.9%), depicted a comparatively low growth rate of government schools (4.3%) when compared with the earlier period. However, the same period has seen an increase in the percentage of private aided schools. The improved growth rate of private aided schools in Maharashtra and Uttar Pradesh is the result of clearing of the backlog of private schools to be taken over by the government. As discussed earlier, the higher enrolment growth is Kerala can be linked to the process of de-linking of secondary schools, demand for science streams and the market driven approach towards education.

The decade of 1993-2002 witnessed changes in the percentage share of schools under different managements at all India level. Importantly, during this phase bilateral and multi-lateral donor agencies, along with state governments, invested in improving the access and quality of elementary education. Similarly, the nutritional support system of the government at primary level too helped in increasing the base of primary education. In the light of these changes and interventions, it can be assumed that the increased base of elementary education combined with the economic benefits, created an additional demand for secondary education. In this context, there was differential growth rate of institutions under government, private aided and private unaided sectors. Though there has been considerable expansion of the system both at lower and higher secondary levels, this was not reflected in the share of government and private aided schools, especially at lower secondary level as both have declined at least by 5 percentage points at all India level. The decline in the percentage share of government and private aided schools, however, varied among the states. Similarly, the proportion of private unaided schools increased in many of the states, the increase ranging from 59.2 per cent as the highest to 0.2 per cent as the lowest (see Annexure, Table A12).

In the period of 1993-2002, 14 out of 17 major states, have shown marginal to significant decline in the share of both government and private aided schools at lower secondary level. Interestingly, states, which had traditionally supported private aided schools, witnessed a sharp decline (see Annexure, Table A13). Though there was a general decline of government and private aided schools, only in three states a marginal increase in their share could be found which was largely due to the dynamics of interplay between the government and private aided sector. In the meanwhile, the private unaided sector continued to increase its share, often rapidly and significantly in some of the states. As a result of this change, there were 9 states where government schools had higher share and in seven other states private aided sector had the major proportion while in one state the private unaided schools constituted majority. Interestingly, higher proportion of private unaided schools is more conspicuous in educationally and economically backward states along with a few developed states (see Annexure, Table A11).

The states can be divided into three different categories on the basis of domination of secondary schools managed by different agencies. The first level consists of the states where the lower secondary and higher secondary are under complete control and management of the state (e.g. Bihar, Orissa Punjab, Himachal Pradesh, Haryana, Assam, Jammu and Kashmir, Tamil Nadu, Rajasthan, and Andhra Pradesh), though the state of Andhra Pradesh has majority of government schools only at lower secondary level. The second category comprises states where the schools are established and managed by private bodies but funded through grant-in-aid system by the governments. In this list, along with the three sample states i.e. Maharashtra, Uttar Pradesh and Kerala, some other states like West Bengal and Gujarat too have similar pattern. However, Kerala has a mix of both government and private aided schools and also is unique in the sense that it has considerable proportion of higher secondary and more than one-third of lower secondary schools managed by the state government itself. The third type consists of states which have higher proportion of private unaided school than the other management types; this trend is observed in Madhya Pradesh both at lower and higher secondary levels whereas in Andhra Pradesh, this trend is seen only at higher secondary level. Some other states have shown a propensity towards this trend with more than one-third of secondary schools being unaided and under private management, which can be attributed to the liberalization phenomenon. The states falling under different categories cut across differential levels of educational and economic development.

While economically and educationally backward states present varied scenario in terms of extent of provision of secondary schools by different agencies, several factors explain the mixed trends. The state's policy, economic condition, social demand, political dynamics etc. need to be considered as possible reasons for such a scenario. It is worth noting that some of the backward states have adopted a conscious policy of nationalizing secondary schools by withdrawing grant-in-aid to privately managed schools on the pretext of quality control. Contrary to this, in some less developed states, private unaided sector was encouraged to meet the emerging demand for secondary education as a policy of the state. In case of sample states, Uttar Pradesh showed a higher preference towards private unaided sector in the last few years. Growing influence of private sector in providing schooling facilities on the one hand and on the other the fast receding grant-in-aid system, exemplified by the dwindling number of private aided schools, found in many states, except a few states. In all the states, except Maharashtra, there has been a perceptible increase in the share of private unaided sector's involvement in secondary education. The percentage of increase in unaided schools varies among states.

Table 3.10: Percentage of Secondary Schools by Type of Management in Sample States in 2001-02

State	*Lower Secondary*			*Higher Secondary*		
	Govt	*PA*	*PUA*	*Govt*	*PA*	*PUA*
Andhra Pradesh	65.0	7.8	27.2	25.4	10.8	63.9
Kerala	35.2	50.5	14.4	46.9	42.7	10.4
Maharashtra	8.3	66.2	25.5	5.9	87.5	6.6
Uttar Pradesh	8.8	54.8	36.4	5.8	82.5	11.7
India	43.5	30.9	25.5	40.1	40.7	19.3

Source: Selected Educational Statistics 2001-2002, MHRD, GOI, New Delhi, 2003.

At lower secondary level, there has been change in many states especially among the four sample states in the extent of provision of schools by different agencies.

Educationally and economically advanced Maharashtra shows different scenario compared to other three sample states. In this state nearly 75 per cent of lower secondary schools and 93 per cent of higher secondary schools are funded by the government although majority of them are in private aided sector (Table 3.10). The proportion of private unaided schools in this state at lower secondary level has declined while at the higher secondary level it maintained the similar proportion.

Though the state followed a time bound policy and discouraged grant-in-aid system, the percentage share of private aided schools had increased and proportion of private unaided schools has declined marginally at lower secondary level. However, this phenomenon was not due to proactive policy of state government to invest in lower secondary education and supporting private aided schools. Rather the state government was striving to cover backlog of large number of schools established by private agencies prior to 1987 under grant-in-aid system despite fiscal constraints. As such the state adopted a policy of according permission to private bodies to establish secondary schools with a condition of permanent no grant-in-aid, besides no opening of any new schools by the government. As a result the proportion of government schools had declined marginally during the same period in Maharashtra.

In Kerala, while the proportion of private aided and government schools had reduced marginally, the percentage share of private unaided schools had increased almost three times at lower secondary level during post liberalisation period. However, the share of private unaided schools in Kerala still continues to be a small segment. At higher secondary level the proportion of private aided schools has increased rather steeply and the proportion of government schools have declined. At the initial phase of de-linking process during early 90s, the government took the major responsibility of operating the higher secondary schools itself as the private aided schools lacked infrastructure. However, from mid-90s onwards as the private aided schools added up infrastructure, and the government encouraged private bodies to run the schools with grant-in-aid support, especially after completion of the process of de-linking of higher secondary education. The same period saw a marginal increase in the percentage share of private unaided schools. In the state more or less equal proportion of schools are managed by the government and the private aided sector. In case of Kerala, it can be said that despite the effects of liberalization the government continues to play a major role in provisioning of secondary education.

In Uttar Pradesh, while the proportion of government schools at lower secondary level had declined steeply, the percentage of private aided and unaided schools had increased during the same period. At higher secondary level also, the percentage of government schools had declined, but the share of private aided schools had grown, though marginally. However, Uttar Pradesh showed more inclination towards private unaided schools as its proportion has doubled. Despite this change, the government continues to be the major provider of higher secondary education either directly or through grant-in-aid (90%).

The state of Andhra Pradesh witnessed a decline in the proportion of government and private aided schools and an increase in the percentage share of the private unaided schools both at lower and higher secondary level. In fact, the proportion of government schools declined rather sharply during this period. However, the proportion of private unaided schools has increased at both levels in general and especially at higher secondary level (63.9%). While at lower secondary level, the state government continues to share major responsibility of meeting the demand but at higher secondary level the government takes care of the demand partially. This has increased the scope for private unaided sector in meeting the emerging demand.

The four sample states, standing as they do at differential levels of educational and economic development represent different scenarios in terms of providing schools by different agencies during the last decade. While Maharashtra and Uttar Pradesh belong to the second category with maximum private aided schools, Andhra Pradesh represents the other side with maximum lower secondary schools under the government (including local bodies) and more than one-fourth of schools under private unaided category. Again in A.P., a majority of higher secondary schools were provided by private unaided sector. The case of Kerala is slightly different with more than one-third of its lower secondary schools being managed by the government directly while more than 50 per cent being private aided schools (see Table 3.10). The state has 14 per cent private unaided schools, which is the lowest proportion compared to other three states. In general it has observed that all the sample states have depicted a rapid growth of private unaided schools at lower secondary level, except Maharashtra. However, at higher secondary level, the share of private unaided schools has been less prominent in all the sample states, except Andhra Pradesh in comparison to other types of schools. By the turn of the century, Andhra Pradesh has established the predominance of private unaided schools at higher secondary level and a favourable ratio at lower secondary level. During this period Uttar Pradesh too has shown an increased tendency towards private unaided schools both at lower and higher secondary level. Kerala on the other hand continued to maintain the supremacy of state funded schools.

The above discussion is limited to the changes that took place during the first phase of liberalization and till the beginning of this decade. However, the results accrued from the first phase of liberalisation and structural adjustments on the one hand and fast spreading globalisation process on the other have resulted in several economic and policy changes both at the national and the state levels. Naturally, these changes have affected the education in general and secondary education in particular after 2002. In order to capture these developments and look at the future of secondary education, an attempt has been made to trace the recent changes in the following section.

GROWTH TRENDS FROM SAMPLE STATES TO SAMPLE SCHOOLS

The changing scenario of secondary education in terms of demand and supply patterns accelerated during the first half of the first decade of the new millennium. This increased pace of change can be seen from the changing proportion of schools belonging to different managements in a very short span (2001-04). In continuation of the trend of previous decade, the proportion of private unaided schools has increased across all the states (see Annexure, Table A13). At secondary and higher secondary levels, all other states, except Madhya Pradesh, have shown an increase in the growth rate of private unaided school. In the backdrop of the national and state trends on the expansion of education vis-à-vis the role of public and private sector in secondary education, this section attempts to inter-weave the analysis by examining the trends and patterns of public and private sector in sample states, regions and to institutions in sample districts. In doing so, it attempts to capture the impact of these macro changes at the micro level, viz. schools and students through specifically designed case studies using the most recent available information.

Trends in Sample States

The growth and expansion of secondary schools in the beginning of the new millennium (2001-02) would be significantly influenced with federal interventions/initiatives and enhanced plan allocation for achieving universalisation of elementary education, viz. Sarva Shiksha Abhyan (SSA), Education For All programme (EFA). Further, with improved economic growth, burgeoning middle class, restricted family size, enhanced social awareness, etc on the one hand and the policy shift in the macro economic context on the other would play a contributive role in impacting the trends and patterns of public and private sector in secondary education. In this light, this section attempts to examine the latest scenario of provision of schools by types of management and their enrolment in secondary education among the sample states.

The preference towards the private unaided sector that has begun during early 1990s, in the first phase of liberalization, accelerated in its second phase during the first half of the decade. The declining state funding combined with the increasing pressure from the lower levels of education spurred the increase of private unaided sector. However, the proportion of institutions under different managements in the sample states, during 2004-05, shows that in all the four sample states, except Maharashtra, the private unaided schools have increased in proportion than other management types (see Table 3.11). Within a period of four years (2001-04), the secondary educational scenario in the state of Uttar Pradesh has entirely changed as the demand and supply of secondary education has skewed in favour of private unaided sector. As a result, both the proportion of institutions and enrolment under the private unaided sector has increased at both levels of secondary education. Maharashtra has not shown any significant change in terms of demand and supply pattern, except a slight increase in the proportion of government schools at secondary level. Further this state continued with the same pattern as in the nineties wherein supply was exceeding the demand in private unaided sector. However, government run and funded schools continued to meet most of the demand for lower secondary education in the state. Kerala too maintained pattern like Maharashtra in institutional growth under different managements as in the beginning of 2000s.

At higher secondary level, in the span of four years the proportion of private unaided schools has doubled while Maharashtra has maintained the status quo. Andhra Pradesh continued to have a higher proportion of private unaided schools, Uttar Pradesh also displayed a remarkable increase in their proportion. In a short span time the proportion of private unaided schools in Uttar Pradesh had doubled. Sixty percent of private unaided school were covering 34 per cent of enrolment.

Table 3.11: Proportion of Secondary Schools by Management Type and their Enrolment in Sample States

State	Schools				Enrolment			
	Govt	PA	PUA	Total	Govt	PA	PUA	Total
	Lower Secondary (2004-05)							
Andhra Pradesh	62.5	6.1	31.1	100	62.5	6.1	31.4	100
Kerala	35.7	51.4	15.9	100	34.3	60.5	5.2	100
Maharashtra^	7.7	63.1	29.2	100	8.6	76.1	15.3	100
Uttar Pradesh@	6.6	38.1	53.1	100	3.71	45.63	50.5	100
India*	40.8	27.5	30.7	100	38.48	41.35	20.17	100
	Higher Secondary (2003-04)							
Andhra Pradesh	22.8	13.8	63.4	100	--	--	--	--
Kerala	33.2	39.4	27.4	100	--	--	--	--
Maharashtra	6.4	86.5	7.1	100	--	--	--	--
Uttar Pradesh	5.7	33.7	60.6	100	6.0	60.0-	34.	--
India#	36.1	31.2	31.2	100	36.2	44.0	19.8	100

^ Data refer to the period 1993 to 2002-03.

* Data refer to the period 1993 to 2003-04 for schools and enrolment data refer to the period 1993 to 2001-02.

Data refer to the period 1993-2001-02.

@ Data for Uttar Pradesh corresponds to 60 districts at the lower secondary level, while the state has 70 districts as per 2001 census—Data on enrolment by management not available.

Sources:

(i) All India Educational Survey, 1993, NCERT, New Delhi.

(ii) Directorate of School Education, GOAP, 2004-05.

(iii) Education Since Independence, Directorate of School Education, Govt of Kerala, 2004.

(iv) Directorate of Secondary Education, Govt of Maharashtra, 2004-05.

(v) Board of Secondary and Higher Secondary Education, Govt of Uttar Pradesh, 2005.

(vi) Selected Educational Statistics, 2003-04, MHRD, Govt of India.

A number of interesting trends and change in the size and pattern of different types of management can be observed from Table 3.11.

- Private unaided schools had higher growth rate than other management schools in all sample states, except Maharashtra.
- Educationally backward states Andhra Pradesh and Uttar Pradesh show higher proportion of unaided schools at secondary level compared to other two states. In these two states the proportion of enrolment in unaided schools is same as in proportion of schools at lower secondary level.
- In Kerala and Maharashtra, the extent of coverage of students by unaided schools was lower as compared to the proportion of unaided private schools in the states.
- Small proportion of enrolment in private unaided schools suggests the demand for differential education in Kerala and Maharashtra.
- Higher proportion of students covered by unaided schools in Uttar Pradesh and Andhra Pradesh not only signifies less investment by state government on secondary education but also mass spread of private schools into rural areas and also across income groups.
- The increased pace of expansion of unaided schools indicates the demand and changing aspirations of parents with regard to choice of schools and the apathy of states' commitment and investment to expand and improve the system. Unfortunately, in economically and educationally disadvantaged states, the demand for secondary education is largely met by private sector. This also shows a market driven growth of private unaided schools in all the states.

Regional Diversity in Sample States

The response to the demand and supply mechanism in the secondary education also reflects the regional disparity at state levels. An attempt is made here to examine the role of different management types across regions[3]. Andhra Pradesh can be categorised into three regions, viz., Coastal–developed, Rayalaseema-medium developed and Telangana–the backward region. During 1987-88, the A.P. government was the major provider (above three-fourth) of lower secondary schools in all the three regions. Distribution of government schools was more or less similar across regions. About two decades later, during 2004-05, the government is still the major provider (ranging from 56% to 72%) of lower secondary education followed by private unaided sector; the presence of aided schools being marginal. However, considerable difference can be found in terms of distribution of government schools across the regions. Developed Coastal Region accounts for higher percentage of government and private aided schools, while the backward Telangana Region has less percentage of government and private aided schools but high percentage of private unaided schools. The state government plays an important role in the expansion of education in the developed regions of the state while the private entrepreneurs are responding to the educational needs of the backward regions. The highest, that is double-digit growth, is found in the private unaided sector, especially in the backward region. Growth of government sector is marginally better than the private aided sector; it is higher in the backward regions. This shows that an expansion of schools is taking place in the backward regions and all the managements have responded to the demand, especially the private unaided sector in a much bigger way (see Annexure, Table A14).

The percentage share of students enrolled in government schools is higher than that of private unaided and aided schools. However, there is region-wise variation in terms of enrolments in government schools. For example, in A.P., while the percentage share of enrolment in government schools in developed coastal area and moderately developed Rayalaseema region, is over 70 per cent, it is less than 60 per cent in the backward Telangana region. Similarly, both the developed and the medially developed regions have higher percentage of enrolment in private aided schools than the Telangana region. On the contrary, the backward Telangana region has the highest percentage of students enrolled in private unaided schools, almost equalling to the combined strength of the other two regions. In other words, while in the developed and medially developed regions the demand for lower secondary schools is largely met by government sector, in the backward regions considerable percentage of students flow into unaided sector. During the last decade, the proportion of private unaided schools remained stagnant in the developed region while there has been an exponential growth in their proportion in the backward regions. This dimension of the preponderance of private unaided sector both in terms of percentage of educational institutions and enrolment in a most backward region needs to be critically looked at. Hence, a further look at the sample districts too exhibits the regional differences and differential growth of schools belonging to these managements, more so the private unaided sector (see Annexure, Table A15).

Maharashtra presents a unique perspective in our current analysis. There are six regions in Maharashtra with one metropolis and five other important towns. However, it needs to be mentioned that each region consists of some developed and some backward districts, except Aurangabad, which is largely a backward region. For analytical purpose, we have categorized Mumbai, Nasik and Pune regions as developed, Amravati and Nagpur as developing, and Aurangabad as backward.

The state policy of funding the privately managed schools to ensure public-private partnership is reflected in higher percentage of private aided schools in the state and across the regions. There is more number of private aided schools, amounting almost 70 per cent, in various regions. However, interestingly, the percentage of private aided schools is less in the most developed Mumbai region and the backward Aurangabad region. The percentage of government schools is higher in backward Aurangabad region, though their overall percentage in Maharashtra is quite less and it varies from region to region. When we look at the spread of private unaided sector, it provides quite a different picture. It has a maximum percentage in Mumbai (30.2%), the developed urban region, and minimum of 15.7 per cent in the medially developed Amravati. However, the backward region of Aurangabad supports private unaided sector almost equal in share with that of developed Nasik and Pune regions. Thus, the fast growth of private unaided sector is happening *de facto* in the developed regions. Comparable data between 1990 and 2000-01 reflect that there is a slight decline in the percentage of government and private unaided sectors in the state and increase in the share of private aided sector. This trend is further substantiated by the drastic reduction in the percentage of private unaided sector from 29.1 per cent to 18.5 per cent in the developing region of Nagpur and the backward region of Aurangabad, and a considerable decline in the developing Amravati regions. This encouraging trend further suggests the state priority of giving grant-in-aid to schools located in the backward and developing regions. This may be attributed to the state commitment on education towards developing educational infrastructure in backward areas, an important corrective initiative as Maharashtra has extreme inter-district inequalities.

The demand for secondary education in terms of enrolment in all the regions, by and large, is met by the private aided sector. However, in case of Mumbai, an industrially, economically and educationally developed region, 30.2 per cent of private unaided schools cater to 12.9 per cent of students. But in all the other cases, the percentage of enrolment in private unaided schools ranges from 5.67 per cent to 8.69 per cent and is concentrated in developed regions; otherwise, there has been a decline in the enrolment percentage of private unaided schools in developing and backward regions which corresponds to the decline in the institutions over the years.

In Kerala, during the period of 2000-01, the state had 39.5 per cent government, 54.1 per cent private aided, and only 6.4 per cent private unaided schools. Despite government and private aided schools being in majority, or in other words the government being directly or indirectly involved in the provisioning of education, an inter-regional variation is found in terms of types of management. In the underdeveloped northern region, the percentage of government schools is more in comparison to the other two regions, which is in contrast to the backward regions of Andhra Pradesh. The backward northern region of Kerala has an equal proportion of government and private aided schools. In relatively developed southern and central regions, private aided schools are in higher proportion than the government schools. In the developed regions, private aided sector is a major player in making educational provisions, but this sector is not as prominent in underdeveloped areas. As a result, the government has taken up the responsibility of opening more schools in backward regions. More interestingly, there are more private unaided schools in the backward northern region just like in the backward regions of Andhra Pradesh. In the last decade, there had been a decline in the proportion of government schools in the medium developed and backward regions and a corresponding increase in private unaided sector. In fact, the percentage of private unaided schools has doubled during this period in the backward region.

Though the highest percentage of institutional growth has taken place in the backward northern region, it has not been supported by increased percentage of enrolment. However, there has been identical increase in the percentage of enrolment in private unaided schools in all the regions, which is almost double than that in the previous decade.

Uttar Pradesh is one of the least developed states in India with a per capita income that is marginally higher than that of Bihar and Orissa. Like other states, Uttar Pradesh also has regional imbalances. Uttar Pradesh can be categorized into five regions namely, Eastern, Western, Central, Bundelkhand and Hills. The Western Uttar Pradesh is agriculturally prosperous; it is relatively more industrialized and has seen greater degree of urbanization. At the other end is Bundelkhand, with low agricultural growth, and having less number of industrial units, etc.

Uttar Pradesh has also regional variations in terms of provision of lower secondary schools by different management types. In all the regions of the state, private unaided schools are in majority, irrespective of the level of development of the region. However, in the backward region of Bundelkhand, their presence is marginally lower in percentage, though it is still higher than the two states of Kerala and Andhra Pradesh. The percentage of government schools is quite low in the state, and their distribution is rather unevenly with a significant proportion being in backward Bundelkhand region, like in other sample states, except Andhra Pradesh.

As discussed earlier, the proportion of private unaided schools is rapidly increasing in most of the states in general, and in Uttar Pradesh in particular. During 2004, a majority of lower secondary schools in Uttar Pradesh were private unaided, comprising 53.1 per cent of total number of schools, which is the highest among the sample states. However, the percentage share of private unaided schools varies from region to region, the highest being in the relatively developed central region (65.38%). In the backward region of Bundelkhand, the percentage of private unaided schools though is less than the other regions in the state, their proportion is substantial and much larger than in the backward regions of other sample states and also of many other states.

Regional scenario clearly underlines the variations and imbalances at regional levels, similar to that at the state level. At times these regional variations are sharper than the inter-state variations and point out to the unequal sharing of benefits. Such extreme variations highlight the role of socio-economic and political forces in determining the structure, function and pace of educational provision by different agencies. However, this regional analysis has facilitated in identifying critical inferences, besides brining out the similarities and dissimilarities at regional level across sample states.

First of all, Government is the major provider of secondary education either directly or indirectly (private aided) in almost all the regions across the sample states, except Andhra Pradesh. Secondly, there has been an increase in the percentage of private unaided schools in all the regions but more pronouncing in backward regions in all the sample states. Interestingly, in educationally and economically developed Maharashtra and educationally developed Kerala, the percentage of government schools is higher in backward regions. Thirdly, as a corollary to point one, even though private unaided sector is growing rapidly and substantially, yet its share is lower to that of government and private aided schools in all the regions, except Telangana region of Andhra Pradesh. Another fact is the significant role of private aided sector in Maharashtra and Kerala and its conspicuous absence in Andhra Pradesh. While backward regions are showing higher level of demand for secondary education in terms of higher growth rate of enrolment, on the supply side unaided sector is growing at a higher pace in all the sample states. However, government too has responded to this demand from backward regions in Maharashtra, Kerala and Uttar Pradesh along with private aided sector, though the intensity varies from state to state and region to region.

Inter-District Variation

In India not only the states, even the regions are also quite large and diversified. Therefore, for all implementing purposes, like revenue and educational management, district is the basic unit of administration. The four sample states differ from each other in terms of number of districts and their level of development (see Annexure, Table A16 to A19). In all the four states, inter-district variation is quite striking (see Appendix, Note on Sample Districts). These imbalances do get reflected in terms of distribution of schools and enrolment under different managements, particularly of private unaided sector at the district level. As discussed earlier, the state of Uttar Pradesh has undergone a rapid educational transformation in the last 3 years, especially in terms of increase in the private unaided sector. The data for the year 2004 shows that (see in Annexure, Table A19) the growth of private unaided sector is unprecedented; it ranges from a high of 77.0 per cent to a low of 2.8 per cent among various districts. In a little less than half of the districts, private unaided schools constitute the majority, having more than 50 per cent of share. These districts cut across developed and underdeveloped areas. A sharp decline of private aided sector at lower secondary level in the state reflects that only in 12 districts, private aided schools are in larger proportion compared to other management type schools. However, the highest and the lowest proportion varies from 75.3 per cent to around 11 per cent in different districts. While the proportion of government schools varies from a relatively high 46 per cent in one of the most backward districts, to abysmal low of 0.6 per cent in a relatively developed agro-industrial district. Only in two districts, the government schools outnumber the other management type schools.

In case of Andhra Pradesh, the inter-district disparities are conspicuous among 14 districts across different regions. The inter-district differences come out rather clearly in case of private unaided schools, whose proportion ranges from as high as 65 per cent to as low as 8.5 per cent among the fourteen districts. The number of schools run by the government varies between 91 per cent in a relatively underdeveloped district (Srikakulam) of developed coastal region, to only 23 per cent in a district of backward Telangana region. These are the two districts, which also account for the lowest and the highest percentage of private unaided schools respectively. In four districts, of the less developed Rayalseema region, the percentage of private unaided schools varies from 40 per cent to 20 per cent, which shows disparities among the districts even within a particular region (see Annexure, Table A17). However, except in two districts, in all others the government schools formed the largest percentage.

Though the overall percentage of private aided schools is pretty low with 6.1 per cent in the state, it does provide a window to the general inter-district disparity. Further, the highest percentages of these schools are found in a few developed districts and the capital city, while their presence in other districts is marginal.

A greater degree of similarity could be observed in the share of government schools in Andhra Pradesh and enrolment in them in all districts, except two districts. In the capital city of the state, there is a higher percentage of government schools, though there is no matching enrolment in them, thus showing the case of lower demand and higher supply. However, there is higher demand for private unaided schools in the city. The reversal trend is different all other districts, that is, the presence of higher percentage of private unaided schools without the corresponding coverage of enrolment.

Among 34 districts, the share of government schools in

Maharashtra ranges from a maximum of 27.3 per cent to a minimum of zero percent (see Annexure Table A16). However, their concentration can be found in backward districts. Private aided sector, being the major provider of the secondary education, is predominant in all the districts with a presence of about 90 per cent to 40 per cent across 34 districts. Share of private aided sector exceeds 50 per cent, except in one district. Similarly, although found in all the districts, the extent of private unaided schools varies from 40 per cent to 8 per cent. Only three districts, out of which two are highly urbanized and industrially developed (Mumbai and Thane), have a concentration of private unaided schools above 30 per cent. Even though private unaided schools have made a good entry in all the districts, only in three big industrial and developed districts of Mumbai, Thane and Pune, their percentage is more than the percentage of other management schools.

In case of Maharashtra, there is not only a dominance of the private aided sector, but also this sector has spread across in almost all the districts. Even the backward districts of the developed regions have substantial percentage of private aided sector, which is quite different from the other two states. Further, looking at the spread and coverage of various types of schools in general and private unaided schools in particular, it can be surmised that there is low inter-district disparity. Despite this observation, one can still find a relatively higher degree of concentration of private unaided schools in backward districts of the state.

In Kerala, demand for lower secondary education is largely met either by the government or private aided sector. However, inter-district variation is still prevalent as government schools have a higher percentage in backward districts while private aided schools are mostly located in developed and medium developed districts (see Annexure, Table A18). Interestingly, though the percentage of private unaided schools is negligible in the state, much lower than 10 per cent, their distribution is most unequal. The developed capital and port city of the state, for obvious reasons, has comparatively higher percentage of private unaided schools, but this percentage is below the proportion of private unaided schools located in one of the most backward districts. Like in other states, except in a few developed cities, higher percentages of private unaided schools in the backward districts of Kerala, however, account for low enrolment coverage.

We have examined the percentage of districts on the basis of proportion of private unaided schools and the extent of their enrolment. The districts have accordingly been categorized into four groups, namely moderate, high, higher and predominant. Out of 131 districts of four sample states, Uttar Pradesh has the distinction of having districts belonging to all the four groups (see Table 3.12). However, the enrolment share of private unaided schools was very high compared to the share of schools in the high category range of 26 to 50 per cent. Uttar Pradesh is the only sample state that has districts with the predominant presence of private unaided schools and enrolment. On the contrary, Kerala reports a moderate presence of private unaided schools and enrolment. While Maharashtra reports more than 50 per cent schools in the high presence category, but enrolment is almost within the moderate presence type. In Andhra Pradesh, the distribution of schools is almost the same in moderate and high presence categories, while two thirds of enrolment is within the moderate category, which matches the national average.

Table 3.12: Distribution of Districts with Different Range of Private Unaided Lower Secondary Schools and Enrolment in Sample States

Range of % of School/ Enrolment	Andhra Pradesh (23) % of		Kerala (14) % of		Maharashtra (34) % of		Uttar Pradesh (60) % of	
	Schools	Enrolment	Schools	Enrolment	Schools	Enrolment	Schools	Enrolment
	Moderate Presence of Private Unaided Sector							
Below 25	47.83	69.57	100.00	100.00	44.12	94.12	6.67	25.00
	High Presence of Private Unaided Sector							
26 and 50	43.48	26.09	0.00	0.00	52.94	5.88	26.67	51.67
	Higher Presence of Private Unaided Sector							
51 and 70	8.70	4.35	0.00	0.00	2.94	0.00	61.67	20.00
	Predominant Presence of Private Unaided Sector							
Above 70	0.00	0.00	0.00	0.00	0.00	0.00	5.00	3.33

* Data for Uttar Pradesh corresponds to 60 districts, while the state has 70 districts as per 2001 census.

Note: Figures in parenthesis indicate the number of districts in each state.

Source: (i) Directorate of School Education, GOAP, 2004-05.

(ii) Education since Independence, Directorate of School Education, Govt of Kerala, 2004.

(iii) Directorate of Secondary Education, Govt of Maharashtra, 2004-05.

(iv) Board of Secondary and Higher Secondary Education, Govt of Uttar Pradesh, 2005.

- In Kerala all the districts have moderate proportion of private unaided schools as well as enrolment (below 25%)
- In Maharashtra all the districts except a few have moderate proportion of enrolment in private unaided schools. More than 50 per cent of the districts have high presence of private unaided schools.
- In Andhra Pradesh highest percentage of districts have moderate proportion of enrolment in private unaided schools
- Uttar Pradesh has districts belonging to all categories having proportionate of institutions as well as enrolment.

Uttar Pradesh has a high percentage of districts with very high proportion of institutions and one-fifth of districts with very high proportion of enrolment in private unaided schools. The high and higher categories of districts are above 25 per cent in Andhra Pradesh.

Provision of secondary education by different management mechanisms at the district level highlights a few important aspects reflecting the state policies. First, inter-district variations are common to all states. Kerala and Maharashtra are both educationally developed states and show if not identical but similar trends. Both in Kerala and Maharashtra, percentage of government schools is higher in backward districts. However, in Kerala the percentage of private aided schools is higher in developed districts, while in the case of Maharashtra, the percentage of private aided schools is more in backward areas as well. In Kerala, both the developed and the backward districts share a common characteristic in terms of having higher percentage of private unaided schools. On the contrary, in Maharashtra, private unaided schools are found in higher percentage in industrial and capital towns than in the backward districts. Educationally and economically backward Andhra Pradesh and Uttar Pradesh, show different trends. In Andhra Pradesh government is the major provider of education in all the districts, except two highly developed urbanized districts. The percentage of government schools is higher in backward districts than in developed districts. Private unaided schools are found in higher percentage in some of the developed as well as backward districts. The distinct feature of Uttar Pradesh is the large shift towards private unaided schools in recent years. However, government schools are slightly more number in backward regions than the private aided schools. Private unaided schools though found in all the districts, also occupy a sizeable proportion in backward districts.

From the above analysis, it emerges that the role of different management types in secondary education at the national and state levels appears to be the natural and logical consequence of the dynamics at the district level. However, an attempt is made here with the proposition that the same trend may be applicable at the institutional, that is, school level.

MICRO LEVEL EVIDENCES FROM SAMPLE SCHOOLS

An attempt has been made to look at micro level evidence among different management schools in rural and urban locations by using the specifically designed case studies in 48 schools in four sample districts each from four sample states. These four districts were Nalgonda (A.P.), Thiruvanthapuram (Kerala), Pune (Maharashtra) and Varanasi (U.P.). Out of these four, Thiruvanthapuram is a capital city, Pune is a developed educational centre, Nalgonda is a fast growing commercial centre of Andhra Pradesh and Varanasi is an important historical, religious and educationally medium developed district of Uttar Pradesh. A brief description of the four districts is given in Appendix. The purpose of such case studies was to obtain valuable information at disaggregated level by different categories, viz., rural-urban; gender and social based, in terms of their participation in different types of management of schools (see Table 3.13).

During 1998-2003, there has been an increase in enrolment at secondary level, especially at higher secondary level. The private unaided schools had higher growth rate of enrolment than the government schools. The rural-urban disparity can be found in enrolment, for example, at the lower secondary level, though there has been an overall increase in the percentage of enrolment, it is lower in rural than in urban areas, particularly due to the steep decline of enrolment; of boys in government schools in rural areas. More interestingly, in rural areas, the growth of enrolment in private unaided schools was not only higher but twice the percentage of increase in the urban localities.

At the higher secondary level, the government schools continued to retain the level of enrolment, largely due to availability of particular

Table 3.13: Percentage Change in Enrolment by Management Type in Sample Schools During 1997-98 and 2001-02

Management Type	Rural			Urban			Total		
	Boys	Girls	Total	Boys	Girls	Total	Boys	Girls	Total
				Secondary (N=48)					
Government	-23.1	15.7	-12.2	9.4	8.0	8.4	-4.7	8.8	3.6
Private Aided	10.6	1.7	5.6	35.2	17.6	21.4	20.6	12.2	14.8
Private Unaided	69.5	24.7	44.7	54.7	12.5	22.8	55.3	12.7	23.3
Total	-0.6	4.3	1.8	32.1	13.1	17.8	17.9	11.4	13.5
				Higher Secondary (N=28)					
Government	10.4	103.9	36.9	-5.0	0.3	-2.1	0.3	16.2	7.7
Private Aided	-20.4	51.5	-13.1	9.9	44.9	42.6	-9.8	45.0	36.0
Private Unaided	69.5	24.7	44.7	-8.6	-8.6	-8.6	-2.8	-3.4	-3.0
Total	-0.1	83.1	19.7	-4.1	30.5	20.9	-2.7	33.7	20.7

Source: Field Survey in Four Sample States, 2003-04.

subjects only at government schools. On the contrary, there has been a decline in the enrolment percentage of private aided schools in rural areas; The enrolment, on the other hand, has increased substantially in private unaided schools. Similarly, in urban areas, whereas the enrolment percentage in sample government schools has declined, an increase in the same is found in private aided sector. This suggests a trend towards migration of rural students to urban private aided schools in search of subjects like Science, Commerce and Mathematics. Interestingly, the decline in the enrolment percentage of private unaided schools in urban areas is quite conspicuous.

Evidence from case study schools indicates that increase or decrease in the proportion of enrolment is not entirely dependent on management or performance of the school. Out of 48 case studies, enrolment has increased in more than half of the schools, while a little less than half have shown a decrease. A majority of schools with decreasing enrolment were good performing[4] schools, which included management of all types from both rural and urban areas. Similarly, a majority of poor performing schools, suffering from decreasing enrolment, belonged to government and private aided managements. Interestingly, some government and private aided schools have shown an increase in the enrolment, despite being poor performers (see Case Studies). The reason for this can be attributed to scholarships and other benefits available as well as gender preference (see case study of Uttar

Pradesh), religious and community affiliations. However, some good performing government and private aided schools, despite performing well, attracted less number of students, which may be explained in terms of preference for differential schools and a shift towards private unaided schools, especially to such schools as were having English as medium of instruction.

Based on the pattern of enrolment among the case study schools, an important question was addressed regarding the demand for education in different social groups, including gender. The data from the case studies of lower secondary schools suggest that there has been tremendous decline in the enrolment of boys in government schools in rural areas, and increase in enrolment of boys during the same period in private unaided case study schools; it was more than three times than that of girls. Similarly, in urban areas, the percentage of enrolment increased for boys by over 9 per cent, and that of girls was slightly less than that. Interestingly, during the same period, the growth rate of enrolment of boys in private unaided schools in rural areas, was more than three times, and nearly four times of enrolment of girls in urban areas. The comparison brings out an interesting fact, that is, a significant portion of rural boys are shifting out from government schools to private unaided schools. In the higher secondary schools, growth rate of the enrolment of boys has increased in private unaided schools, and a significant increase in enrolment of girls is found in government schools.

Unlike the national pattern found in Table 3.7 that expansion in private unaided sector is universal across social groups, the micro level school data depicted that private unaided schools have the lowest representation of these communities with just over 6 per cent and the figure touches barely 15 per cent in private aided schools (see Table 3.14). It is in the government schools that these deprived communities have a sizeable presence, which is just about one-fifth of total enrolment of the schools.

An observation of the socio-economic background of students attending different management schools reveals an interesting fact. However, it needs to be mentioned that the information was ascertained from school records and personal assessment of heads of schools and teachers. It has been found that the students attending private unaided schools are largely from better socio-economic background, while the students enrolled in government schools, are from lower-middle income groups. This means affluent parents are

Table 3.14: Proportion of Enrolment by Social Groups and Type of Management in Sample Schools (in %)

Type of Management of School	Location	Scheduled Castes			Scheduled Tribes			Other Backward Castes		
		Boys	Girls	Total	Boys	Girls	Total	Boys	Girls	Total
Govt	Rural	16.8	10.2	12.4	3.3	2.7	2.9	37.7	13.3	21.7
	Urban	15.7	20.3	17.5	11.7	25.1	17.1	44.4	44.0	44.3
	Total	16.4	11.7	13.6	6.2	6.2	6.2	40.0	18.1	26.9
Pvt Aided	Rural	8.9	12.8	10.8	7.5	9.1	8.3	36.1	34.3	35.2
	Urban	11.7	10.2	10.6	4.0	2.2	2.6	14.4	15.7	15.4
	Total	10.1	11.0	10.6	6.0	4.2	4.8	27.0	21.0	23.1
Pvt Unaided	Rural	5.3	7.2	6.0	0.5	0.2	0.4	65.4	57.6	62.6
	Urban	3.7	3.0	3.4	2.7	0.6	1.8	28.1	29.7	28.8
	Total	4.4	4.6	4.5	1.7	0.5	1.2	45.5	40.5	43.5

Source: Field Survey in Four Sample States, 2003-04; (N=48).

gradually switching over their wards from government to private schools. This trend has a serious social implication that over a time, schools could likely to represent a particular class character and as a result instead of becoming diverse centres of learning, these would turn into exclusive learning centres.

The socio-economic profile of students studying in sample schools further reinforces the categorization of schools and their distinct student profiles. As the data indicate, maximum percentage of government schools cater to students belonging to low socio-economic status and only an insignificant proportion of government schools have students from higher socio-economic backgrounds. Even these are government schools which have fewer students from middle socio-economic group; this group also seems to be preferring private aided schools. In contrast to this, maximum percentages of private unaided schools are catering to students coming from higher socio-economic background. There has been a concentration of students from poor socio-economic status in government schools. The same trend is observed by Karan and Pushpendra (2005) at elementary schools in Bihar, that 'Dalitisation (socially deprived community in India) of government schools is taking place only in terms of students.... This has implications not only for the students enrolled ... but also for their (schools) overall functioning' (p.115, Karan and Pushpendra, 2005). Such trends are visible in Uttar Pradesh as well (Jeffery, 2005).

Like the concentration of different socio-economic groups in particular management types of schools, there are evidences that schools are also divided on the basis of caste, community and religious affiliations. Though we do not have individual student data, analysis of data from all sample schools indicating the background of students does prove the point. For example, in Kerala, three of the private aided sample schools show that majority of students belonged to a particular community, that is, Hindus, Muslims and even converted Hindus. The trend is not limited to private unaided schools; rather it exists in schools belonging to all management types[5]. Government schools are, however, as discussed earlier, gradually being concentralized with students belonging to SC/ST and low economic-status groups. In fact, it would not be wrong to say that often government directly creates such segregation by creating special schools exclusively for children belonging to these communities.

The Phenomenon of Privatisation and Explanation

State intervenes selectively in other areas but universally in education (Erickson 1989). However, this intervention differs from state to state and more often than not is guided by political processes and socio-economic conditions. Of late, a large number of private entrepreneurs are coming forward to participate in the secondary education provisioning. As a result, in the last few decades, educational scenario has undergone significant transformation not only in terms of expansion of educational facilities, but also in terms of types of educational provisioning. Despite the plurality of players, government continues to be the main provider of education, either directly managing schools or funding the privately managed schools (private aided schools). However, their proportion has declined both at national and state levels, including in three of the sample states. While in some states, the private aided schools have declined steeply, loosing primacy, but in a few others they continue to be in majority with marginal increase or decrease. Similarly, government (including local bodies) schools continue to be in majority in some of the states, but in some other states, their share has declined considerably. However, in almost all the states, the presence of private unaided sector has grown positively though its proportion has varied from a significant level to marginal. The four sample states under study represent the varied picture described above. In the following section we will discuss the changing management scenario of the secondary schools.

Declining Share of Private Aided and Government Schools: Reasons

In consonance with the national trend the growth rate and percentage share of government and private aided schools have steeply declined in Uttar Pradesh. The steady and significant decline of proportion of private aided schools can be attributed to a number of factors; the most important being the state policy and its financial constraints.

Initially, nationalistic and philanthropic motives were responsible for the mushrooming growth of private aided sector which also received political patronage. This trend had its moorings first in freedom movement of Indian independence, it continued till 70s and 80s. However, this unfettered growth of private aided schools created large financial burden for the states, forcing many state governments, including the Government of Uttar Pradesh, to initiate new regulations. During the late 80s, the Government of Uttar Pradesh took a conscious decision on the private aided schools where it stipulated that the government would not give recognition to such new schools. Interestingly, the state government took over most of the schools established prior to 1986, which is the landmark year from the perspective of educational policy, under grant-in-aid system in order to improve quality of provisions.

This important shift in the policy, according to state administration, has emanated from the National Policy of Education (1986) which has envisaged consolidation of secondary schools and encouraging private participation. This about turn in policy indicates the government's total withdrawal from funding the private enterprises in education in Uttar Pradesh (Jeffery, 2005). A similar situation is found in the context of Maharashtra in the form of its 'permanent no grant policy'. However, there is some variation of the policy in Maharashtra in relation to tribal and backward areas. This important dimension of educational change needs to be explained.

There are a few reasons: first, the private aided sector had expanded to such an extent and the demand was increasing so much that the government was unable to fund all the private managed schools at the state level due to financial constraints. Over the years, the private contribution to education had dwindled, consequently, the share of the government expenditure on education increased substantially (Varghese and Tilak, 1985). As a result, making further expansion of the system became difficult on the part of the government, thus reducing the possibility of further assistance to private schools through grant-in-aid. Secondly, the adoption of National Education Policy in 1986 and subsequent Programme of Action (1992) envisaged higher resource flow to the education sector through diverse sources, including private participation. Although the policy did not call for establishment of private schools *per se,* some state governments used this argument as an open support for the policy of '*no more grant-in-aid*' to private schools, especially those opened after 1987 (Uttar Pradesh and Maharashtra). This policy of the states had directly affected the growth of private aided schools, especially after 1990. Another plausible explanation for the decline of the share of private aided schools could be that under the impact of globalization, the state has been gradually withdrawing itself from the sphere of large public investment, thereby letting the space, including of education to be occupied by market.

As a part of its National Educational Policy in post-1986 period, the state of Uttar Pradesh insisted on provisions regarding the financing of the new ventures, though it would not fund them. This strict vigil into the financial viability of new ventures discouraged many initiatives in terms of opening new schools. Secondly, the new state policy also took away the privilege of recruitment of teachers, payment of salaries and other apparently lucrative aspects from the private management, thus making the stipulations least attractive to the private management. Though this is not the case with Maharashtra and Kerala, but is a strong reason to describe the decline of private aided schools in Uttar Pradesh. Thirdly, though there has been growing social demand for 'differential education', the private aided schools have not been able to tap this opportunity because they have little option in adopting new curriculum, design new courses or follow alternative pedagogy.

Kerala, however, is a unique case, where private aided schools continue to be the major player in delivering secondary education; this can be attributed to a number of reasons. Primarily, unlike Maharashtra and Uttar Pradesh, the state government has not followed 'no grant-in-aid' policy; therefore, as a state policy, the practice continues. Secondly, this is the only state which strictly follows the principle of additional section and teaching post when enrolment increases above the required norm. Coupled with this are the powers of the private management in recruiting the teachers. Further, it can be said that this has been possible in Kerala where there is not much scope for institutional expansion due to the declining enrolment trend at lower levels. Besides the nexus between private managements and politics is a very important factor. Many of the private aided schools are directly or indirectly connected with politicians and their families.

Why Private Unaided Sector is Growing?

Based on the macro and micro level analysis on the extent of privatisation of secondary education, an attempt is made in this section to explore several possible reasons for the fast growth of private unaided sector in general and in backward areas in particular[6]. In doing so, we have also attempted to look at its nature and dimensions. Also attempt is made to explore the implications of this rapid change on the education system, economy and the society at large.

Generally, two kinds of explanations for this phenomenon of privatisation are put forth namely: (i) excess demand; and (ii) differentiated demand (James, 1991). Besides these two, yet another explanation most often put forth for the genesis and growth of private unaided schools is the disenchantment with the government schools (Erickson: 1986). It is generally believed that failure of government schools has led to the genesis of private schools; that failure can be in meeting demand, quality or heterogeneous education and in the pretext of both factors (ibid). Many perceive that the increasing private initiatives in education, especially in the recent past, are more in response to differentiated demand than excess demand for education in the Indian context (Varghese: 1993). However, in the Indian context in general and more closely in the context of four sample states in the recent decade, private unaided schools have proliferated for variety of reasons. Privatization of secondary education in this study is examined from different perspectives namely, government failure, excess demand, differential demand, stratification of differential demand, economic and sociological dimensions.

Government's lack of focus on secondary education has led to invest inadequately both on meeting the expanding demand and on improving the quality of secondary education. But, most states in India claim to have fulfilled the minimum essential access norms of distance; it is also true to a large extent in many states. However, following the National Policy on Education, 1986, which envisaged consolidation of existing schools and encouraging private participation at secondary level coupled with financial constraints, most of the states have stopped further expansion of secondary education by way of establishing new schools. Instead, the existing schools and private sector were expected to accommodate the additional demand. So, the *government's failure* to expand has resulted in both excess demand and dilution of quality which in turn leads to differential education.

Excess demand is an outcome of the simple economic theory of demand and supply. It operates when the state is not in a position to provide enough number of places in schools for all those who demand it. In this case, those who are not getting admission in the state sector may be seeking places in the private sector, as the 'second best' solution (Erickson, 1986). This is a phenomenon largely specific to developing counties. However, in case of India the situation is quite different. India does not have restricted admission policy up to lower secondary level; rather it has open admission policy that refuses none and accommodates, all in the state managed and funded schools. However, excess demand on state-run schools indirectly promotes the growth of private unaided schools. Increasing demand often results in crowded classrooms with children from heterogeneous groups in government schools. Such a situation generally encourages certain sections of parents to shift their children to private unaided schools which leads to the need for differential education.

Fiscal constraints of states result in limited expansion of secondary educational provision in some states. In fact, low governmental investment in secondary education, despite the growing number of students, has given rise to private unaided schools. The unprecedented growth of private unaided secondary schools and their enrolment in the last half a decade in few states, including the economically and educationally backward states of Uttar Pradesh and Madhya Pradesh, can be attributed largely to excess demand. Similarly, the excess demand at higher secondary level and the availability of limited seats due to restriction clause in government and aided schools have led to the emergence of private unaided schools in some of the states including Andhra Pradesh and Madhya Pradesh. The rise of private schools in backward regions may be attributed to lower base, increased number of unemployed youths and poor quality of teaching in government schools, vitiated further by teacher absenteeism, and the growing demand with low supply.

Differential education is in demand broadly by two sets of

consumers. One, the conventional types, who always distinguish themselves from the commoners in general and educational opportunities in particular. The second set of consumers are the neo-rich class which prefers differential education as an outcome of either demonstrative or imitative practices of the conventional class. Many consumers now aspiring for differential education were otherwise using the government schools. As a result of increasing differential demand from a variety of social groups and consequent desertion of government schools has indeed changed the social composition of these schools. The growth of private schools in educationally and economically developed states like Maharashtra, Tamil Nadu, Karnataka, Kerala, Himachal Pradesh and Punjab can be explained as a response to differential demand. Further examination shows that this demand for differential education through private unaided schools is not confined to educationally and economically developed states; rather it has spread to the backward regions with a few exceptions viz. the state of Bihar, thereby highlighting the dominance of market forces in the supply of educational commodity across the states.

Differential demand has resulted in different forms, viz., preference for a particular medium of instruction–use of English; to a limited extent variation in curriculum or adoption of national curriculum (different from state curriculum); outcome-oriented in the form of better performance in public examinations (not necessarily better learning); demand for exclusivity; quality of teaching-learning process, etc.

Private providers used this opportunity to their advantage in responding to such varied demand. The response of market mechanism to this particular form of educational demand varies from place to palace and also depends on the nature of providers. Consequently, the differential demand gets stratified within the private sector. As a result, private unaided sector has shown the tendency of stratification in its quality, cost and clientele group, emerging with a popular belief that private unaided schools are more in demand by all sections of the society.

Economic Reasons

An important economic consideration in the growth of private unaided school is the impact of economic liberalization. Economic liberalization in the early 1990s boosted the income level of people with better job opportunities and higher disposable income. These factors have facilitated higher household expenditure on education. This capacity to pay, coupled with the awareness that quality education can only lead to better livelihood opportunities either in the form of better employment or earning or geographical mobility, has encouraged the growth of private sector. The economic dimension of privatization of education received a boost from the technological boom that came along with the rapid strides in information technology, particularly at the higher secondary level.

Economic reasons viz. fiscal deficit and structural adjustment, have constrained the growth of government and private aided school in many states including Uttar Pradesh and Maharashtra. The policy of discontinuing grant-in-aid provision to private schools established after 1986 in some states resulted in the growth of private unaided schools to cater to the demand. Apart from this, another important economic aspect that requires an understanding is the theory of 'monopoly rent'. It states that as long as private schools continue to maintain their quality and exclusiveness and equip their students with better skills enabling them perform better in labour market, this puts them in an advantageous position over the rest. The quality of exclusiveness that translates into better labour market performance has been responsible for the growth of private aided schools and can be put in the context of demand for differential education.

Educational Reason

An educational reason behind the growth of private unaided schools could be explained in terms of private tuition. Initially, private tuition evolved as a supplementary process to support either the weak students in coping with the demands of the education or to help good students do better especially for entering into technical and professional streams. As the system became widespread and government schools failed in providing quality education and investment on private tuition increased, parents opted for private schools as an alternative. Consequently, many of the institutions involved in private tuition have turned into private unaided schools.

Sociological Reasons

There are important sociological dynamics that play an important role in privatization of secondary education. In fact, despite good performance, enrolments in some of the government schools have declined because parents wanted to segregate their wards from the mixed social climate of government schools* . The micro level evidences from the case studies reveal that due to growing heterogeneity and crowding of classrooms in government/government aided schools, parents from better socio-economic groups have preferred private unaided schools. There were parents who were earlier sending their children to government schools. This tendency of segregation is related to issues of class, caste, age old discriminations, preferred process of socialization and other cultural preferences. This feature was earlier found among the higher socio-economic groups and among boys; now the trend has caught up with low income groups as well. Consequently, the government and private schools are becoming exclusive schools for different segments of society. Especially the government schools are getting 'ghettoized' with a large concentration of students from scheduled castes, scheduled tribes and other backward classes (for detail see case studies), as well as girls.

Ghettoization of Government Schools

The school was established in 1948 and catered to a large segment of rural population around the catchments area. The students of the school were generally of higher caste and higher income groups. In the last decade the government has established three hostels for boys and girls of scheduled caste, scheduled tribes and other backward classes. As a result students belonging to higher caste and higher income groups have gradually shifted to private unaided schools thus changing the social profile of the school. Presently out of 648 students, 98 per cent of students belong to scheduled castes, scheduled tribes and other backward communities. Only 11 students belong to upper caste but from extremely poor families. Though enrolment has increased, it has only increased the proportion of disadvantaged students. (Government High School, Tirumalagiri, Nalgonda, Andhra Pradesh).

However, in the context of India with so much diversity and complexities in secondary education system, it is difficult to strictly categorize the phenomenon of private unaided schools strictly in terms of excess and differential demand because more often they overlap each others. Differential education is often rooted through the channel of excess demand. In fact, there is a mixed trend that can be found in India which

* In Andhra Pradesh and Uttar Pradesh, most of the government/local body/ private aided schools have higher concentration of students belonging to lower socio-economic groups, thus creating a climate of segregation.

can be explained in typical circumstances of Andhra Pradesh. The ICT revolution though had spread all over India, some of the states like Andhra Pradesh took it seriously, both as a challenge and opportunity. Consequently, this changed the educational profile of the state, especially at higher secondary level with increased demand and supply of differential education across areas and different socio-economic groups. For example, within a short span, enrolment in technical and professional education was raised to the highest in Andhra Pradesh during 2002-03[7], which was a distant fourth in 1995-96 among the major states in India. The increased enrolment in technical and professional education from this sample state makes a case for government failure and excess demand because, most government schools do not have science section and even if they have, the seats are restricted. Thus, government failure led to excess demand which was met by the private unaided sector in Andhra Pradesh. In addition to science and math streams, these private schools prepared the students for public examinations, and for entry to the technical and professional education. The excess demand thus delineated into differential demand in higher secondary education in Andhra Pradesh.

The enabling capacity of technical and professional education has facilitated the movement of professionals to abroad, largely to USA, in search of better opportunities. This phenomenon of moving out of the country had its impact on social sector, particularly in the marriage market. The preference for working wife with the possibility of an employment in the same sector enforced the decision on girls to seek technical and professional education. As a result, the choice for professional education and great 'American Dream' created a sort of 'social obsession' among the ambitious parents and aspiring students. Hence, excess demand and differential education explain the higher increase in the private unaided schools at higher secondary level in Andhra Pradesh.

Implications

Looking at the growth, expansion and coverage of private unaided sector especially after 1990s, particularly its preponderance in economically and educationally backward regions, raises several issues and concerns in addition to a few positive implications.

Despite the government being the major player in secondary education sector, the onset of private unaided schools has definitely provided the parents with more school choices. As a result of such choices, private unaided sector has brought along an important dimension of competition. Competition and efficiency are the key features of market economy and the private unaided schools have brought this principle into the fore in the education system. The better performance of private unaided schools, to some extent, has ensured that government schools have to follow suit. In this context, one can cite the examples from Andhra Pradesh, Maharashtra and Kerala, which necessitated the government and private aided schools to critically look at their results. The state governments have linked the performance of government schools in public examinations to promotion, increment and postings in recent years. As a result, public accountability has entered into educational system, which was hitherto absent[8]. This can be evidently seen in the improvement of public examination results.

Further, in all probability, in the absence of private schools, the higher demand and low supply would have meant higher discrimination in the admission process in the government and private aided schools which could had led to further widening of inequities and social tension. The private unaided schools have reduced to some extent the government responsibility to meet either excess demand or differential education.

Apart from these perceived benefits, the private unaided sector has created a number of problems for the system. The high percentage of growth of private unaided schools in general and backward areas in particular, as explained earlier, led government schools serving exclusively the lower socio-economic groups and deposing diversity from the government system. In addition, it also created stratification within the private system. This stratification means that there are different types of schools within the private unaided sector i.e. good, bad and average performing schools, thus creating systems within the system. As such, the private unaided schools tend to segregate the learners on the basis of ability to pay. In such conditions, the quality and performance of the private schools reduces rather drastically. This, in turn, will create low quality private schools for the poor children, reduce their performance, aspiration and capabilities to enter into the specialized labour market. It has been found from our field study that poor are gradually entering the private schools that not only lack basic infrastructure but also have equally poor record in public examinations.

The private unaided schools segregate the community and adversely affect the social composition of the schools. The homogenization of schools, in such circumstances, will help in conglomerating the religion-caste-class-nexus and contribute towards the perpetuation of the hegemony and new forms of inequalities. For example, as explained earlier, the exclusiveness of private schools has ensured the 'ghettoization' of government schools with a large concentration of students from poor socio-economic background especially of scheduled caste, scheduled tribes and other backward classes. However, this trend is more prevalent in those states where private unaided schools are in large percentage. The consequences of this development have several implications for the provisioning of education in terms of government schools losing their diversity, quality of education and more importantly the social inclusiveness. This in turn leads to social segregation and children moving away from the government and private aided schools. As a result the accountability of the government schools and bargaining power of stakeholders get adversely affected. Interestingly, this social inclusivity also affects the private unaided schools by undermining the importance of diversity and social responsibility. It is pertinent to cite the performance and quality of Cotton Hill School of Kerala, which has been of course of very high standard and exemplary because the school has students from all sections of the society and is a government school. Similarly, the government schools in our sample states are also doing pretty well in terms of their performance.

Interestingly, micro level data from the case study schools have shown that despite good performance of some of the government schools, enrolment has declined as the students have moved out of the school as parents want segregation from a mixed social climate of government schools (Huzuar Nagar, Andhra Pradesh)[9]. As a result, the government and private aided schools are becoming exclusive schools for poorer sections of the society with a large concentration of students from scheduled caste, scheduled tribes and other backward classes (for detail see case studies). Similarly, the penetration of private schools in rural areas has brought new forms of gender equity. As discussed in the previous section, the enrolment figures at micro level evidently show the gender and social inequity where not only students from lower caste and lower class are being concentrated in government schools but increasing number of girls are also being enrolled in government schools, while upper caste students and boys from lower class, given the opportunity, are shifting to private unaided schools. In this context, it can be inferred that there is a social hierarchy in accessing schooling opportunity in private unaided schools which can have serious long term implications. Although selecting private unaided sector as schooling opportunity is slowly percolating down to the lower economic strata but it definitely would have an adverse impact on the household economy as they would be called upon to spend a major portion of their meagre income on education.

The penetration of this phenomenon into all parts of India has resulted in a 'stratification of the system' in terms of quality, cost and clientele group. For example, tuition fees among seven private unaided schools in Pune (Maharashtra) show that they vary from ₹ 100-₹ 700 per month. As the economic theory of rational behaviour would tell us, this different fee structure essentially highlights the differences of quality among these schools. This, in turn, demonstrates the hierarchy and stratification within the private unaided schools and consequently, their varying status of quality provision.

Since this growth is concentrated in backward regions, which is also divided with feudalism, points to the tendency of privileged class to move out of government schools for other alternatives as a response to 'social segregation'. In fact, it has been found that government schools have higher percentage of low caste students as a result of the pulling out of upper caste students from the these schools[10]. However, the demand for private unaided schools at lower secondary level has a different explanation as these are more concentrated in backward regions. This is like Uttar Pradesh where private bodies are finding it profitable to open such schools and it also means that higher demand and awareness of benefits of education may be gradually spreading to the lower levels.

As explained earlier, the growth of private unaided schools can be attributed to the tradition of private tuition. The gradual transformation of organized private tuition to the modern day coaching centers and private schools has certainly increased the enrolment of students in private schools from lower and middle income families. However, despite increase of private unaided schools and more students entering into these institutions, private tuition still remains a supplementary system. Rather it has increased with more and more students preferring private tuition for entering into technical and professional education. Consequently, it has increased the household expenditure on education especially of low income groups and by implication furthering the gap of economic inequality.

Equity is a major casualty. Inequity in its various stratifications, viz. economic, social, gender, regional, etc. would further widen, in addition to creating new forms of inequities both at the societal and at the family levels between siblings and gender, etc. which will have severe repercussions on the household economy of poorer sections of the society.

Education is a social good and, therefore, the state has the responsibility not only of providing quality education but also ensuring quality education for all. In a country like India, with so much diversities and inequities, it is difficult to assume that private unaided schools will be able to create a qualitatively better and sustained future for all. Private schools have their benefits but handing over the future of education to market forces is not the panacea for our ills. Indeed, a concerted effort is required to balance the system and allow the best practices to flourish.

The latest available data from statistics of School Education 2007-08 shows a marginal increase in the proportion of unaided schools though it varied among the states.

NOTES

1. Local Bodies refer to municipalities, district level councils, and village panchayats etc. which are all elected bodies. As a consequence of 73rd and 74th Constitutional amendments, managements of the schools are decentralized to local bodies.
2. Government schools include schools run by local bodies. Government provides funding for local body schools.
3. Reference years vary from state to state, depending upon the availability of comparable regional data. Brief details on regions are given in Appendix in the chapter on 'Access and Coverage'.
4. Sample schools for the case studies were drawn both from among the high and poor performing schools. Here performance denotes results in public examinations.
5. For details see Appendix which provides details of schools.
6. The share of private unaided schools from primary to higher secondary level at 1986, 1993 and 2001-02 is reported in Annexure, Table A11.
7. Selected Educational Statistics for the Year 1985-86, 1990-91 and 2002-03. Ministry of Human Resources Development, Government of India, New Delhi.
8. This aspect has been discussed in detail in the chapter on Teacher Management.
9. In Andhra Pradesh, most of the government/local bodies' schools have a higher concentration of students belonging to lower socio-economic groups, thus, creating a climate of segregation.
10. Based on enrolment data of the sample schools.

REFERENCES

Chopra, R. and Jeffrey, P. (ed.) (2005): *Educational Regimes in Contemporary India.* Sage: New Delhi.

Erickson, D.A. (1989): A Libertarian Perspective on Schooling; *in* W. L. Boyd and James G. Cibulka (Eds.), *Private Schools and Public Policy: International Perspectives* (pp. 21-42). The Falmer Press, London.

James, Estella (1991): *Private Finance and Management of Education in Developing Countries-Major Policy and Research Issues,* IIEP, Paris.

Kingdon, G and Muzammil, M. (2003): *The Political Economy of Education in India-Teacher Politics in Uttar Pradesh,* Oxford University Press, New Delhi.

Karan, A.K. and Pushpendra (2005): "Bihar-Including the Excluded and Addressing the Failures of Public Provision in Elementary Education'; *in* Santosh Mehrotra (ed): *The Economics of Elementary Education in India: The Challenge of Public Finance, Private Provision and Household Costs.* Sage, New Delhi.

Government of India, (1986): *National Policy on Education (1986).* MHRD, Government of India, New Delhi.

Government of India, (1992): *Programme of Action, (1992).* MHRD, Government of India, New Delhi.

Shah. J. Parth: "New Education Policy: Choices and Competition"; *in* Bibek Debroy and Parth J. Shah (eds): *Agenda for Change Action Plan for the Economy.* Centre for Civil Society, 1998.

Tilak, J.B.G. (1992): 'Public and Private Sectors in Education in India'; *in* R.F. Arnove, P.G. Altbach and G.P. Kelly (Eds.): *Emergent Issues in Education-Comparative Perspectives.* (SUNY Series in Frontiers Education), Abany, NY, State University of New York Press, pp. 173-185, 331-34.

Tilak. J.B.G. and Varghese. N.V. (1985): Discriminatory Pricing in Education. *Occasional Paper*, No.8, NIEPA, New Delhi.

Tooley, James and P. Dixson (2003): Private Schools for the Poor-A Case Study from India. C/BT, London, available at www.cfbt.com

Varghese, N.V. (1993): 'Private Schools in India: Presumptions and Previsions'; *in* R. P. Singh (ed.): *Private Initiatives and Public Policy in Education.* Federation of Management of Educational Institutions, New Delhi.

Annexure

Table A1: Proportion of Schools and Enrolment by Type of Management at Elementary Levels in India (in %)

Year	*Primary*			*Upper Primary*		
	Govern-ment	*Private Aided*	*Private Unaided*	*Govern-ment*	*Private Aided*	*Private Unaided*
			Schools			
1973-74	93.3	5.0	1.6	77.6	17.8	4.7
1978-79	94.0	4.4	1.6	78.4	16.9	4.7
1986-87	93.1	4.3	2.6	75.1	16.3	8.6
1993-94	92.1	3.8	4.1	79.5	9.5	11.0
1996-97	91.7	3.3	5.0	75.5	10.3	14.2
2001-02	90.9	3.1	6.0	76.4	7.8	15.8
			Enrolment			
1978-79	84.41	12.59	3.00	53.44	41.47	5.08
1986-87	83.03	11.85	5.13	58.33	33.21	8.46
1993-94	80.84	10.58	8.58	58.03	30.94	11.03
2001-02	76.01	9.03	14.96	53.80	27.87	18.33

Note: Government schools include schools run by local bodies

Source: Selected Educational Statistics 2001-2002, MHRD, GOI, India, 2003; p. 14-15.

Table A2: Share of Schools at Primary and Upper Primary Levels by Type of Management across Major States in India at Selected Points of Time

States	Primary Level						Upper Primary					
	1993			2000-01			1993			2000-01		
	Govt	PA	PUA	Govt	PA	PUA	Govt	PA	PUA	Govt	PA	PUA
Andhra Pradesh	92.9	4.1	3.0	94.5	3.4	2.2	79.9	6.9	13.2	72.7	3.5	23.8
Kerala	39.7	58.4	2.0	38.0	59.7	2.3	33.5	64.5	2.0	32.2	62.8	5.0
Maharashtra	91.5	4.5	4.0	90.4	5.1	4.5	91.4	5.9	2.7	87.7	7.9	4.5
Uttar Pradesh	87.1	1.5	11.4	91.9	1.0	7.2	57.1	9.5	33.4	58.4	9.0	32.6
Assam	98.6	0.2	1.2	96.4	2.4	1.2	95.8	3.4	0.8	88.2	11.8	0.0
Bihar	99.4	0.6	0.1	100.0	0.0	0.0	97.7	1.8	0.5	99.4	0.5	0.1
Gujarat	95.0	1.3	3.6	69.0	4.9	26.2	86.4	5.1	8.5	82.8	3.9	13.3
Haryana	98.0	0.8	1.2	77.0	1.6	21.4	81.9	1.4	16.7	63.7	1.3	35.0
HP	97.5	0.5	2.0	97.0	0.0	3.0	91.2	2.5	6.2	92.8	0.3	6.9
J&K	98.3	0.3	1.4	87.2	0.8	11.9	90.3	0.9	8.8	66.6	0.9	32.5
Karnataka	94.9	1.7	3.4	93.0	1.1	5.9	80.5	10.2	9.2	79.0	7.9	13.2
MP	92.0	1.5	6.4	82.6	1.2	16.2	77.2	2.6	20.1	69.2	1.0	29.8
Orissa	99.0	0.8	0.3	99.4	0.7	0.0	91.9	5.0	3.1	86.2	6.0	7.8
Punjab	98.1	0.5	1.4	93.2	0.6	6.2	92.5	1.9	5.6	93.8	1.2	4.9
Rajasthan	92.1	1.0	6.9	90.4	0.5	9.0	81.4	2.7	15.9	80.6	1.9	17.5
Tamil Nadu	83.5	16.1	0.3	83.6	16.1	0.3	66.4	32.6	1.0	66.4	32.6	1.0
West Bengal	92.0	8.0	0.04	100.0	0.0	0.0	26.0	73.8	0.2	0.0	100	0.0
India	92.1	3.8	4.1	90.9	3.1	6.0	79.5	9.5	11.0	76.4	7.8	15.8

Source: All India Educational Survey, 1993, NCERT, New Delhi Selected Educational Statistics, 2001-02, MHRD, Govt of India

HP: Himachal Pradesh; J&K: Jammu and Kashmir; MP: Madhya Pradesh.

Table A3: Share of Enrolment at Primary and Upper Primary Schools by Type of Management Across Major States in 1993

States	*Primary Level*			*Upper Primary*		
	Govt	*PA*	*PUA*	*Govt*	*PA*	*PUA*
Andhra Pradesh	*80.70*	*8.98*	*10.31*	*73.48*	*13.82*	*12.70*
Kerala	39.34	56.98	3.68	38.46	60.71	0.82
Maharashtra	72.85	19.67	7.48	33.51	58.14	8.35
Uttar Pradesh	77.78	4.20	18.02	34.11	37.17	28.71
Assam	97.77	0.84	1.39	93.32	5.67	1.01
Bihar	97.59	1.60	0.81	94.79	3.22	2.00
Gujarat	84.45	3.93	11.62	55.88	31.95	12.16
Haryana	89.63	2.91	7.47	81.49	8.46	10.05
HP	93.97	1.05	4.99	93.60	1.71	4.70
J&K	88.43	2.40	9.18	87.94	3.51	8.55
Karnataka	78.37	11.24	10.39	60.86	26.45	12.69
MP	84.45	2.94	12.61	79.20	4.57	16.23
Orissa	97.60	1.23	1.17	72.60	20.10	7.30
Punjab	89.66	4.73	5.61	80.07	13.20	6.74
Rajasthan	80.47	3.77	15.75	80.84	6.45	12.71
Tamil Nadir	67.49	29.45	3.06	61.01	34.90	4.09
West Bengal	82.29	17.29	0.42	24.05	74.63	1.32
India	80.75	10.68	8.57	58.03	30.94	11.03

Note: Enrolment by type of management data for 2002 is not yet available by states.

Source: Sixth All India Educational Survey, 1993, NCERT, New Delhi.

Table A4: Share of Secondary and Higher Secondary Schools and Enrolment by Type of Management in Selected States, 1986

States	Lower Secondary						Higher Secondary					
	Schools			Enrolment			Schools			Enrolment		
	Govt	PA	PUA	Govt	PA	PUA	Govt	PA	PUA	Govt	PA	PUA
AP	54.89	22.66	22.45	76.49	16.39	7.12	65.94	25.46	8.60	78.00	5.84	16.16
Kerala	38.89	57.09	4.02	39.80	57.36	2.85	65.48	17.86	16.67	45.25	46.87	7.87
Maharashtra	11.08	60.15	28.77	14.47	73.72	11.81	10.64	82.92	6.44	5.45	87.39	7.16
U P	19.80	65.07	15.13	11.50	82.25	6.25	16.57	82.12	1.30	13.51	85.62	0.86
Assam	66.23	32.15	1.61	83.62	15.83	0.55	99.18	0.27	0.55	93.21	6.28	0.51
Bihar	93.88	5.10	1.02	82.21	4.22	13.57	34.19	5.93	9.88	81.51	12.60	5.89
Gujarat	7.21	91.85	0.94	10.13	89.03	0.83	10.79	88.24	0.97	12.52	86.30	1.18
Haryana	84.57	12.37	3.05	77.88	18.76	3.36	31.67	14.44	3.89	81.31	13.91	4.78
HP	87.77	7.74	4.49	93.13	4.02	2.85	93.28	4.20	2.52	95.00	2.59	2.41
J & K	88.53	7.33	4.14	86.92	8.40	4.68	88.89	6.11	5.00	93.05	5.01	1.94
Karnataka	31.66	47.37	20.97	34.89	53.58	11.53	44.13	41.77	14.10	38.95	50.03	11.03
MP	72.46	10.28	17.26	79.91	13.08	7.02	77.36	14.25	8.39	72.90	18.56	8.54
Orissa	15.17	60.23	24.60	28.02	53.82	18.16	46.67	0.00	53.33	100.00	0.00	0.00
Punjab	83.44	12.19	4.36	75.16	18.57	6.27	55.83	40.28	3.89	59.22	34.44	6.33
Rajasthan	93.01	4.58	2.41	72.24	21.35	6.40	75.48	20.15	4.37	78.70	17.82	3.47
Tamil Nadu	69.94	17.22	12.83	59.18	35.90	4.92	48.96	39.01	12.03	48.15	46.02	5.83
West Bengal	0.60	97.95	1.45	1.46	95.63	2.90	3.61	93.63	2.75	3.46	94.31	2.22
All India	43.48	43.86	12.66	43.30	50.19	6.51	41.69	52.36	5.96	33.38	61.30	5.31

Source: Sixth All India Educational Survey, 1993, NCERT, New Delhi.

Table A5: Share of Secondary and Higher Secondary Schools and Enrolment by Type of Management in Selected States, 1993

States	*Lower Secondary*						*Higher Secondary*					
	Schools			*Enrolment*			*Schools*			*Enrolment*		
	Govt	*PA*	*PUA*	*Govt*	*PA*	*PUA*	*Govt*	*PA*	*PUA*	*Govt*	*PA*	*PUA*
Andhra Pradesh	76.05	10.56	13.39	72.3	15.7	12.0	37.46	16.33	46.21	46.0	23.2	30.8
Kerala	36.14	58.60	5.26	41.7	55.9	2.4	74.58	18.31	7.12	73.4	21.3	5.4
Maharashtra	10.64	56.76	32.60	10.9	77.7	11.4	10.20	84.15	5.65	8.4	87.7	4.0
Uttar Pradesh	29.37	47.49	23.13	13.6	77.2	9.2	18.88	75.23	5.89	15.6	79.2	5.3
Assam	84.48	13.80	1.72	89.2	9.7	1.1	98.49	1.01	0.50	97.6	1.7	0.8
Bihar	94.63	3.79	1.58	93.9	3.8	2.3	65.20	11.60	23.20	50.8	16.5	32.7
Gujarat	9.10	87.90	3.00	8.6	89.5	2.0	8.17	88.94	2.89	9.4	88.5	2.2
Haryana	79.31	5.20	15.49	73.9	13.3	12.8	71.46	17.91	10.63	76.5	16.9	6.6
HP	85.56	4.88	9.56	90.4	3.7	5.9	71.37	8.30	20.33	87.5	5.4	7.2
J & K	88.18	4.42	7.40	89.7	4.7	5.7	98.00	0.03	1.99	93.7	3.5	2.9
Karnataka	29.98	40.24	29.78	33.3	53.0	13.7	46.08	42.55	11.36	42.5	49.6	7.9
Madhya Pradesh	58.93	3.18	37.89	71.1	8.8	20.2	65.57	10.54	23.89	69.1	12.0	18.9
Orissa	26.40	50.83	22.77	31.4	51.0	17.6	31.33	32.11	36.55	20.5	41.5	38.0
Punjab	83.43	10.26	6.31	74.7	19.1	6.3	68.41	22.72	8.87	71.8	23.3	4.9
Rajasthan	87.99	3.39	8.62	84.6	9.0	6.5	72.67	16.53	10.80	80.2	14.5	5.3
Tamil Nadu	69.84	20.35	9.81	59.2	36.3	4.5	50.31	37.56	12.13	52.1	42.3	5.7
West Bengal	22.72	76.48	0.81	23.9	74.3	1.9	25.93	71.15	2.92	25.2	71.6	3.2
India	48.75	35.17	16.08	45.2	46.0	8.7	42.37	44.99	12.64	42.2	47.6	10.2

Source: Sixth All India Educational Survey, 1993, NCERT, New Delhi.

Table A6: Growth Rate of Institutions at Lower Secondary Level by Type of Management Across States between 1986 and 1993 (in %)

States	Govt	Private Aided	Private Unaided	Total
Andhra Pradesh	10.9	-5.1	-1.7	5.8
Kerala	-2.1	-0.7	2.8	-1.1
Maharashtra	4.0	3.7	6.5	4.6
Uttar Pradesh	6.1	-4.1	6.5	0.3
Assam	7.6	-7.9	4.8	3.9
Bihar	1.7	-2.7	8.1	1.6
Gujarat	5.4	1.3	20.3	1.9
Haryana	1.0	-9.9	28.6	2.0
HP	3.2	-3.0	15.4	3.6
J&K	2.9	-4.2	11.9	3.0
Karnataka	4.0	2.4	10.3	4.9
MP	4.1	-9.0	20.3	7.4
Orissa	12.9	1.8	3.2	4.3
Punjab	-0.6	-3.0	4.8	-0.6
Rajasthan	5.2	1.6	27.3	6.1
Tamil Nadu	3.3	5.8	-0.5	3.3
West Bengal	68.5	-3.2	-7.7	0.3
India	5.0	0.1	6.9	3.3

Source: Fifth and Sixth All India Educational Surveys, 1992; 1998, NCERT, New Delhi.

Table A7: Growth Rate of Institutions at Higher Secondary Level by Type of Management Across States between 1986 and 1993

States	Govt	Private Aided	Private Unaided	Total
Andhra Pradesh	3.1	4.9	42.1	11.8
Kerala	21.9	20.1	6.0	19.7
Maharashtra	7.4	8.2	6.0	8.0
Uttar Pradesh	5.5	2.2	28.5	3.5
Assam	7.2	29.2	6.0	7.3
Bihar	6.3	21.3	24.5	10.2
Gujarat	1.6	5.9	23.6	5.7
Haryana	14.7	20.5	34.9	16.9
HP	6.5	21.9	49.0	10.6
J&K	4.9	1.3	-10.9	4.2
Karnataka	5.3	4.9	1.5	4.6
MP	4.5	2.5	24.3	7.0
Orissa	50.1	na	50.5	58.9
Punjab	18.2	5.8	29.2	14.8
Rajasthan	3.1	0.7	17.9	3.6
Tamil Nadu	4.7	3.7	4.4	4.3
West Bengal	34.1	-2.7	2.1	1.2
India	6.5	4.0	18.3	6.2

Source: Fifth and Sixth All India Educational Surveys, 1992; 1998, NCERT, New Delhi.

Table A8: Growth Rate of Enrolment at Lower Secondary Level by Type of Management Across States between 1986 and 1993

States	*Govt*	*Private Aided*	*Private Unaided*	*Total*
Andhra Pradesh	3.31	3.48	12.26	4.15
Kerala	4.34	3.27	1.42	3.66
Maharashtra	0.32	5.31	3.96	4.51
Uttar Pradesh	4.84	1.42	8.10	2.34
Assam	6.24	-1.80	15.81	5.26
Bihar	1.43	-1.91	-22.72	-0.47
Gujarat	2.53	5.11	18.97	5.04
Haryana	4.53	0.29	27.42	5.31
HP	6.68	5.72	18.85	7.13
J&K	2.95	-5.82	5.26	2.49
Karnataka	3.99	4.50	7.30	4.67
MP	5.77	1.60	25.06	7.55
Orissa	5.32	2.81	3.18	3.61
Punjab	4.59	5.09	4.71	4.69
Rajasthan	7.85	-6.82	5.57	5.45
Tamil Nadu	3.90	4.07	2.46	3.89
West Bengal	53.47	-0.67	-3.44	2.99
India	4.71	2.78	8.50	4.06

Source: Fifth and Sixth All India Educational Surveys, 1992; 1998, NCERT, New Delhi.

Table A9: Growth Rate of Enrolment at Higher Secondary Level by Type of Management Across States between during 1986 and 1993

States	*Govt*	*Private Aided*	*Private Unaided*	*Total*
Andhra Pradesh	1.68	33.50	20.25	9.65
Kerala	14.02	-4.97	0.70	6.40
Maharashtra	5.25	-0.93	-8.88	-0.97
Uttar Pradesh	2.02	-1.13	29.51	-0.02
Assam	1.18	-16.98	6.96	0.52
Bihar	0.72	11.94	37.64	7.75
Gujarat	7.63	12.51	22.14	12.12
Haryana	25.72	30.44	32.90	26.84
HP	30.06	46.07	53.94	31.62
J&K	5.72	0.30	11.62	5.62
Karnataka	3.55	2.15	-2.47	2.27
MP	26.22	19.50	42.53	27.20
Orissa	47.57	NA	NA	85.10
Punjab	25.28	15.25	17.65	21.89
Rajasthan	14.83	11.22	21.53	14.52
Tamil Nadu	10.26	7.71	8.52	9.03
West Bengal	36.08	-1.46	7.86	2.49
India	10.16	2.74	16.95	6.50

Source: Fifth and Sixth All India Educational Surveys, 1992; 1998, NCERT, New Delhi.

Table A10: Growth Rate of Institutions at Lower Secondary Level by Type of Management Across States between 1993 and 2001-02

States	Govt	Private Aided	Private Unaided	Total
Andhra Pradesh	3.9	2.2	14.4	5.7
Kerala	2.5	1.1	15.0	2.8
Maharashtra	-0.5	4.0	-0.5	2.2
Uttar Pradesh	-10.0	4.6	8.2	2.9
Assam	1.4	1.8	37.5	4.0
Bihar	-3.2	-14.9	-21.8	-3.6
Gujarat	0.1	0.6	23.2	2.2
Haryana	0.7	-7.1	15.7	4.2
HP	1.3	-5.2	10.1	2.2
J&K	0.3	-1.5	13.9	1.0
Karnataka	6.7	2.7	9.6	6.3
MP	0.6	1.9	10.8	5.5
Orissa	10.7	-14.5	6.5	1.9
Punjab	-0.3	-0.7	7.6	0.4
Rajasthan	1.4	-8.1	22.2	4.9
Tamil Nadu	4.2	4.2	4.2	4.2
West Bengal	-41.0	7.1	26.2	4.5
India	2.5	2.3	9.2	3.8

Source: (i) All India Educational Survey, 1993, NCERT, New Delhi.
(ii) Selected Educational Statistics, 2001-02, MHRD, Govt of India.

Table A11: Growth Rate of Institutions at Higher Secondary Level By Type of Management Across States between 1993 and 2001-02

States	Govt	Private Aided	Private Unaided	Total
Andhra Pradesh	4.3	4.0	12.9	8.9
Kerala	13.7	31.5	24.9	19.7
Maharashtra	-38.4	6.6	8.0	-16.7
Uttar Pradesh	-9.3	4.4	11.5	3.3
Assam	1.8	0.0	-100.0	1.7
Bihar	8.4	-25.7	-41.0	3.4
Gujarat	2.7	0.4	19.3	1.7
Haryana	10.1	5.8	23.1	11.6
HP	13.7	-0.6	12.5	12.7
J&K	0.4	8.0	18.9	1.5
Karnataka	6.1	6.1	6.2	6.1
MP	-0.4	-4.9	13.2	4.0
Orissa	27.0	-100.0	-100.0	11.6
Punjab	11.7	0.4	6.6	9.4
Rajasthan	7.7	-1.4	14.4	7.5
Tamil Nadu	5.4	5.4	5.4	5.4
West Bengal	-22.8	11.9	14.7	8.5
India	5.9	5.4	11.7	6.6

Source: (i) All India Educational Survey, 1993, NCERT, New Delhi.
(ii) Selected Educational Statistics, 2001-02, MHRD, and Govt of India.

Table A12: Share of Private Unaided Schools by Levels of School Education Across Major States in India

	Primary			Upper Primary			Secondary			Higher Secondary		
	1986	*1993*	*2001*	*1986*	*1993*	*2001*	*1986*	*1993*	*2001*	*1986*	*1993*	*2001*
Andhra Pradesh	1.4	3.0	2.2	7.4	13.2	23.8	5.4	13.4	27.2	17.3	46.2	63.9
Kerala	1.7	2.0	2.3	1.3	2.0	5.0	4.0	5.3	14.4	16.7	7.1	10.4
Maharashtra	3.4	4.0	4.5	2.1	2.7	4.5	28.8	32.6	25.5	6.4	5.7	6.6
Uttar Pradesh	6.8	11.4	7.2	35.5	33.4	32.6	15.1	23.1	36.4	1.3	5.9	11.7
Assam	1.3	1.2	1.2	0.4	0.9	0.0	1.6	1.7	21.2	0.5	0.5	0.0
Bihar	0.0	0.1	0.0	0.5	0.5	0.1	1.0	1.6	0.2	9.9	23.2	0.2
Gujarat	2.7	3.6	26.2	6.3	8.5	13.3	0.9	3.0	16.1	1.0	2.9	12.1
Haryana	0.5	1.2	21.4	3.8	16.7	35.0	3.1	15.5	39.9	1.7	10.6	25.7
HP	0.4	2.0	3.0	1.4	6.2	7.0	4.5	9.6	18.7	2.5	20.3	19.9
J & K	1.0	1.4	12.0	3.3	8.8	32.5	4.1	7.4	20.2	5.0	2.0	6.9
Karnataka	3.2	3.4	5.9	6.2	9.2	13.2	21.0	29.8	39.3	14.1	11.4	11.5
MP	3.6	6.4	16.2	11.2	20.1	29.8	17.3	37.9	59.2	8.4	23.9	51.0
Orissa	0.4	0.3	0.0	3.8	3.1	7.8	24.6	22.8	33.8	53.3	36.6	0.0
Punjab	0.5	1.4	6.2	4.6	5.6	5.0	4.4	6.3	11.8	3.9	8.9	7.0
Rajasthan	3.9	6.9	9.0	8.1	16.4	17.5	2.4	8.6	34.1	4.4	10.8	18.9
Tamil Nadu	0.0	0.3	0.3	0.6	1.0	1.0	12.8	9.8	9.8	12.0	12.1	12.1
West Bengal	0.0	0.0	0.0	0.0	0.2	0.0	1.5	0.8	4.4	2.8	2.9	4.8
India	2.6	4.1	6.0	8.6	11.0	15.8	11.1	16.1	25.5	6.3	12.6	19.3

Source: (i) Selected Educational Statistics 2001-2002, MHRD, GOI, New Delhi, 2003.

(ii) Fifth and Sixth All India Educational Surveys, 1986 and 1993, NCERT, New Delhi.

Table A13: Percentage of Secondary and Higher Secondary Schools by Management Type Across Major States in India in 2001-02 and 2003-04

State	*2001-02*						*2003-04*					
	Lower Secondary			*Higher Secondary*			*Lower Secondary*			*Higher Secondary*		
	Govt	*PA*	*PUA*	*Govt*	*PA*	*PUA*	*Govt*	*PA*	*FUA*	*Govt*	*PA*	*PUA*
Andhra Pradesh	65.0	7.8	27.2	25.4	10.8	63.9	63.0	6.6	30.4	22.8	13.8	63.4
Kerala	35.2	50.5	14.4	46.9	42.7	10.4	34.6	49.5	15.9	33.2	39.4	27.4
Maharashtra	8.3	66.2	25.5	5.9	87.5	6.6	7.7	63.1	29.2	6.4	86.5	7.1
Uttar Pradesh	8.8	54.8	36.4	5.8	82.5	11.7	6.6	38.4	55.0	5.7	33.7	60.6
Assam	67.4	11.4	21.2	97.8	0.9	0.0	60.5	13.8	25.7	88.4	3.4	8.2
Bihar	98.5	1.2	0.2	99.3	0.6	0.2	96.5	1.6	1.9	98.1	0.6	1.3
Gujarat	7.5	76.4	16.1	9.0	78.9	12.1	7.1	69.6	23.3	7.7	74.2	18.1
Haryana	58.3	1.9	39.9	63.2	11.1	25.7	53.4	1.6	45.0	57.7	8.8	33.5
HP	78.8	2.5	18.7	77.4	2.7	19.9	72.8	1.8	25.4	71.7	2.8	25.5
J & K	76.6	3.3	20.2	84.4	8.7	6.9	66.3	0.0	33.7	84.0	0.0	16.0
Karnataka	31.2	29.5	39.3	46.0	42.5	11.5	33.6	29.1	37.3	34.0	25.7	40.3
MP	38.5	2.3	59.2	44.3	4.7	51.0	49.8	1.4	48.8	48.6	5.6	45.8
Orissa	55.7	10.5	33.8	100.0	0.0	0.0	52.2	9.6	38.2	100.0	0.0	0.0
Punjab	78.9	9.3	11.8	82.6	10.5	7.0	77.3	9.1	13.5	76.6	10.3	13.2
Rajasthan	64.9	1.0	34.1	73.5	7.6	18.9	53.8	0.6	45.6	65.7	5.9	28.4
Tamil Nadu	69.8	20.4	9.8	50.3	37.6	12.1	42.7	13.3	44.0	39.6	22.0	38.4
West Bengal	0.1	95.5	4.4	1.2	94.0	4.8	0.2	93.7	6.1	1.1	95.5	3.4
India	43.5	30.9	25.5	40.1	40.7	19.3	40.9	27.5	31.7	36.1	31.2	32.7

Source: Selected Educational Statistics 2001-2002; 2003-04, MHRD, GOI, New Delhi, 2003; 2006.

Table A14: Growth Rate (in percent) of Institutions by Regions and Types of Management at Secondary Level in Sample States

State/Region	*Govt*	*PA*	*PUA*	*Total*
AP			1987-88 to 2004-05	
Costal	3.9	1.3	18.8	4.7
Royalaseema	3.8	2.4	19.9	5.6
Telangana	5.4	2.2	16.6	7.5
Total	4.5	1.8	17.4	6.2
Kerala			1990-91 to 2002-03	
South	0.1	-0.6	5.4	0.0
Midle	1.1	1.6	4.0	1.6
North	-1.2	-1.4	8.9	-0.7
Total	-0.1	0.2	5.7	0.4
Maharashtra			1990-91 to 2002-03	
Mumbai	1.6	-1.3	0.7	-0.4
Nashik	4.5	-0.9	2.7	0.3
Pune	-0.1	-0.6	3.9	0.7
Kolhapur	NA	NA	NA	NA
Aurangabad	-5.2	-0.3	-1.8	-1.8
Amravati	-6.8	1.6	3.3	1.3
Nagpur	-4.6	4.3	-2.0	1.7
Latur	NA	NA	NA	NA
Total	-1.1	2.7	2.9	2.5

Note: Government includes local bodies.

Sources: (i) Directorate of School Education, GOAP, 2004-05.
(ii) Education Since Independence, Directorate of School Education, Govt of Kerala, 2004.
(iii) Directorate of Secondary Education, Govt of Maharashtra, 2005.
(iv) Board of Secondary and Higher Secondary Education, Govt of Uttar Pradesh, 2005.

Table A15: Share of Institutions and Enrolment by Region and Type of Management in Sample States

States/Regions	Institutions						Enrolment					
	Govt	Aided	Unaided	Govt	Aided	Unaided	Govt	Aided	Unaided	Govt	Aided	Unaided
Andhra Pradesh		1987-88			2004-05			1987-88			2004-05	
Costal	82.7	15.1	2.2	72.3	8.7	18.6	NA	NA	NA	74.19	11.06	14.74
Royalseema	87.8	8.7	3.5	64.5	5.2	29.9	NA	NA	NA	70.43	7.11	22.46
Talangana	78.8	11.4	9.8	56.1	4.8	38.9	NA	NA	NA	57.85	5.81	36.34
Total	82.0	12.4	5.7	62.5	6.1	31.1	NA	NA	NA	65.24	7.93	26.1
Maharashtra		1990-91			2002-03			1990-91			2002-03	
Mumbai	4.2	59.8	36.0	5.3	53.4	41.3	7.96	76.33	15.71	6.8	65.9	27.2
Nasik	5.7	74.8	19.6	9.3	64.7	26.0	4.48	87.88	7.64	6.5	84.7	8.8
Pune	3.9	72.6	23.5	3.5	62.2	34.3	4.38	87.26	8.36	3.7	79.0	17.2
Kolhapur	0.0	0.0	0.0	0.5	73.0	26.4	0.00	0.00	0.00	0.9	87.2	11.9
Aurangabad	26.0	44.9	29.1	17.0	54.0	29.1	36.25	53.54	10.21	24.6	64.4	11.0
Amravati	12.8	65.9	21.3	4.7	68.4	27.0	15.30	76.39	8.31	6.5	82.2	11.3
Nagpur	14.4	53.6	32.1	6.7	72.8	20.6	15.24	75.42	9.34	7.9	81.9	10.2
Latur	NA	NA	NA	14.5	66.3	19.3	NA	NA	NA	23.1	69.7	7.1
Total	10.3	62.2	27.5	6.8	64.1	29.2	12.2	77.4	10.4	8.6	76.1	15.3
Kerala		1990-91			2000-01			1990-91			2000-01	
South	38.6	57.4	4.0	38.3	57.0	4.7	37.35	59.87	2.78	35.47	59.63	4.89
Middle	31.8	62.1	6.1	32.6	60.7	6.7	29.02	67.71	3.27	25.15	68.79	6.07
North	50.6	46.4	3.0	47.8	44.7	7.6	49.22	49.74	1.04	45.17	52.18	2.65
Total	40.0	55.6	4.5	39.5	54.1	6.4	39.7	58.1	2.2	37.4	58.5	4.1

States/Regions	Institutions						Enrolment					
	Govt	Aided	Unaided	Govt	Aided	Unaided	Govt	Aided	Unaided	Govt	Aided	Unaided
Uttar Pradesh		—			2003-04			—			2003-04	
Western	NA	NA	NA	3.53	37.95	47.74	NA	NA	NA	3.49	43.54	36.79
Central	NA	NA	NA	4.36	30.26	65.38	NA	NA	NA	4.01	39.36	55.93
Bundelkhand	NA	NA	NA	14.69	42.19	43.12	NA	NA	NA	14.37	51.99	33.35
Eastern	NA	NA	NA	3.80	41.81	53.71	NA	NA	NA	2.97	49.01	44.37
Total	NA	NA	NA	4.20	38.13	53.12	NA	NA	NA	3.71	45.63	43.11

Note: Government includes local bodies.

Sources: (i) Directorate of School Education, GOAP, 2004-05.
(ii) Education Since Independence, Directorate of School Education, Govt of Kerala, 2004.
(iii) Directorate of Secondary Education, Govt of Maharashtra, 2005.
(iv) Board of Secondary and Higher Secondary Education, Govt of Uttar Pradesh, 2005.

* Data for Uttar Pradesh includes only 60 districts.

Table A16: Share of Lower Secondary Schools and Enrolment by Type of Management and Districts in Maharashtra 2002-03

Districts	*% of Lower Secondary Schools, 2003-04*			*% of Enrolment in Lower Secondary Schools, 2003-04*		
	Govt	*PA*	*PUA*	*Govt*	*PA*	*PUA*
Mumbai	5.2	57.1	37.7	8.7	65.4	25.9
Thane	6.3	45.1	48.5	4.3	63.3	32.4
Raigad	3	62.3	34.7	1.9	78.4	19.7
Ratnagiri	0.7	75.7	23.6	0.5	86.7	12.8
Sindhudurg	0.6	87.7	11.7	0.6	93	6.4
Nasik	8	62	30	6.4	83.3	10.3
Dhule	9	73.1	17.9	4.1	87.5	8.4
Nanddarbar	27.9	40.2	31.8	19.1	67.8	13.1
Jalgaon	4.3	72.5	23.2	4.8	89.1	6.1
Ahmednager	2.6	58.9	38.5	2	82.8	15.2
Pune	5.6	59.4	35	6.5	71.3	22.2
Satara	0.4	73.5	26.1	0.3	86.4	13.3
Sangh	0.2	71.1	28.6	1.2	88.2	10.6
Solapur	1.7	69.8	28.6	1.6	85.8	12.6
Kollhapur	0.6	69	30.4	1.3	86.2	12.5
Aurangabad	15.2	57.6	27.2	23.7	65.9	10.4
Jalna	15.7	49.2	35.1	25.1	61.9	13
Parbhani	21.6	50.8	27.6	26.5	63.7	9.8
Hingoh	26.7	45.8	27.5	35	53.7	11.3
Beed	14	56.7	29.3	21.1	67.8	11.1
Nanded	16.8	67.5	15.7	25.3	69.7	5
Osmanabad	16.2	56.1	27.7	23.3	65.3	11.4
Latur	11	72.6	16.5	21.1	72.4	6.5
Buldhna	3.5	64.5	31.9	4.1	85.1	10.8
Akola	2.4	64.8	32.8	7	76.9	16.1
Washin	1.8	65	33.1	4.9	81.4	13.7
Amravati	5.9	75.1	19	7.7	83.5	8.8
Yavtmal	6.9	68	25.1	7.7	82	10.3
Wardha	2.4	80.4	17.3	1.8	88.4	9.8
Nagpur	4.9	71	24	7.2	81.6	11.2
Bhardara	1.7	77.8	20.5	1.8	89.8	8.4
Gondia	9.4	72.4	18.2	12	77.3	10.7
Chandrapur	6.6	74.8	18.5	7.1	82.6	10.3
Godchi	20.3	61.4	18.3	24.6	67.9	7.5
Maharashtra	6.8	64.1	29.2	8.6	76.1	15.3

Source: Directorate of Primary Education, Statistical Division, Govt. of Maharashtra, Pune, 2004.

Table A17: Share of Lower Secondary Schools and Enrolment by Type of Management and Districts in Andhra Pradesh, 2004-05

Districts	*% of Lower Secondary Schools, 2004-05*			*% of Enrolment in Lower Secondary Schools, 2004-05*		
	Govt	*Pvt. Aided*	*Pvt Unaided*	*Govt*	*Pvt. Aided*	*Pvt Unaided*
Srikakulam	91.0	0.5	8.5	94.9	0.1	4.9
Vizianagaram	76.0	5.9	18.2	76.5	9.5	14.0
Visakhapatnam	69.4	5.4	25.2	69.9	8.5	21.6
East Godavari	70.8	6.5	22.7	80.0	7.6	12.3
West Godavari	77.7	8.6	13.7	80.4	11.1	8.6
Krishna	69.2	12.8	18.0	66.9	14.9	18.1
Guntur	65.7	18.2	16.1	62.2	24.7	13.1
Prakasam	68.1	12.9	19.0	67.3	12.6	20.1
Nellore	72.8	5.4	21.7	69.4	9.8	20.8
Chittoor	69.1	3.2	27.7	74.6	5.0	20.3
Cuddapah	53.6	6.3	40.1	49.8	10.0	40.1
Anantapur	76.3	3.1	20.7	83.5	3.3	13.1
Kurnool	60.1	9.1	30.8	66.4	11.9	21.7
Mahabubnagar	71.4	3.9	24.7	77.3	3.8	18.9
Ranga Reddy	39.5	2.6	58.0	46.7	2.7	50.7
Hyderabad	41.6	10.7	47.8	15.5	17.2	67.4
Medak	74.4	0.9	24.7	80.4	1.0	18.6
Nizamabad	69.3	5.2	25.5	66.8	6.2	26.9
Adilabad	61.9	2.8	35.2	63.0	5.6	31.3
Karimnagar	54.1	2.6	43.2	62.4	3.6	34.0
Warangal	60.5	5.1	34.4	62.0	3.6	34.4
Khammam	69.6	3.8	26.7	72.9	7.3	19.8
Nalgonda	23.0	11.8	65.1	67.4	3.8	28.8
AP	62.8	6.1	31.1	66.0	7.9	26.1

Source: Directorate of School Education, GOAP, Hyderabad, A.P. 2004-05.

Table A18: Share of Lower Secondary Schools and Enrolment by Type of Management and Districts in Kerala in 2003-04

Districts	*% of Lower Secondary Schools, 2003-04*			*% of Enrolment in Lower Secondary Schools, 2000-01*		
	Govt	*Pvt. Aided*	*Pvt Unaided*	*Govt*	*Pvt. Aided*	*Pvt Unaided*
Thiruvananthapuram	49.4	39.3	11.3	51.17	39.31	9.51
Kollan	35.7	59.6	4.7	41.33	53.32	5.34
Pathanamthitta	28.5	67.3	4.2	28.05	64.35	7.60
Alappuzha	30.2	66.1	3.6	32.13	64.26	3.61
Kottayam	24.5	68.9	6.6	21.59	70.17	8.25

Contd.

Districts	*% of Lower Secondary Schools, 2003-04*			*% of Enrolment in Lower Secondary Schools, 2000-01*		
	Govt	*Pvt. Aided*	*Pvt Unaided*	*Govt*	*Pvt. Aided*	*Pvt Unaided*
Idukki	39.0	53.7	7.4	32.65	62.91	4.44
Ernakulam	29.4	59.1	11.5	25.49	64.45	10.07
Thrissur	32.0	59.6	8.4	25.35	69.39	5.27
Palakkad	38.6	51.0	10.5	35.12	60.48	4.40
Malappuram	42.9	41.9	15.2	41.08	57.38	1.54
Kozhikkode	37.4	53.6	8.9	30.42	67.37	2.21
Wayanad	59.7	34.3	6.0	51.96	45.32	2.72
Kannur	48.5	45.6	5.9	26.54	71.52	1.94
Kasargod	65.0	28.2	6.8	58.05	39.68	2.28
Kerala	37.7	54.0	8.2	35.36	59.87	4.77

Source: (i) Educational Statistics Since Independence, 2004, Department of General Education, Govt of Kerala.

(ii) Selected Educational Statistics 2000-01. Directorate of Public Instruction, Thiruvananthapuram.

Table A19: Share of Lower Secondary Schools and Enrolment by Type of Management and Districts in Uttar Pradesh, 2003-04

Districts	*Lower Secondary Schools*			*Enrolment in Lower Secondary Schools*		
	Govt	*PA*	*PUA*	*Govt*	*PA*	*PUA*
Agra	3.2	35.9	60.9	1.3	43.7	49.1
Firozabad	46.7	42.2	11.1	0.8	47.8	17.0
Mainpuri	7.4	40.2	52.5	4.7	45.7	47.2
Etha	3.9	30.2	65.8	1.5	19.6	73.7
Mathura	19.6	53.9	26.5	1.1	57.8	24.9
Aligarh	25.8	22.5	51.7	1.2	9.5	32.3
Bulandshahar	19.9	50.2	30.0	2.5	63.4	22.3
Ghaziabad	45.5	32.2	22.3	2.2	53.9	22.3
Meerut	18.8	54.7	26.5	2.8	63.0	24.2
Bagpat	4.1	75.3	20.6	1.0	82.8	15.2
Muzaffar Nagar	1.7	44.6	53.6	2.4	61.0	32.7
Shaharanpur	22.2	47.0	30.8	2.7	70.5	11.6
Moradabad	3.7	26.8	69.5	3.5	42.0	37.5
Bijnor	7.1	32.4	60.5	9.1	48.8	28.0
Rampur	20.5	31.8	47.7	28.4	48.7	19.1
Bareilly	1.8	40.7	57.5	2.5	56.0	34.5
Badaun	4.5	35.6	59.8	4.7	53.1	36.5
Shahjahanpur	30.2	27.2	42.6	6.2	32.3	43.2

Contd.

Districts	*Lower Secondary Schools*			*Enrolment in Lower Secondary Schools*		
	Govt	*PA*	*PUA*	*Govt*	*PA*	*PUA*
Pilibhit	29.9	11.7	58.4	21.3	8.6	56.0
Farrukhabad	2.7	39.5	57.8	5.4	47.2	47.4
Kannaoj	0.8	43.8	55.4	0.7	47.9	51.4
Etawah	5.3	43.0	51.7	7.3	50.9	41.8
Lakhimpur Kheri	7.5	45.2	47.3	7.8	58.4	32.6
Sitapur	11.5	37.4	51.1	10.2	40.1	42.7
Hardoi	4.0	34.3	61.7	2.4	24.8	72.8
Lucknow	2.7	19.9	77.4	4.8	34.0	61.2
Unnao	7.1	36.8	56.1	5.9	54.3	39.8
Rae Bareili	6.1	31.9	62.0	2.9	44.1	53.0
Kanpur Nagar	1.9	24.3	73.8	1.6	37.8	60.6
Kanpur Dehat	0.7	42.0	57.3	0.6	37.0	62.4
Fatehpur	2.7	39.6	57.7	3.4	51.5	44.7
Barabanki	14.9	34.0	51.1	11.9	42.4	42.9
Jalaun	7.8	50.0	42.2	4.0	54.4	41.6
Hamirpur	21.6	41.2	37.3	19.2	47.9	32.9
Jhansi	10.9	40.3	48.7	9.9	55.6	33.5
Lalitpur	24.1	37.9	37.9	41.9	43.7	14.4
Mahoba	25.7	25.7	48.6	40.3	35.6	24.1
Banda	19.4	41.8	38.8	16.2	54.9	29.0
Shahu JiM Nagar	13.2	42.1	44.7	9.7	61.6	28.7
Pratapgarh	5.7	41.1	53.1	5.1	55.9	38.9
Allahabad	2.2	29.4	68.4	2.1	37.3	59.9
Sultanpur	9.8	43.2	47.0	9.5	53.1	33.6
Faizabad	5.2	41.4	53.4	6.3	48.5	32.2
Bahraich	7.8	45.1	47.1	5.7	51.0	43.3
Gonda	2.8	42.1	55.1	4.6	54.2	41.2
Balrampur	9.5	57.1	33.3	4.1	79.1	14.6
Basti	2.3	59.1	38.6	5.2	58.5	34.9
Siddhartha Nagar	29.6	67.6	2.8	8.5	82.7	4.0
Gorakhpur	7.9	58.4	33.7	4.5	66.8	24.3
Maharaj Ganj	5.3	52.0	42.7	3.7	69.1	16.7
Deoria	1.2	49.2	49.6	0.6	41.2	58.1
Padrauna	1.9	51.9	46.3	0.6	55.3	40.5
Azamgarh	10.4	37.2	52.4	1.6	50.8	42.0
Mau	0.6	40.0	59.4	0.1	55.1	44.8
Ballia	4.3	47.3	48.4	1.9	49.7	48.0
Jaunpur	1.4	54.7	43.8	0.5	64.2	35.2
Ghazipur	2.1	21.5	76.4	1.5	18.3	65.7
Varanasi	3.0	46.0	50.9	3.9	51.7	44.4
Bhadohi	3.3	56.7	40.0	6.2	74.6	19.2
Mirzapur	5.1	44.4	50.4	3.5	56.3	33.4
Uttar Pradesh	8.8	38.1	53.1	3.7	45.7	43.2

Source: State Board of Secondary Education, Allahabad, U.P., 2004.

ANNEXURE I

NOTE ON SAMPLE DISTRICTS

Four districts from the four sample states were chosen as sample districts for micro level school case studies. These four districts were Nalgonda (A.P.), Thiruvanthapuram (Kerala), Pune (Maharashtra) and Varanasi (U.P.). Out of these four, Thiruvanthapuram is a capital city, Pune is a developed educational centre, Nalgonda is a fast growing commercial centre of Andhra Pradesh and Varanasi is an important historical, religious and educationally medium developed district of Uttar Pradesh.

Nalgonda is a medium developed district, consisting of backward areas. The district has higher percentage of government schools with corresponding percentage of enrolment. However, the district has a substantial number of private unaided schools. They form a little less than one-third of the total number of schools in the district covering one-third of students. The private aided schools constitute a very small segment, covering an equal proportion of students.

Thiruvanthapuram is the capital city of Kerala and is the hub of political activity, relatively developed and well connected with other parts of India. In consonance with the state level pattern, there are higher percentages of government and private aided schools with matching percentages of enrolment. The district has a little more than ten percent of private unaided schools with an enrolment of less than 10 per cent of students. The city has some of the best government schools with higher enrolment and bigger school size and importantly these schools have done well over the years. The demand for private aided schools here is often determined by loyalties to caste, class and religion. Despite the district being capital city, with urbanization and higher socio-income groups, yet the extent of private unaided schools is not high in proportion, like in case of other sample districts in the other three states.

Pune is one of the important cities not only of Maharashtra but also of India. It is a major commercial, educational and industrial town. In conformity with the general trend of the state, the city has a meagre percentage of government schools with equal percentage of enrolment. However, the district has higher percentage of private aided schools with a slightly better percentage of enrolment, thus underlining the state and regional educational characteristics. Interestingly, in the district, more than one-third schools are under the private unaided sector, covering only slightly more than one-fifth of total student enrolment.

Varanasi is one of the oldest towns of India, famous for its religious fervour and tourist attraction. This medially level developed district has a negligible presence of government schools with a slightly better enrolment percentage. The private unaided schools account for more than fifty percent, covering a high percentage of students followed by private aided schools with higher percentage of enrolment than their proportion. The trend in Varanasi is quite different from the other three sample districts. It points to the general state and regional educational features.

4

Gender and Social Equity Perspective in Secondary Education

The educational expansion and the dynamics of development and the delivery mechanism of secondary education is well examined in the earlier chapters. Does this expansion entail equity? It is equally essential to look at the question of equity while delineating the demand for secondary education. Hence, this chapter attempts to examine the gender and social equity in the demand for secondary education. It also attempts to look at various interventions by the Government of India and state governments to improve the participation of girls and children from the socially deprived sections of the population.

The first section of the chapter attempts to examine the demand for secondary education by gender and social groups. Subsequently, the interventions to improve the participation of both gender and the deprived social groups are attempted further.

Demand for Secondary Education: Gender Perspective

Gender perspective in participation has been examined using a number of indicators from simple share of girls to total enrolment to a little sophisticated gender parity index bedsides, the growth rates of boys and girls enrolment in secondary and higher secondary education. Growth rate of enrolment at various levels in general and in the context of lower and higher secondary level in particular provides an interesting insight into emerging trends of demand for secondary education from gender perspective (see Table 4.1).

Table 4.1: Growth Rate of Girls' Enrolment at All India Level

Year	Primary		Upper Primary		Lower & Higher Secondary		Lower Secondary		Higher Secondary	
	Boys	Girls	Boys	Girls	Boys	Girls	Boys	Girls	Boys	Girls
1950-51 to 1960-61	5.5	7.8	7.0	12.3	7.6	13.3	–	–	–	–
1960-61 to 1970-71	4.2	6.5	6.3	9.3	7.8	10.5	–	–	–	–
1970-71 to 1980-81	2.4	3.0	4.0	5.7	2.9	6.0	–	–	–	–
1980-81 to 1990-91	2.3	3.6	4.5	6.3	5.4	6.4	6.9	8.3	3.5	6.5
1990-91 to 2001-02	1.0	2.0	1.8	3.7	2.5	5.2	2.1	4.5	3.5	6.7

Source: Selected Educational Statistics for various years, MHRD, GOI, New Delhi.

When we examine the gender equity, there has been a consistent higher growth rate in girls' enrolment, compared to boys at all levels. After having higher growth rate during initial decades, it has steadily declined which has nevertheless been obvious. However, at lower and higher secondary levels, still the growth of girls' enrolment is higher than at the lower level and among boys indicating that girls still have to reach an optimum level of equal enrolment. In other words, though the demand for secondary education among girls had a positive growth rate, yet there is a gap between boys and girls.

The growth rate of enrolment among girls is more than double compared to that of boys in lower and higher secondary levels at all India level during the last decade (see annexure Table A2). There has been a considerable variation among states with regard to gender disparity in education based on socio-cultural and economic development context. When we compare the growth rate of girls' enrolment among major states, it is interesting to find that all the states had the national pattern of having higher growth rate among the girls, except in two states at lower secondary level, where both boys and girls have the same growth rate. However, the extent of growth rate varied from 9.3 to 0.3 during 1990-2001.

Similarly, in all the major states the growth rate of enrolment at secondary level was higher among the girls than the boys. This shows increased participation of girls in education than earlier decades (see annexure Table A1). At lower secondary level the highest growth rate of enrolment among girls was in Madhya Pradesh (9.3%) closely followed by other backward states. However, economically and educationally developed Haryana has also shown higher growth rate in girls enrolment where traditionally girls education had been neglected. This higher growth rate of girls' enrolment in the backward states symbolizes the lower base size of girl's education besides indicating the increasing participation of girls.

However, the growth rate of enrolment at higher secondary level among girls has been higher than that of lower secondary nationally and across the states. The similar trend can be seen like the lower secondary level among the states. At higher secondary level, the states, which had consistently higher growth rate of enrolment at lower secondary level, proved to have better and higher growth rate of girls' enrolment. Once again, these states cut across both developed and under developed states. The growth rate of girls' enrolment during 1990-2000 varied between 13.2 and 3.3 per cent as the highest and the lowest among Haryana and Uttar Pradesh. Most states had higher growth rate of girls enrolment compared to national average growth rate. Some of the states like Punjab, Orissa, Madhya Pradesh and Rajasthan have shown significant improvement in girls' enrolment at higher secondary level during 1990-2000, even though they were having negative growth rate of enrolment in the earlier decade.

Among the four sample states, while Kerala has a distinction of gender parity both at lower and higher secondary levels with similar growth rate, even though girls out-number boys at higher secondary level. Maharashtra, at lower secondary level, and Andhra Pradesh, at higher secondary level, have higher growth rate of girls' enrolment. The most backward state, that is, Uttar Pradesh lags behind others.

The data depicting the growth rate of enrolment at secondary and higher secondary level puts some light on the participation of girls in education as well as inter-state variation. However, it is quite clear that both at the national level as well as state level there has been increase in the enrolment rate in comparison to previous decade. Some states have a higher growth rate of enrolment at primary level, in fact during the last decade most of the states have shown a perceptible increase in the enrolment of girls. But few states have been able to sustain it over a period of time as well as carrying it forward to next level. States like Madhya Pradesh, Haryana, and Rajasthan had shown much higher percentage of increase in the rate of girl's enrolment not to that of respective states total but also higher than the national average. While at the higher secondary level Andhra Pradesh, Karnataka, Haryana and Orissa have better participation rate. On this basis we can divide the states into three categories. One category of states shows the tendency of higher enrolment at secondary level and maintain rate for transition to higher secondary level. The other states belong to category of moderate level of increase in the enrolment and transition and the third category of states have lower enrolment and lower transition.

The striking phenomena is the relatively higher enrolment of girls in some of the backward states like Rajasthan, Uttar Pradesh and Jammu and Kashmir but when this growth rate is compared to higher secondary level the results are poor. Even a developed state like Haryana shows promising growth rate at secondary level and dipped down at higher secondary level. This forces us to ask the reasons behind this difference.

However, there is not much to rejoice about at the higher growth rate of girls for the simple reason that the base for girls is low and their previous participation rate has been poor thus a general increase in the rate means little unless it is connected to higher retention rate at higher levels of education. Secondly, it may be added that a genuine growth in the participation of girls in education suggests not only the economic development of the state but the general status of women in that locality.

Gender Parity

At the backdrop of growth of girls' enrolment, we have examined the gender parity in terms of proportion of girls to total enrolment at different points of time. During 1950-51, girls' enrolment to the total enrolment was 28.1, 16.1 and 13.3 at primary, upper primary and secondary levels respectively indicating a wide gap of participation among boys and girls in education (see Table 4.2). The extent of girl's participation decreases with the increase in the levels of education.

Table 4.2: Percentage of Girls Enrolment at Various Levels

Year	*Primary*	*Upper Primary*	*Secondary*	*Hr. Sec/Intermediate*
1950-51	28.1	16.1	13.3*	–
1960-61	32.6	23.9	20.5*	–
1970-71	37.4	29.3	25.0*	–
1980-81	38.6	32.9	29.86	29.8
1990-91	41.5	36.7	32.54	29.4
2001-2002	44.1	41.8	39.4	39.8
2007-08	47.5	45.8	43.4*	–

Source: Selected Educational Statistics 2001-2002, Department of Education, MHRD, GOI, New Delhi

It has taken over five decades of efforts to increase the proportion of girls' enrolment although the variation in the proportion of girl's participation in education continues at various levels. The cumulative efforts have brought the proportion of girls up to 43.4 per cent in lower and higher secondary by 2007-08. Ideally, the ratio should be equal and the existing scenario shows the levels of inequality.

The unequal participation of girls can be gauged at all levels from primary to higher secondary levels. However, the gender inequality not necessarily be uniform across the country. The state levels analysis of gender inequality in participation reveals the degree of difference.

Except Kerala no other state has a higher proportion of girls' enrolment in secondary education than that of the boys though it is not the case at the lower level. However, some of the educationally and economically developed states have made strong strides in the direction following Kerala (see annexure Table A2). In addition to this a few of the backward states too have made considerable progress in this regards but many of the backward states are still far away from achieving equality in girls enrolment to that of total enrolment. For instance, in one of the sample states, that is, in Uttar Pradesh, girls constitute a slightly more than one-fourth in secondary and one–third in higher secondary level despite showing an increase from the earlier period, followed by Bihar and Rajasthan during 2001-02.

There is conspicuous disparity among the socio-economically backward northern states and other parts of the country in the percentage proportion of girls at lower secondary level. The states, which are economically poor, educationally backward, pervasiveness of rigid castes and feudal system, coupled with larger rural areas, the proportion of girls is perceptibly very low. The BiMARU states (Bihar, Uttar Pradesh, Rajasthan and Madhya Pradesh) are the ones matching with all these characteristics of backwardness and having apparently very low proportion of girls to total enrolment. Not only these states have lower proportion of girls but the progress of girls' enrolment in these states has also been very slow compared to other states in the last two decades. Among the BiMARU states, Madhya Pradesh showed better performance in terms increase of proportion of girls in the last one decade, compared to other three states, as this state also has exhibited the highest growth rate of schools and enrolment during the same period. In case of Rajasthan, though institutional and girls' enrolment growth rates were reasonably higher, yet the proportion of girls to total enrolment remained low due to a large backlog of gender parity. In other two states (Bihar and Uttar Pradesh), the growth rate of institutions has been very low, coupled with low enrolment growth rates which led to low gender parity.

Contrary to this, interestingly some of the states like Haryana, Himachal Pradesh and Orissa, which were having very low proportion girls, have significantly improved during 1980-90 consistently even in last decade to catch up with other advanced states. In fact, the state of Himachal Pradesh which was occupying 14th place in terms of proportion of girls to total enrolment during 1980s has been able to achieve second place next to Kerala by 2001. While Haryana, though belonging an economically well off state, with a large rural base and a feudal culture, is yet to make progress unlike Uttar Pradesh which has remained still at bottom level. The political and social commitment as well as financial capability of the states plays an important role in improving gender parity in education which is evident from the above states.

Ten of the seventeen major states showed less gender parity at higher secondary level compared to lower secondary level enrolment. At higher secondary level, the gender parity is not an issue in case of Kerala where girls constitute 55 per cent of total enrolment, clearly showing rather a bias towards girls. The liberal state policy of free education for girls, the high pass percentage and higher divisions obtained by girls in X grade public examinations, higher female ratio among the state population etc may be the possible reasons for such a favourable representation of girls. Kerala is closely followed by Tamil Nadu with 49 per cent, showing a marked improvement of percentage proportion of girls at higher secondary level compared to lower secondary level. The state of Himachal Pradesh, like in the case of lower secondary, and Maharashtra and Karnataka showed impressive improvement in gender parity in the last two decades, it was followed by few other states. However, some of the states which showed better gender parity at lower secondary level failed to do so at higher secondary level. Interesting observations emerge from the gender parity pattern among different states. While Rajasthan occupies the lowest position among all the states with only 28 per cent girls in total enrolment, the other three BiMARU states showed better gender parity at higher secondary level compared to lower secondary level improving significantly in the last two decades.

The improvement in the proportion of girls' enrolment can be attributed to increased improved access and enrolment in terms of institutional growth. Many states have adopted a conscious policy of prioritizing opening of schools in rural areas and especially for girls which effected the girls' enrolment.

Three patterns emerge from the analysis of participation and representation of girls in schools at secondary level in the states. First, a group of developed states which have shown higher representation of girls consistently at all levels of school education. The same group of states has marginally lower proportion of girls at higher levels of school education. Contrary to this the backward states have not only lower proportion of girls in secondary level but also their proportion declines significantly from lower to higher levels of school education which constitute the second category. In the third groups of states the proportion of girls are lower at the lower level but found to be higher at lower/higher secondary grades. Interestingly this is not only common to some of the backward states but also found in Kerala.

This shows gender disparity varies at different levels of education. One possible explanation to the trend visible among the third category of states is that, less number of girls usually comes to lower secondary schools than boys and if they continue in the system they have a better chance to complete than the boys, many of whom drop out at higher secondary level. Generally, the girls have the lesser chance to survive in the system and in case of backward states the girls who sustain the system are comparatively from better off families than boys, therefore, are more likely to continue in the higher levels of schools education. However, in case of Kerala there are several reasons behind the lower representations of boys at higher secondary level which includes poor economic background, low performances/ failure in public examination at lower secondary level, inability to get admission in higher secondary level, preference of boys for technical and vocational education, drop out etc.

Gross Enrolment Ratio

Besides the growth rate and proportion of girls enrolment, which indicates the expansion in absolute numbers but not relate it to the relevant age groups population. Hence, it is pertinent to examine the gross enrolment ratios. The gender parity[1] in gross enrolment ratio during 2002-03 in at national level was ranging from 1.08 to 0.49 (see Annexure Table A2). Educationally backward like earlier indicators have shown very low gender parity compared to educationally developed states. Further the gender parity is very low in rural areas in general and across the states and especially in BiMARU states. It can be mentioned that though the enrolment trend have conclusively proved that the demand is more in rural areas which have low access, demand is increasing among girls yet the gender parity is very low particularly among rural women. This further illustrates the social disparity in the country.

As discussed earlier girls education in India has a lot to do with prevailing socio-cultural context rather than economic factor, which is of course an important one. The states like Uttar Pradesh, Rajasthan, Bihar and even Haryana have this gender discrimination well entrenched in their social system. All these states have significant rural population and are generally patriarchal in nature, which are amply reflected in various social practices viz. sati, untouchability, dowry, child marriage, high maternal mortality rates, etc. Child Marriage and female infanticide is a major problem in Rajasthan that unequivocally states the low participation of women and due to child marriage and early marriage practices many girls could not transit to higher secondary level. Early marriage, early pregnancy and poor maternal health record is a vicious circle that keeps girls from the boundaries of higher secondary education even though they manage to enter the lower secondary education level. These states also suffer from the 'son preference syndrome' with a higher premium on boys and their overall development than girls. As level of education improves and cost of education also goes up including the opportunity cost hence girls tend to be treated less favourably than boys resulting in their overall lower participation in higher secondary level.

There are other social and sociological reasons behind the poor representation of girls in the higher secondary schools apart from the reasons given above. One of them is lack of availability of separate toilets for girls in many of the schools in these backward regions which constraints both the parents and the girls from enrolling themselves in these schools. Further, lower percentage of female teachers at higher secondary level who acts not only as role models for these girls but also reassure them and their parents for continuing education. Though over the years one can find an improvement in this aspect at the national level but in case of these states it is still low. Even at the national level the figure is still below the mark. Another reason that affects participation of girls in higher secondary education is the distance, the respective state governments may have fixed the norms both population and distance keeping in mind of the general characteristics but it certainly does not suit to girls in many a cases. For example, lack of travelling facility and longer travel time force many a girls from discontinuing education and in case of tribal areas and difficult geographical terrain without hostels and adequate facilities the chance of girls continuing in the system is lesser. Therefore, it can be said that location, socio-economic condition and cultural context play a much larger role in the participation of girls in education in general and higher secondary education in particular. The equity provisions concerning the aspects of access and participation have been discussed in the separate chapter.

In Indian context disparities are not limited to gender alone rather its spread over to various social groups defined in terms of caste, communities and families. As caste and class tend to converge into one in Indian social context, giving it a distinct look becomes imperative to examine this peculiarity and its impact on secondary education.

Social Disparity

Indian population comprises of a large number of groups belonging to various castes, communities, linguistic divisions and ethnic varieties. Base of these diversities resolves around their level of economic growth and social opportunities placing them into different levels of development. But from general perspective, it is easy to observe that the privileges and penalties are differentially distributed, creating essentially an unequal society. As a result of this historical legacy, the Constitution of India has identified some groups as Scheduled Castes (SC) and Scheduled Tribes (ST) and set the agenda before the state to provide them more concessions and opportunities. One of the most disadvantaged groups of Indian society are the SC and ST communities and they constitute nearly one-fourth of India's population out of which SCs are 16 per cent and the ST population is around 8 per cent.

Any educational development strategy therefore needs to sufficiently address their problem if it has to succeed at national level. Further, the framers of Indian Constitution had kept in mind the social and civil disabilities encountered by these groups and there made adequate space for their welfare. Based on these constitutional commitments both at national and state levels affirmative actions were incorporated into state policy, particularly to enable them to achieve educational and economic standards (these pro-equity and other facilities providing policies are discussed in detail in a separate chapter). In view of these mechanisms and special measures, it becomes imperative to look at the nature of demand, and participation of these groups in education (see Table 4.3).

Table 4.3: Proportion of Enrolment of Schedules Cates and Scheduled Tribes in India

Years	*Primary*	*Upper Primary*	*Secondary*	*Hr Secondary*
		Scheduled Castes		
1981-82	15.4	11.7	10.6	11.4
1990-91	15.9	12.5	11.9	9.7
2001-02	18.9	16.7	14.7	13.1
		Scheduled Tribes		
1981-82	6.7	4.0	3.3	2.4
1990-91	7.9	5.1	4.2	3.0
2001-02	10.3	7.5	5.9	5.0

Source: Selected Educational Statistics, Govt. of MHRD, New Delhi, 1981-82, 1990-91, 2001-02.

In the last two decades, the proportion of SC and ST enrolment to that of total enrolment has increased at all levels of school education. However, the data reveals that this increase is more at the lower level of education than at the lower and higher secondary stages. In the last two decade there has been nearly one and half percent increase in the enrolment rate of SCs and almost doubled for STs. It also shows that while the SC students at lower and higher secondary levels constituted 14.7 and 13.1 per cent of the total enrolment at all India level during 2001-02, the percentage of ST students at the same level was only of 5.9 and 5.0 per cent respectively for the same period. In case of SCs the percentage share of their enrolment is equivalent to their total share of population while in case of STs it is less than to their proportion of population.[2]

Since the SC and ST population is spread over different states across the country while ST population is concentrated in some pockets of India. But the level of development of these populations varies substantially from one another. These averages generated at national level provide an understanding, yet they do not explicate the situation too clearly, as there has been considerable diversity in local contexts.

The growth rate of enrolment among the SCs and STs during 1990-2001 was higher than that of national average growth rate (for all communities) both at the secondary and higher secondary levels (see annexure Table A4). This higher growth rate apparently represents the lower base of their enrolment therefore, attests to their educational underdevelopment. Despite the apparent higher growth rate among SCs and STs they still lag behind the general population. Further, their enrolment growth rate varies from states to state. But it is important to note that in most cases the growth rate of SCs was higher than the growth rate of the concerned states.

The growth rate of Schedule Castes is higher in states where their population is of higher proportion and the state is relatively developed. This argument is difficult to prove as the growth rate of SC communities at lower secondary level is considerably low in some developed states. However, the growth rate of enrolment for SC community is lower in backward states.

Growth rate of enrolment does not indicate the exact nature of participation. Therefore, it is important to examine the percentage share of enrolment to the total population in order to arrive at the general assessment of their participation in education (see annexure Table A3). At national level the percentage share of the enrolment of scheduled castes was lower to their proportion of population during the last two decades and in both levels of secondary education. The proportion their enrolment for both levels of secondary education is same though the proportion of enrolment during 1990s has increased at a higher pace at higher secondary level. Among the major states the proportion of their enrolment ranges from 25.4 per cent to 5.5 per cent.

Few of the states with significant SC population have not only shown higher percentage of enrolment of SC but it is higher than their population proportion. Further analysis of this trend shows that these states are different from other states in terms of their approach to SC populations which are rooted in history of social movements, political agenda, and general economic development of the state resulting in pro-active state policy with special equity programmes. Alternatively this highlights to the increasing demand for secondary education from these communities when given with appropriate incentives. However, these equity programmes either in the form of scholarships or hostels have been discussed in the next section.

Similarly, ST population had the higher growth rate than the national average with 6.2 per cent though they occupy the lowest position in the educational ladder. The growth rate for ST communities at the state level has been better than the average growth rate of the concerned states irrespective of their levels of development. Interestingly the highest and the lowest growth rate of enrolment of STs were found in backward states which incidentally have higher concentration of these communities. However, an important fact that needs to be noted is that the states with higher proportion of ST population happened to be backward states in general and especially in education. SCs the proportion of ST students to the total enrolment ranges from 18.1 to 0.5, which should be taken as an indicator in order to assess their real participation. Though there has been increase in the growth rate enrolment of tribals except Maharashtra and Assam in no other state it is comparable to the proportion of their population. However, some of the backward states with higher concentration of tribal population have shown substantial increase in the proportion of their enrolment of tribal students especially in last decade. Despite this they are far away from any significant rate of enrolment especially in states where they are in large number.

Among the four sample states while Maharashtra and Andhra Pradesh substantial SC and ST population, Uttar Pradesh has a negligible population of STs and more than one-fifth of SC population. Kerala on the other hand has only 10 per cent of SC and ST population (see Table 4.4).

Table 4.4: Percentage of SC/ST Enrolment to the Total Enrolment

States	*1990-91*		*2001-02*		*1990-91*		*2001-02*	
	SC	*ST*	*SC*	*ST*	*SC*	*ST*	*SC*	*ST*
	Primary				Upper Primary			
Andhra Pradesh	19.71	6.94	20.12	9.94	16.48	3.92	18.48	5.15
Kerala	11.57	1.33	10.24	1.33	10.86	0.85	10.43	1.0
Maharashtra	14.56	8.95	15.19	11.06	13.17	5.75	14.94	7.6
Uttar Pradesh	17.43	.24	26.06	0.26	9.4	.16	18.16	0.26
India	15.93	7.94	18.88	10.3	12.5	5.13	16.72	7.5
	Secondary				Higher Secondary			
Andhra Pradesh	15.47	3.38	16.9	4.41	11.4	1.63	10.3	4.73
Kerala	10.18	0.66	9.8	0.79	11.12	0.59	9.86	0.59
Maharashtra	13.58	4.79	14.64	6.56	7.6	1.96	12.22	4.14
Uttar Pradesh	12.2	0.25	14.38	0.25	12.8	0.25	11.35	0.26
India	11.86	4.22	14.69	5.89	9.65	3.02	13.09	4.96

Source: Based on the actual enrolment figures taken from Selected Educational Statistics–1990-91 and 2001-2002, MHRD, GOI, New Delhi.

Like all India pattern in all the four sample states the proportion of SC and ST students was higher at primary level and it steadily goes down with increase of level of school education. In all the four states in primary and except Uttar Pradesh at upper primary level the enrolment for SC and ST students were higher than the proportion of their population. In fact over the years the enrolment rate of these groups have shown consistent rise which can be attributed to the efforts of various policies and programmes for universalization of elementary education including DPEP. At the lower secondary level though the proportion of enrolment for SCs had remained higher in all states except Uttar Pradesh, there was perceptible decline in the proportion of enrolment for tribals. This was particularly visible in case of Andhra Pradesh and Maharashtra, the states with significant percentage of tribal population.

This indicates that though at the primary and upper primary level tribal students have higher representation they tend to have drop out rate at these levels resulting with low demand for secondary education reflecting in the form of lower proportion of enrolment to their population size. However, considering the percentage increase in the proportion of enrolment it must be admitted that demand has consistently increased for secondary education from SC and ST community, which may not be comparable to primary level but certainly much higher than the earlier decade. The improvement may be attributable to various policy measures and interventions by both the national and state governments. The following section attempts to highlight various interventions on gender and social equity.

POLICIES AND PROGRAMMES FOR GENDER AND SOCIAL EQUITY

One of the dimensions in educational development is equity particularly in a multi-layered and highly stratified society like India. Constitution of India guarantees right to equality to all its citizens but in reality equal opportunities, rarely get translated into equality, in view of large scale disparities at various levels. These disparities are more pronounced in terms of social grouping viz. caste, gender and community and come from socio-economic inequalities. There are various historical, socio-economic and psychological forces those operate both at individual and societal level denying equal opportunities as these groups suffer from deep-rooted discrimination. In this section an attempt is made to examine equity programmes related to gender and social groups (scheduled castes and scheduled tribes). We have examined various equity programmes and strategies adopted in India in general and sample states in particular at secondary level.

The policies and programmes to safeguard the interest of the marginalized groups and efforts to rehabilitate them have evolved since Independence. There are certain common programmes existing across the country, however, not only vary among the states but also in terms of quality and extent of coverage. In fact, empirical evidences have pointed out that despite a universal scheme being ideal incentive schemes vary from state to state (K. Sujatha: 1998). In our discussion on equity we have limited our focus on schemes those are implemented at the center as well as available in four sample states.

Constitutional Provisions

Article-14 of the Indian Constitution guarantees right to equality and attempts to provide equality of opportunity and equality before law for all citizens thereby creating legal safeguard of provisions and mechanisms to combat discrimination and inequality. Further, Article-46 of the Constitution directs the state to create facilities and make special efforts for providing educational opportunities to children belonging to weaker sections of the society especially scheduled castes and schedules tribes. In fact, the fifth schedule of the Constitution is devoted to protect the interest of these communities.

At the all India level periodically Five Years Plans and other plan documents specifically look at polices which will alleviate the problems of these communities and empower them. Similarly, the Ministry of Social Justice and Empowerment, Tribal Welfare and Rural Development as nodal agencies operate from the central level and are engaged in planning, policy formulation and programme implementing. Both at the union and state level there are social welfare and tribal welfare departments to look after the progress and development of schedules castes and scheduled tribes. These departments apart from functioning on their own join the education department in supplementing the efforts to improve the educational progress of the weaker sections of the population. This section covers the concept of incentives, different incentive schemes operated by central government and incentives and special programmes for education of girls, scheduled castes and scheduled tribes in four sample states.

Incentive Schemes and Programmes

As a part of Constitutional guarantee, free education is provided to children of scheduled castes and scheduled tribes at all levels of education including professional courses in all the states and union territories in the country. Similarly, many states offer free education to girls up to secondary level and some states up to higher education in government and government funded private institutions. In addition to free education several other incentives, institutional arrangements, financial support are provided to facilitate education of girls and scheduled castes and tribes. The Central government plays a significant role in extending financial support through scholarships and stipends from higher secondary level to higher and professional education, in addition to funding to establish hostels, residential Ashram schools and remedial coaching at school level etc. The state governments have devised different incentives and equity programmes for school education up to secondary level. These include provision of scholarships, incentives, exclusive institutional arrangement like hostels, Ashram schools, residential schools, flexible norms in providing access to secondary education etc.

All the special schemes and programmes initiated to ensure equity can be broadly classified under four heads, viz., (i) Incentives (ii)

Special Institutional Provision; (iii) Improvement in Quality; and (iv) Waivers and concessions. These schemes are directed either to individuals belonging to a particular stratification for instance scholarships, free uniforms, free textbooks etc or through institutional equity measures in terms of free hostels, special schools, residential schools, building and infrastructure, creation of model schools etc. While the quality improvement scheme can benefit the individuals (provision of remedial and extra coaching) or/and institutions (computers, laboratories, creation of special institutions etc). Institutional arrangements have been made to draw scheduled castes and tribal children to schools. Waivers or Concession refer to affirmative action in the West and Reservation policy in India. The concession includes reservation of seats in educational institutions and government jobs, reimbursement of fee etc. The scheme benefiting the individual can be of monetary and non-monetary in nature. Except scholarships, which involve financial transfer from the government to students through institutions, all other schemes directed to individuals are in kind.

However, these scholarships are given to students studying in government and private aided schools. Similarly, some states provide attendance scholarships to scheduled castes and scheduled tribe girl students. This provision exists in one of our sample states viz. Maharashtra. Similar facility exists for backward Muslim girls in Kerala. A special scholarship is given to children of parents engaged in unclean occupation. The extent of coverage of scholarships in the states depends on availability of funds. Both central and state governments have combined to provide these schemes.

In a federal country like India, both central and state governments launch many such equity schemes. One of the major central schemes is Post-Matric scholarships to Scheduled Caste and Tribes. National Rural Talent Search scheme is another one, which identifies talented students from rural India and supports them up to higher education. Central government provides funding to the state governments for construction of hostel for SC/ST students. Further, it directly undertakes the responsibility of establishing girls' hostels. The central government also provides few other quality improvement schemes like, coaching facilities to meritorious students; coaching facilities for appearing the competitive examinations by Union Public Services Commission and the Reserve Bank of India. Provision of remedial coaching and teaching facility for students belonging to SC/ST and

Book Bank scheme for supporting the academic interest of students are two other central schemes of quality improvement.

In pursuant to above description it can be said that equity schemes and programmes are provided both at central and state level. In this context, it is pertinent to divide these schemes into two parts namely, central and state schemes.

Central Government Sponsored Incentive Schemes

Among the other schemes, Post–Matric scholarships to Scheduled Caste and Tribes is the major scheme, which covers universally and supplies are equitably distributed across all the sates. This scheme starts at the higher secondary stage and continues up to higher level of education including professional education. Another important initiative of central government is National Rural Talent Search (NRTS) scheme, which identifies talented students from rural India and supports them for higher education. However, there are reservations in this scheme for students belonging to weaker sections as per constitutional norms[3] and girls. Similarly, another initiative of central government is National Talent Search Scheme managed by NCERT. This scheme is based on a competitive examination and has 1000 scholarship out of which 15 and 7 per cent are reserved for SC and ST students. Like NRTS this scholarship also continues up to higher and professional education. The scholarship has a quota for each state in proportion to the number of secondary school students. Central government provides funding to the states governments for the construction for hostel SC/ST students and also directly undertakes the responsibility of establishing girls' hostels.

The central government too provides coaching facilities to meritorious students for higher levels of education and achievement, the coaching facilities for Union Public Services Commission conducted examination and for the posts in Reserve Bank of India as examples. Provision of remedial coaching and teaching facility for students belonging to SC/ST communities is also another important central government scheme intended to upgrade the merits of weak students (Grade IX-XII). For supporting the academic interest of students the central government also sponsors the Book Bank schemes that enable the students to borrow the books from the bank.

Institutional Interventions

Institutional Interventions are pursued through *Ashram Schools and Hostels* administered by Department of Tribal Welfare, Government of India. The government of India has consistently tried and, to quite an extent, has been successful in providing residential schools for tribal students in tribal localities known as Ashram Schools. This effort has allowed tribal children to access approach to the school without being worried of physical barriers and quite importantly it has provided them with a conducive atmosphere to learn and study.

Establishing Girls' Hostel is another important institutional intervention. The central government, through its ministries of Social Justice and Empowerment and Tribal Welfare, since many decades, has been providing assistance and help to the girls hailing from SC, ST and economically backward communities. One of their major activities has been providing support to state governments in creating facilities for girl students belonging to these sections in the form of hostels without which many of them would not have been in a position to complete their studies. Of course, the number of hostels in each state and the number of students residing in them vary from state to state.

Other Incentives for Girls Education

Private participation has been sought to improve educational access in tribal and rural areas. As an equity measure the state has followed the practice of providing hostels for girls, recruiting female teachers to provide incentives to rural girls, free bus concessions to girls at secondary stage, attendance stipend for tribal students, scholarship for SC and ST students, etc. Andhra Pradesh and Maharashtra has also a policy of providing by-cycle to rural and tribal girls in order to improve their accessibility to school enabling them better transport of facilities.

The state of Maharashtra has discontinued the practice of grant-in-aid for schools established by private management and allowed a more open policy of promoting secondary education through private participation only; hence one can find strong political and economic content in educational policy undoubtedly exercised by private bodies.

Pace Setting Schools

In a bide to achieve equity with excellence the central government introduced the concept of pace-setting schools in the name of *Jawahar Navodaya Vidyala* (JNV) to improve quality of education and provide opportunity to rural students from lower socio-economic group. The Scheme was introduced as a part of National Education Policy, 1986 in order to provide a pace setting school in each district. There are 508 JNVs covering 506 districts with student strength of 0.16 millions.

At least 75 per cent of the seats in a district are filled by candidates selected from rural areas and remaining seats are filled from the urban areas of the district. Reservation of seats in favour of children belonging to scheduled caste and scheduled tribes is provided in proportion to their population in the concerned district provided that no district, such reservation will be less than the national average but subject to a maximum of 50 per cent for both the categorizes taken together. Efforts are made to ensure that one-third of the total seats are filled up by girls. These schools admit students through an open entrance examination. The test of quality that comes out with the success in public examination has been excellent, much better than many government and private schools. A large number of students of JNVs have successfully entered into technical and professional colleges and have competed with the best.

New Initiatives

The Union Ministry of Human Resource Development has recently introduced a scheme known as 'Kasturba Gandhi Girls' Residential Schools, under which the ministry funds both state government and Non Governmental Organization to run the free residential schools/ hostels for girls in blocks where the female literacy is lower than the state/district average. Largely these areas correspond with scheduled castes and scheduled tribe concentrated localities.

However, the major weakness of central government schemes are their poor implementation and dependency on state government who more often than not divert the funds and fail to act on schemes. Since the post-matric scholarship is the major central government scheme which focus on higher education which has been very meaningful and relevant at that level in supporting higher education among the students of weaker sections. However, this scheme addresses a very small segment of students who could reach at that level. This leaves the major burden of providing incentives and facilities for weaker sections at school level education to the relative capacities of the state government. Therefore it is important to look at state level incentive and interventions for the education of SC/ST and girls students.

State Schemes

Considering the federal structure of the country and the status of education as a joint responsibility of central and state governments it is safe to assume a degree of variety and differences in schemes initiated at state level. In this part of the section we are focusing on schemes those are common among the states and more particularly among the sample states.

Free Education

SC/ST students receive free education at all levels while education for girls is free up to secondary and higher secondary level. In Kerala however, girls education is free even at higher education level. In addition to these many states have merit scholarships for students of SC/ST based on their performance at the end of primary, upper primary and continues till higher secondary level. These scholarships are higher in amount than stipends and administered at district and state level. Maharashtra government conducts merit scholarship examination at district/state level where they reserve a few scholarships for SC/ST students based on their proportion at the district level, this ensure better coverage (see annexure). These schemes ensure in identifying meritorious students at an early level and help them in pursuing higher education.

Free Uniforms and Text Books

Provision of free school uniforms exists in Andhra Pradesh, Maharashtra in addition to few other states. All the states including all sample states follow the practice of supplying free textbooks to children belonging to scheduled castes and scheduled tribes though some discontinue the facility to students beyond primary level.

Pre-matric scholarships are one of the major schemes at the school level. Under this scheme no fee is charged from students belonging to SC/ST category. They are also provided with some amount of stipend. This amount varies from state to state and from level to level. It ranges from ₹ 20-75 between primary, upper primary to secondary level. Among the four sample states the stipend of pre-matric scholarship varies from ₹ 50-75 for ten months. The girls belonging to SC/ST community are given attendance scholarship by some states. In case of Maharashtra the value of attendance scholarship for SC girls is ₹ 100/p.m. for ten months at the lower secondary level. The state also provides merit based scholarship where it has an inbuilt mechanisms to protect equity. There are reservation for rural general, rural SC/ST, girls etc.

Bright Students Scheme

The sample states of Andhra Pradesh and Maharashtra have adopted a novel scheme to promote and recognize the merits of students belonging to weaker sections. Under this scheme known as 'Bright Students Scheme' where if a student performs well in the public examination or entrance test at district level is rewarded by this scheme. An award of ₹ 20,000 per annum is given to one child in a family which comes under the below poverty line to enable him/her to study in one of the best private school. Similarly, under Upgradation of Merit scheme a student belonging to SC/ST category if manages to score more than 500 marks in class X (public examination) is given ₹ 15,000 per year to study in a residential school. Maharashtra state implements a scheme called admission into best available schools, admission in private schools (quality private unaided school), e.g. more than 6,000 students belonging to SC community have been provided with this facility. The expenditure in such schools is around ₹ 12,000 p.a. at lower secondary level.

Institutional Arrangements (Hostels)

In addition to scholarships and incentive the welfare departments at the state government's level have established hostels so that students belonging to weaker sections can reach up to secondary level. Recognizing the levels of discrimination and difficulties faced by the students of weaker sections in accessing secondary education the states governments have established hostels. This provision of hostels are for weaker section students are common in most of the states but their frequency, facilities, coverage and norms vary from state to state. Many states have these hostels either at district and divisional level while in Andhra Pradesh Kerala and Maharashtra hostels are located at Block/Mandal (sub-district) level which is minimum. These states have a policy of establishing at least two hostels (one for boys and one for girls) at sub-district level for scheduled castes and scheduled tribes. In these hostels besides free boarding and lodging facility the students are paid cosmetics allowances. Along with this in case of Maharashtra some monthly pocket allowance is provided.

In Andhra Pradesh apart from SC and ST students, students from other community viz. socio-economically backward castes are also provided with this facility. In fact, as pressure for education mounts from these communities the hostel facility has been more open. The hostels are however, managed either by the government or private agencies funded by the government. In case of sample states, of Kerala and Andhra Pradesh the hostels are managed by the Welfare departments, in Maharashtra and Uttar Pradesh both Welfare department and private aided managements. Though these hostellers belong to SC/ST category they attend schools in the same locality along with other category students. Sometimes, as a result of this proximity the schools often get crowded with these students leading to homogenization of lower socio-economic groups in government schools.

The number of hostels and management types varies among the four sample states. Andhra Pradesh has the largest number of hostels both for SC and ST both among the sample states as well as the country (see Table 4.5).

Table 4.5: Number of Hostel and Beneficiaries in Sample States

State	*Scheduled Caste*		*Scheduled Tribe*	
	Hostels	*Students*	*Hostel*	*Students*
Andhra Pradesh	2219	236204	505	79912
Maharashtra	2194	119475	320	20127
Uttar Pradesh	173	7250	01	60
Kerala	104	5900	14	608

Source: Directorate of Tribal and Social Welfare of respective states.

Among the four sample states Andhra Pradesh has more hostels and covers larger number of students though it has a lower percentage of SC than Uttar Pradesh and less ST population than Maharashtra. The state Uttar Pradesh has significant SC population it is investing very less on providing hostel facility to access secondary education by disadvantaged students. In Andhra Pradesh per student cost is ₹ 375 for SC hostels while for ST was ₹ 350. In case of Maharashtra if the hostel is run by private aided then the cost is ₹ 500 and for Government run schools it is ₹ 700 for both the SC and ST hostels.

Ashram Schools

One of the key educational initiatives taken by different state governments to spread formal education among tribes was the establishment of Ashram Schools. The concept of Ashram schools owes its origin to the Gandhian philosophy of combining education and work together with residential facility where teachers and students live together. The system has greater significance for tribal students because of their scattered habitation, difficult geographical terrain and different socio-cultural values (K. Sujatha: 1990). The first few Ashram schools were established by philanthropists. Based on their successful functioning later in early 1960s the Education Commission had recommended opening of Ashram schools in tribal areas for improving access and participation in education. Consequently Ashram schools were established as a part of central government scheme which later transformed to respective state governments. These are inter-village schools, serving the tribal areas where it was difficult to open other types of schools. In Ashram schools along with free boarding and lodging facilities are provided to along with education. And the teachers are also expected to reside in the school. Ashram schools follow the same curriculum and textbooks prescribed by the government for other schools.

Ashram schools are present in most of the tribal concentrated states but largely found in Andhra Pradesh, Maharashtra, Gujarat, Madhya Pradesh, Orissa and Rajasthan and a few in Kerala and none in Uttar Pradesh (see Table 4.6). They vary among the states in terms of size, levels of education and provisions. In some states like Andhra Pradesh and Kerala Ashram schools are managed by

Tribal Welfare Department while in Maharashtra most of them are managed by voluntary organizations funded by the state government.

Table 4.6: Number of Ashram Schools and Enrolment in Sample States

States	*No. of Schools*	*No. of Students*	*Per Student Cost (in Rupees)*
Andhra Pradesh	515	101150	350
Maharashtra	677	175000	500
Kerala	02	120	NA
Uttar Pradesh	00	00	00

Source: Directorate of Tribal and Social Welfare of respective states.

Ashram schools follow an open admission policy. However, the sanctioned seats remain limited due to cost factor. The provisions of such schools by these states exemplify their commitment to equity. The role played by Ashram schools in education especially in imparting secondary education to tribal children has been significant which otherwise would not have been possible. Needless to mention, that most of the educated tribals are first generation learners from these schools only. Majority of tribal teaches working in these areas are the products of Ashram schools clearly indicating the direct impact of these schools on education and employment opportunity of tribals.

Residential Schools

In order to nurture excellence while focusing on equity Residential Schools have been set up by the state governments for both scheduled castes and scheduled tribes with boarding and lodging facility. With higher investment, better facilities, structured and rigorous academic schedule, and selecting the students through an open entrance test, these schools have been envisaged to combine equity with excellence. These schools cater to the educational needs of three categories of students, namely, for rural students in general, exclusively for scheduled castes and scheduled tribes.

Table 4.7: Number of Residential Schools and Enrolment by Social Groups in Sample States

States	*No. of Schools for Rural Children*		*Scheduled Caste*		*Scheduled Tribes*		*Stipend per Student*	
	Schools	*Enrol.*	*Schools*	*Enrol.*	*Schools*	*Enrol.*	*SCs*	*STs*
Andhra Pradesh	109	91340	98	22473	60	16680	375	375
Kerala	–	–	14	1680	12	1400	–	–
Maharashtra	–	–	2	280	–	–	500	–

Source: Directorate of Tribal and Social Welfare of respective states.

Andhra Pradesh has not only highest number of residential schools but also expanded the facility to a large section of communities that includes scheduled castes, scheduled tribes and backward castes and rural students (see Table 4.7). Though the process of establishing such schools was started in 70s with one model school it has grown to become one of the largest chains of special schools. This was possible to the active political demand for such schools to accommodate best students from their constituencies. As a result each district has got minimum of four such schools, two for boys and two for girls. Some of the districts have got even six schools. This speaks of the state policy in providing quality education to deprived students. The teachers from these schools are specially selected and receive higher emoluments. All these schools enroll the students at grade-V and they continue up to lower secondary level and some of them have up to higher secondary level. In these schools students receive quality education through rigorous teaching-learning schedule. This has helped them in doing rather well not only public examinations but also in entrance tests for technical, professional and higher education. The results of schools in public examination are considered as an indicator of school performance and in the same indictor the results of these school have been excellent.

The policy in Andhra Pradesh is more progressive and development oriented which has focused not only participation of weaker sections in education but also combining equity with excellence. In fact, it would be appropriate to state that due the proactive policies of the state of late, it has achieved significant success in ensuring participation of deprived communities in education process which is rather evident in statistics. The facilities earlier provided for elementary education has been accorded to secondary education as well. But more importantly the recent policy interventions have looked at improving the quality of education and equipping the students with excellence. This may be more expensive but has long-term policy implications. At the first step it will allow the students from weaker sections to enter into higher job market where there is a paucity of personnel from reserved categories.

As a result of these pro-active policies Andhra Pradesh has the largest number of students at higher secondary level among the SC/ST community and at secondary level Uttar Pradesh and Maharashtra precedes and Andhra Pradesh for the obvious reason of large proportion of SC population[4]. Similarly, at higher levels of education students of SC/ST community from Andhra Pradesh have done exceedingly well particularly, in engineering, polytechnic and other professional course. In fact, Andhra Pradesh has the distinction of having higher percentage of SC/ST students in science stream at higher secondary level, which is a rarity. However, this is not limited to SC/STs alone rather girls in general have done well in Andhra Pradesh in comparison to other states and have a larger representation in engineering and information technology courses.

However, when we compare to the level of educational development of marginalized communities at all India level a dismal picture emerges. The level of operation of equity schemes and uneven spread of incentives has resulted in an uneven development of these communities in across the states. For example, Uttar Pradesh despite having a sizeable population and proportion of SCs have done much for the community though in recent years the number of SC students at appearing at secondary level public examination has crossed well over 0.3 million. But considering the enthusiasm of the community to participate in education the response from the state has been poor. In fact, as the number and percentage of these groups grow along there will be an increase in aspiration thus creating a gap between demand and available opportunities. This often leads to growing unrest among these communities (Jeffery et al.: 2005). In order to avoid such situation it imperative to have equity schemes and safety nets otherwise the social fabric will be lost. For this however, there is a need for strong political commitment and proactive strategies.

Access of weaker sections to higher education and skill will only help them in utilizing this opportunity, which can be obtained through quality education at secondary level. Secondly, due to economic liberalization and globalization the jobs in government sectors are slowly reducing and so is the quota for weaker sections and without quality education the students from weaker section won't be able to compete in open market. Only quality education at the secondary level can improve the employment opportunities of weaker sections in open market thus will serve the real cause of social welfare.

To conclude it can be said that though there are multi-level and multiple programmes for the development of education among weaker sections as they differ from state to state in terms of coverage, quality, nature and number of beneficiaries as well as the intensity. It has to be noted that these polices are largely governed by political commitment and financial constraints and those states who have commitment and resources, have tried to make the pubic institutions work for weaker sections.

NOTES

1. Gender Parity Index (GPI) has been calculated by dividing girl's GER by boy's GER of a given level of education. It measures progress towards gender equity in education. When the GPI shows a value equals to ! at any level of education it shows that there is no gender disparity at that level an learning opportunities are available for girls equally to that of boys.
2. In the absence of age group population for SC and ST we referred to the proportion of their enrolment to their population size
3. The Constitution of India provides 15% reservation for SC and 7.5% for STs in educational institutions and government posts.
4. All these comparative reference were taken from Selected Educational Statistics-2002-03, MHRD, GOI, New Delhi, 2004.

REFERENCES

Government of India (1950), Constitution of India, Ministry of Law and Justice, Government of India.

MHRD (1986), National Policy on Education, Government of India, Ministry of Human Resource and Development, Government of India, New Delhi.

MHRD (1992), National Policy on Education (1986) Programme of Action, Government of India, Ministry of Human Resource and Development, New Delhi.

Sujatha, K. (1999), Education of India Schedule Tribes: A Study of Community Schools in the District of Vishakapatnam, Andhra Pradesh, IIEP, Paris.

Annexure

Table A1: Share of Girls to Total Enrolment by Levels of School Education

(*in %*)

States	Primary			Upper Primary			Secondary			Hr Secondary		
	1980-81	1990-91	2001-02	1980-81	1990-91	2001-02	1980-81	1990-91	2001-02	1980-81	1990-91	2001-02
Andhra Pradesh	41	43	49	33	37	46	30	36	44	27	29	39
Kerala	48	49	49	48	49	48	49	50	50	47	52	55
Maharashtra	43	46	48	36	41	47	32	36	44	29	33	42
Uttar Pradesh	32	36	37	25	28	32	16	22	26	19	28	33
Assam	42	47	45	39	40	43	38	44	44	25	34	37
Bihar	29	33	39	21	26	35	15	21	30	12	17	39
Gujarat	40	43	44	37	40	46	35	38	40	33	39	41
Harayana	34	44	47	26	36	45	23	32	42	26	29	38
HP	43	46	48	32	44	48	25	41	47	26	33	44
J & K	36	39	45	31	35	43	31	34	42	33	29	41
Karnataka	44	46	47	37	41	47	35	37	46	25	27	44
MP	33	39	45	25	34	39		24	35	23	27	36
Orissa	39	40	41	32	44	39	28	35	41	18	29	30
Punjab	45	46	47	39	43	47		41	47	37	40	43
Rajasthan	24	30	36	19	22	30		19	28	18	20	28
Tamil Nadu	45	46	49	38	43	48	34	39	44	36	42	49
West Bengal	41	43	48	36	42	43	33	33	40	27	35	37
India	39	41	44	33	37	42	31	33	41	26	32	40

(i) For the year 1980, in case of M.P., Punjab and Rajasthan, the Hr. secondary refers to old pattern (IX-XI). So data for Secondary is not included.

(ii) In the year 2001, the data of Bihar, M.P. and U.P. include the data of Jharkhand, Chhattisgarh and Uttaranchal respectively.

* Includes Inter, Jr. Colleges, pre-degree 2 yr. Course, pre-degree 1 yr. course, 10+2 new pattern and Old pattern (IX-XI).

Source: Selected Educational Statistics, 1980-81, 1990-91 and 2001-02, MHRD, GOI, New Delhi.

Table A2: Gross Enrolment Ratio, Gender Parity Index, per cent Share of Girls at Secondary Level in 2002-03

	GER				Gender Parity Index		Growth Rates* of Lower Secondary			Growth Rates* of Higher Secondary		
	Total	Boys	Girls	Gender gap	Total	Rural	Boys	Girls	Total	Boys	Girls	Total
Andhra Pradesh	40.12	44.69	35.26	9.43	0.79	0.71	1.8	4.9	3.0	7.9	12.3	9.4
Kerala	62.24	59.95	64.57	-4.62	1.08	1.05	1.2	1.2	1.2	4.3	5.7	5.0
Maharashtra	53.08	55.37	50.42	4.95	0.91	0.83	2.7	5.8	3.9	0.6	4.3	1.9
Uttar Pradesh	36.52	42.18	29.61	12.57	0.70	0.63	1.7	3.9	2.2	0.9	3.3	1.7
Assam	29.65	30.71	28.51	2.2	0.93	0.93	3.5	3.5	3.5	5.7	7.0	6.2
Bihar	17.39	22.24	11.39	10.85	0.51	0.48	1.4	6.0	2.6	-5.7	4.8	-3.0
Gujarat	40.20	44.81	34.95	9.86	0.78	0.67	2.6	3.6	3.0	5.3	6.4	5.7
Haryana	47.52	51.25	43.00	8.25	0.84	0.77	3.9	8.3	5.5	9.1	13.2	10.4
HP	68.97	71.79	65.98	5.81	0.92	0.90	0.3	2.8	1.4	1.2	5.8	2.9
J&K	33.38	37.94	28.53	9.41	0.75	0.68	5.8	9.1	7.1	2.5	7.4	4.2
Karnataka	37.95	40.26	35.44	4.82	0.88	0.84	3.0	6.6	4.5	3.1	10.2	5.5
MP	30.61	36.63	23.40	13.23	0.64	0.51	4.2	9.3	5.7	8.0	12.0	9.3
Orissa	31.09	35.33	26.79	8.54	0.76	0.73	-2.0	0.3	-1.2	11.1	11.8	11.3
Punjab	39.12	38.10	40.33	-2.23	1.06	0.96	1.3	3.4	2.2	4.5	5.5	4.9
Rajasthan	29.29	38.37	18.67	19.70	0.49	0.36	4.1	8.9	5.2	5.3	9.6	6.4
Tamil Nadu	55.15	55.28	55.02	0.26	1.00	0.86	2.1	4.1	2.9	4.7	7.4	5.9
West Bengal	30.37	33.44	26.96	6.48	0.81	0.75	0.4	3.2	1.5	2.7	3.6	3.0
India	37.52	41.29	33.21	8.08	0.80	0.72	2.5	5.8	3.7	3.5	6.7	4.6

* Refer to the period between 1990-91 to 2000-01 Compound Annual Growth Rate (CAGR) is (((LY/BY) ^ (1/N)-1)*100).

(ii) For the year 1980, in case of M.P., Punjab and Rajasthan, the Hr. secondary refers to old pattern (IX-XI). So growth at this level is indicated at Higher Secondary Level.

(iii) In the year 2001, the data of Bihar, M.P. and U.P. include the data of Jharkhand, Chhattishgarh and Uttaranchal respectively.

* Includes Inter, Jr. Colleges, pre-degree 2 yr. Course, pre-degree 1 yr. course, 10+2 new pattern and Old pattern (IX-XI).

Source: Selected Educational Statistics, 1980-81, 1990-91 and 2001-02, 2002-03, MHRD, GOI, New Delhi.

Table A3: Share of Enrolment of SCs and STs in The Total Enrolment at Secondary and Higher Secondary Levels in 17 Major States

	Secondary				*Higher Secondary*			
	Scheduled Caste		*Scheduled Tribe*		*Scheduled Caste*		*Scheduled Tribe*	
	1990-91	*2001-02*	*1990-91*	*2001-02*	*1990-91*	*2001-02*	*1990-91*	*2001-02*
Andhra Pradesh	15.5	16.9	3.4	4.4	11.4	16.3	1.6	4.7
Assam	10.8	13.9	14.1	18.1	9.6	12.8	13.8	16.7
Bihar	8.7	9.2	6.6	5.9	0.5	6.7	0.2	1.0
Gujarat	9.6	8.7	8.3	11.1	8.4	10.4	8.2	12.0
Haryana	11.4	14.2	Na	Na	7.2	11.9	Na	Na
HP	9.6	20.8	1.8	3.8	17.1	17.5	2.9	3.9
J & K	8.1	5.5	Na	2.8	Na	4.6	Na	2.5
Karnataka	12.2	16.1	2.8	5.1	12.9	13.7	2.3	4.1
Kerala	10.2	9.8	0.7	0.8	11.1	9.9	0.6	0.6
MP	8.3	15.2	8.5	13.9	16.4	12.9	14.4	11.7
Maharashtra	13.6	14.6	4.8	6.6	7.6	12.2	2.0	4.1
Orissa	8.0	14.3	5.4	10.8	6.9	13.6	3.3	6.4
Punjab	18.3	25.3	Na	Na	13.2	16.7	Na	Na
Rajasthan	12.3	13.0	7.8	9.0	9.3	11.2	5.3	7.9
Tamil Nadu	15.6	23.4	0.6	0.8	12.2	18.8	0.5	0.7
UP	12.2	14.0	0.3	0.5	12.8	10.9	0.3	0.7
W. Bengal	11.5	18.2	2.0	3.5	8.5	17.7	1.7	2.7
India	11.9	13.5	4.2	5.4	9.7	13.1	3.0	5.0

Source: Selected Educational Statistics, 1980-81, 1990-91 and 2001-02, MHRD, GOI, New Delhi.

Table A4 : Growth Rates* of Enrolment of SCs and STs at Secondary and Higher Secondary Levels in 17 Major States

	Secondary	*Higher Secondary*	*Secondary*	*Higher Secondary*
	Scheduled Caste	*Scheduled Tribe*	*Scheduled Caste*	*Scheduled Tribe*
Andhra Pradesh	3.9	5.6	13.0	20.5
Assam	5.9	5.9	8.9	8.0
Bihar	3.1	1.6	22.5	13.3
Gujarat	2.1	5.8	7.8	9.5
Haryana	7.6	Na	15.5	Na
HP	8.8	8.7	3.2	5.5
J & K	3.5	Na	Na	Na
Karnataka	7.2	10.2	6.1	11.0
Kerala	0.8	2.8	3.9	5.0
MP	11.6	10.6	6.9	7.2
Maharashtra	4.6	6.9	6.4	9.1
Orissa	4.2	5.2	18.4	18.4
Punjab	5.3	Na	7.2	Na
Rajasthan	5.6	6.5	8.2	10.4

Contd.

	Secondary	Higher Secondary	Secondary	Higher Secondary
	Scheduled Caste	Scheduled Tribe	Scheduled Caste	Scheduled Tribe
Tamil Nadu	6.8	5.6	10.1	8.1
UP	3.5	8.3	0.1	11.3
W. Bengal	5.8	6.7	10.1	7.8
India	5.0	6.2	7.6	9.5

* Refer to the period between 1990-91 to 2000-01 Compound Annual Growth Rate (CAGR) is (((LY/BY) ^ (1/N)-1)*100).

* Includes Inter, Jr. Colleges, pre-degree 2 yr. Course and 10+2 new pattern.

Note: In the year 2001, the data of Bihar, M.P. and U.P. include the data of Jharkhand, Chhattishgarh and Uttaranchal respectively.

Source: Selected Educational Statistics, 1980-81, 1990-91 and 2001-02, MHRD, GOI, New Delhi.

5

Financing Secondary Education in India

Access, expansion and qualitative improvement of secondary education cannot be realized without adequate financial support. Therefore, its financing is an issue of crucial importance. Government resources form an integral part in the growth and development of education system in a developing country like India. The education system covering the secondary schools managed by government including local bodies and private aided schools accounted for 68 per cent during 2003-04[1]. A vast majority, indeed, every two out of three schools comprised a government funded secondary school, covering an enrolment of 80 per cent during 2002 (NCERT, 2002) at the national level.

The present chapter examines the government/public financing of secondary education at the all India level. The first section of the chapter deals with financing of education in India with a focus on sample states covering several important aspects of financing education, viz. allocation of resources for education–inter-sectoral, intra-secotral allocations. With this background on financing education, the subsequent section examines financing secondary education at the national level focusing on sample states. The third section of the chapter deals with an important aspect of financing secondary education, that is, grants-in-aid system in India *per se* and in the sample states in particular. The fourth section deals with an analysis on unit costs of secondary and also elementary education. The last section presents the emerging trends and issues.

ALLOCATION OF RESOURCES FOR EDUCATION

The issue of allocation of resources for education is crucial because neither qualitative nor quantitative improvements can be effected without adequate provision of resources. Allocation of resources is generally looked at in terms of inter-sectoral, intra-sectroal and inter-functional allocation.

Inter-sectoral Allocation

Share of education expenditure in GDP reflects the relative priority given to education in the economy. India allocated less than one per cent of its GDP for education just after independence, which steadily grew to 3.3 per cent of GDP during 1980s, raised to 4.1 per cent in the beginning of the new millennium. But it declined in the latest years of 2004-05(B), which is a cause for concern. The share of education expenditure in total government revenue expenditure indicates the commitment of the government in financing education. The share of overall expenditure on education ranged between 8 to 10 per cent of the total expenditures except with two peaks crossing above 12 per cent in 1960-61 and 2000-01 (see Figure 5.1).

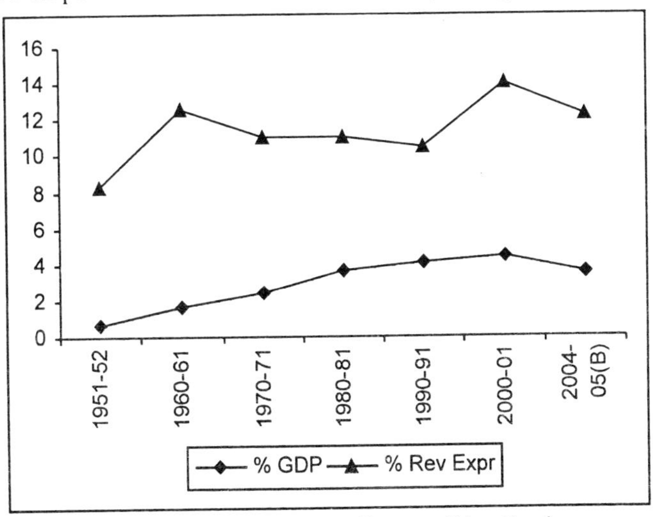

Figure 5.1: Share of Expenditure on Education in GDP and Revenue Expenditure

Source: Based on Analysis of Budgeted Expenditure (various issues).

Inter-state Variations

The national pattern and trend might disguise the disparities across the country. Educationally backward states have lower enrolment vis-à-vis lower investment on education than their counterparts. Vast heterogeneity is mirrored by large differences in the development of education between states. Since, education is a concurrent subject and state contributes majority of the expenditure at all levels of education, it is worthwhile to examine the pattern of financing education across major states at selected points of time.

The purpose of this section is to highlight very briefly the extent of variation across the country (see Tables 5.1 and 5.2 and Annexure Tables A1 and A2). Linking with levels of educational and economic development of major states, four broad patterns of financing of education could be observed, based on the indicators on share of education expenditure in SDP and state budget expenditure. Variations exist even among the broader pattern. Many states in India are geographically vast having huge population. Besides, these states had been formed on the basis of language.

The first category of states includes the one, which allocated a higher share for education even though their SDP or economy is not very strong (Kerala and Himachal Pradesh above 6 per cent of SDP). Tamil Nadu can be included in this category by considering the rapid progress of educational development in that state, even though not much higher resources (only around 4 per cent of SDP) are allocated. It is to be noted that unlike Kerala and Himachal Pradesh, Tamil Nadu has been industrially progressing with a relatively better growth in the state income. Kerala has the distinction of having the highest i.e., above five per cent, share of education expenditures in SDP, among all other states in the country, consistently for a long period of time. Only in the recent years, it has come down to 4 per cent. In terms of relative priority in the government exchequer for education, it has been consistently higher in Kerala compared to many other states and the national average, ranging above 29 per cent, except in the latest year. This decline in education expenditure both in terms of a share of SDP and revenue expenditure is a serious cause for concern. The budget of the government, particularly the revenue budget, has been showing excessive deficits and the state is unable to allocate increasing, or even maintain the same, level of expenditures for education[2].

Table 5.1: Share of Education Expenditures on SDP in Sample States of India

States	*1980-81*	*1985-86*	*1990-91*	*1995-96*	*2000-01*	*2004-05(B)*
Andhra Pradesh	3.98	5.12	3.95	3.30	2.86	3.08
Kerela	6.09	7.13	7.10	6.42	4.11	4.57
Mahrashtra	2.96	3.36	3.50	2.99	4.34	3.00
Uttar Pradesh	2.65	3.44	4.64	4.26	3.71	3.08
India	3.09	3.66	4.07	3.60	4.38	3.52

Source: Analysis of Budgeted Expenditure on Education, various issues.

The second category consists of almost the reverse preposition, that of higher income/economic growth but a lesser allocation to education (Punjab, Haryana, Gujarat, and Maharashtra). Though Punjab and Haryana are prosperous with their fertile agriculture, they have not allocated a higher share for education consistently for a longer period of time. Even during 1990s, they have not raised their allocation. Gujarat and Maharashtra, the two industrially progressive states, also fall in this category but with a little difference, that during 1990s, these states have raised their allocation for education at least marginally. Maharashtra allocated on an average 3.5 per cent during 1980s and 1990s and has marginally increased it to around 3.85 per cent in the beginning of the new millennium. In a progressive state of Maharashtra, even higher expenditure would show a lesser share as income is growing at a faster rate. It is a fact that Maharashtra's economy has demonstrated a strong track record of growth and is a visible success story for the rest of the country (Government of Maharashtra, 2002). Education expenditure as per cent of revenue expenditure ranges between 11 to 33 per cent in the state. This share, though improved in the middle of 1990s, has actually come down drastically in the late 1990s and the beginning of the new millennium.

Table 5.2: Share of Education Expenditure on Education in Total Budget of Selected States of India

States	*1980-81*	*1985-86*	*1990-91*	*1995-96*	*2000-01*	*2004-05(B)*
Andhra Pradesh	25.09	24.72	22.37	20.79	17.39	18.26
Kerela	34.89	32.06	30.58	30.77	24.17	24.21
Mahrashtra	23.38	19.77	23.21	23.74	27.71	20.89
Uttar Pradesh	21.60	22.90	24.07	21.49	20.72	16.97
India	9.27	13.53	10.46	13.34	14.42	12.27

Source: Analysis of Budgeted Expenditure on Education, various issues.

The third category comprises of educationally medium developed states that have been making serious efforts to improve their education in the recent decades. The states such as Karnataka and Andhra Pradesh; Rajasthan and Madhya Pradesh would come under this category. Karnataka and Andhra Pradesh are making serious strides to improve their education systems to withstand their economic progress under globalisation. Indeed, these two states have been pioneers in implementing many of the state reforms from power sector to e-governance. Though their education levels and development are at a disadvantageous position, these states are making serious endeavours. For instance, Andhra Pradesh, one of the sample states, has been moving fast in terms of ICT arena, while its allocation towards education still ranged around only 3.2 per cent with lot of fluctuations in the previous two decades. In terms of relative priority in the government exchequer for education, it increased from 20.45 per cent in 1960-61 to a maximum of 22.84 per cent in 1994-95, much though it declined thereafter, reaching a minimum of 15.08 per cent in the last year. The decline has been more in recent years than earlier. The economic progress or efforts of Rajasthan and Madhya Pradesh present almost a reverse of the situation found either in Karnataka or Andhra Pradesh. These two states are also making some efforts (Lok Jumbish in Rajasthan and Education Guarantee Scheme in Madhya Pradesh) to improve their education and to allocate a higher share for education.

The fourth category includes educationally and economically backward states that do not seem to show any commitment towards improving their levels of education. The states that would fall under this category are Bihar, Orissa, West Bengal and Uttar Pradesh. Uttar Pradesh allocated on an average 3.4 per cent during 1980s and increased it to 4.5 per cent in the 1990s. In a resource-poor state, even a lesser expenditure would show a higher share, as income itself is growing at a slower rate. In Uttar Pradesh, the share ranged between 19 to 25 per cent, which is much lesser compared to Kerala, that allocates above 30 per cent of revenue expenditure to education. It is to be noted that all sample states in the present study encompass all the categories, representing the diversity that the country has.

Intra-sectoral Allocation of Resources

The pattern and size of intra-sectoral allocation within the education sector indicates the relative priority assigned to different levels of education. The pattern of intra-sectoral allocation of resources reflects an unbalanced nature of educational development. The share of elementary education ranged from 43 to 49 per cent of the total expenditure on education, while the share of expenditure on secondary education stagnated at around 30 per cent and that of expenditure on higher education ranged from 9 to 15 per cent and came down further to around 9 to 10 per cent in the 1990s (see Figure 5.2).

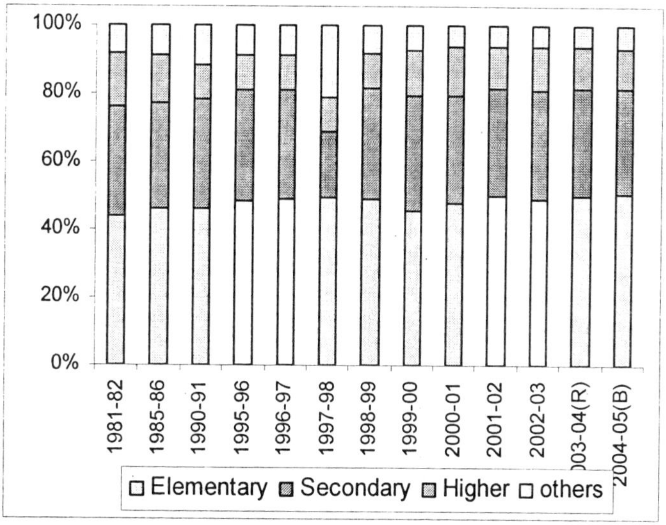

Figure 5.2: Intra-sectoral Allocation of Resources in Education

Source: Based on Analysis of Budget Expenditure (various issues).

Intra-sectoral Allocation in Five-year Plans

From the first to fifth five-year plans, secondary education received less than 20 per cent share in the total education expenditures. Only from the sixth plan, allocation to secondary education improved. But again from seventh plan onwards, it has been fluctuating and in the ninth plan the share has come down to 19 per cent of total education outlay. An apparent shift of resources from higher to secondary education during the 6th to 8th plan can be seen. This further trickled down from secondary to elementary education in the 9th plan and 10th plan outlays (see Figure 5.3). The thrust on improvement of secondary education in the 9th plan has been well charted out but did not reflect on the resources allocated towards secondary education, which was a much less allocation compared to the previous three plans (from 6th to 8th plans). Though there is no mention of secondary education in the approach paper to 10th plan, one could infer, "the regulatory mechanism for private, cooperative and non-profit organisations' supply of education must be modernised and simplified... Oppressive control on fees, teacher salaries, infrastructure and staff strength must be eliminated" (Government of India, 2001). These refer to secondary education also.

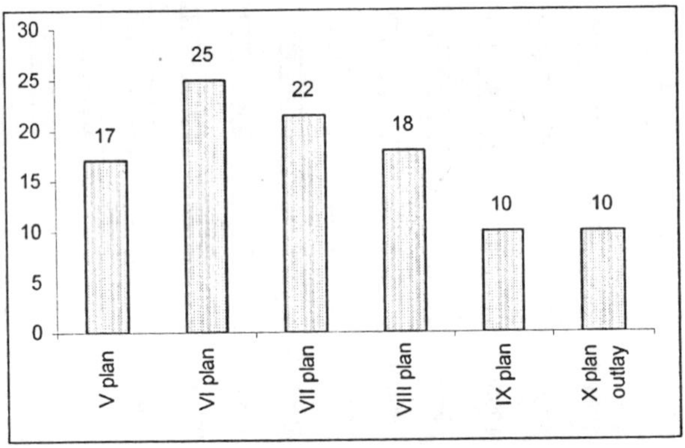

Figure 5.3: Share of Expenditure on Secondary in Education Expenditures on Education under Five-year Plans in India

Source: Annual Financial Statistics of Education Sector, 1997-98, MHRD, New Delhi, and Planning Commission, 2001. Tenth Plan refers to approved outlay.

It could be noticed that the supply of secondary and post-secondary education by non-government or private sector has been encouraged with rationalising the regulatory mechanism. Besides, it supports to recover the cost by removing control on fees, restrictions on teacher salaries and infrastructure in secondary education. One can notice that untill the 9th plan, the cost recovery measures knocked at the doors of higher education only. After a decade of economic reforms, such measures have been encouraged at secondary education as well. Significance of secondary education for the globalised labour market is not yet rightly perceived as is reflected in the trends in financing secondary education. Decline in resources for secondary education from the state has resulted in alternatives emerging in the private unaided sectors.

Intra-sectoral Allocation in Sample States

Allocation of resources within education sector reflects the relative importance accorded to different levels of education. In Andhra Pradesh, the share of inter-sectoral allocation has changed among different levels of education in the last four decades (Report on Secondary Education in Andhra Pradesh). Budget allocations to elementary education varied between 40 and 50 per cent. Initially, the share was around 50 per cent which declined later, reaching a minimum of 33 per cent in 1995-96. But, in the last few years the share has increased considerably due to emphasis on universal elementary education. Secondary education budget varied between 25 and 35 per cent, with a gradual increase till 1980s' but declined in the last few years. Compared to school education, higher education received a favourable treatment in the budget allocation till recently. The proportion of higher education expenditure increased from around 10 per cent in 1960-61 to 23 per cent in 2000-01, with fluctuations. Allocations have declined in the last two years because of policy decision to restrict higher education in the public sector. The allocations for technical education, which is dominated by private sector, declined in the recent years.

In Kerala, little more than half of the total education expenditure was incurred on elementary education during 1980s, which continued till the beginning of 1990s. This high importance gradually declined in the 1990s. Share for secondary education ranged around 30 per cent, which is almost a similar share at the national level. On account of expanding the higher secondary course, on the one hand, and declined resources due to delinked pre-university course from higher education, on the other, would allow for a flow of more resources for secondary education (see Table 5.3).

Table 5.3: Intra-sectoral Allocation of Resources* in Education in the Sample States (in %)

	Elementary	Secondary	Higher	Others	Elementary	Secondary	Higher	Others
	Andhra Pradesh				Kerala			
1985-86	45.88	28.57	19.65	5.90	51.30	29.80	13.00	5.90
1995-96	32.90	23.30	16.40	27.40	47.80	30.80	15.80	5.60
2004-05(B)	46.51	28.94	18.96	5.59	49.88	31.31	12.87	5.94
	Maharashtra				Uttar Pradesh			
1985-86	44.82	38.29	9.96	6.93	43.64	42.12	8.56	5.68
1990-91	40.44	39.80	12.58	7.17	58.22	29.57	7.89	4.32
2004-05(B)	45.50	41.01	9.56	3.93	57.00	31.72	8.31	2.97

* includes expenditure in the revenue account only.
Source: Analysis of Budgeted Expenditure on Education (various years).

In Maharashtra, the sub-sector of elementary education has been allocated between 40 and 45 per cent share in the total expenditure on education. While secondary education between 38 and 40 per cent and in many of the years. It is a much higher share for secondary education compared to many states and also at the national level, which allocated around 30 per cent. Higher education has been getting around the share of 9 to 13 per cent in the total expenditure on secondary education. Technical education in an industrial state is getting around the least significance of around 3 to 4 per cent share in the total expenditure on education in Maharashtra.

In Uttar Pradesh, expenditure on elementary education increased above 50 per cent share during the late 1990s to the new millenium. Secondary education occupied a share of 42 per cent in the middle of 1980s and consistently declined since then. Higher education had a minimal share throughout the two decades in the state. Share of technical education has been fluctuating from a minimum of 4 per cent to a maximum of 15 per cent (see Table 5.3).

Andhra Pradesh followed the national pattern of secondary education budget fluctuating between 23 and 38 per cent, with a gradual increase till 1980s' which, however, declined in the last few years. In Kerala the share for secondary education ranged around 30 per cent, which is almost a similar share at the national level. On the other hand, Maharashtra allocated between 38 and 40 per cent and in many of the years, which is a much higher share for secondary education compared to many states and also at the national level. But in Uttar Pradesh, secondary education occupied a share of 42 per cent in the middle of 1980s which has consistently declined since then.

FINANCING SECONDARY EDUCATION

With this backdrop on few important aspects of financing education in India and across various states with a focus on the sample states, the subsequent section examines financing of secondary education in detail. This section attempts to cover a few important aspects in respect of secondary education viz. centre's role in financing education, inter-sectoral allocation, intra-sectoral plan allocation, etc. However, in the financing of secondary education, the policy and practice of grants-in-aid occupy a major role. For instance, in states like Uttar Pradesh, West Bengal, Maharashtra and Gujarat, the private aided schools and their enrolment in secondary education occupy a predominate share.

In this context, NIEPA commissioned a number of research studies at the state level to examine the grants-in-aid policies and practices adopted in the major states in India. The studies covered several major states, viz., Bihar, (Bhushan, 2003); Tamil Nadu (Duraisamy and Duraisamy, 2003); Kerala, (George et al 2003); Uttar Pradesh (Muzammil 2003); Karantaka (Panchamukhi et al 2003); Delhi (Qamar, 2003); Andhra Pradesh (Reddy and Reddy, 2003); Gujarat, (Shah and Agarwal, 2003); Rajasthan (Sharma, 2003); Maharashtra (Kamdar, 2004); Orissa (Debi, 2005); and Punjab (Gill *et al.*, 2005). The studies covered grants-in-aid to government, local body and private schools and looked into the evolution of grants-in-aid policies towards secondary education; reviewed the strengths and weaknesses of the existing grants-in-aid policies/practices; and suggested measures to improve the system of secondary education. In addition, the studies analysed the trends in financing secondary education with a focus on the last two decades, i.e., 1980s onwards. However, the states covered are irrespective of absence or presence of grant-in-aid schools, for instance, in Bihar there are no private aided schools in the state since 1980. It may be noted all sample states covered in the present study are also part of NIEPA's commissioned studies.

The present chapter attempts to examine the issue in a holistic perspective as per the framework followed in other chapters as well. It examines the pattern of financing education; financing of secondary education; the grants-in-aid policy and practice and unit costs at the national and state level focusing on sample states. It also highlights similarities and disparities within the sample states on financing and grants-in-aid policies and their repercussion on various aspects (viz., access, equity and quality) drawing upon the evidence and analyses made in the relevant chapters.

Role of Central Government in Financing Secondary Education

In the total expenditure on education, the share of secondary education by the Centre ranges from 9 to 26 per cent. States and union territories hold the major responsibility of funding secondary education (see Annexure Figure A1). Though education has been a concurrent subject since 1976, it is only in elementary education, the concurrency between the federal and the state governments is strengthened in the centrally sponsored programmes, namely DPEP and later Sarva Shiksha Abhiyan in fulfilling the goal of universalizing elementary education. Yet another commitment from the central government is realizing the motive of 86th Constitutional amendment on Making Elementary Education a Fundamental Right, besides its international commitment on the goals of Education for All. It is also to be noted that higher education receives a higher priority if not higher allocation of resources from the central government, because of its significance in the country's economic and technological development, spill-over benefits, etc. Secondary education is in the mid-way and the central government's role is neither Constitutional nor it has higher spill-over benefits. The role of the Centre in financing secondary education reveals a trend that, till 1985-86, the share of centre's expenditures was very low. From 1986-87 onwards, the share of centre's expenditure on secondary education increased. Indeed, with the National Policy on Education (1986), the flow of funds from the centre to the states improved in terms of overall expenditure on education and also in secondary education. This may be on account of many centrally sponsored schemes in secondary education viz., the introduction of Navodaya Schools, Educational Technology, Computer Class in secondary schools, etc. But since 1995-95 onwards, the share of central government expenditures has been declining with the states' share remaining stable throughout the entire period. In the total expenditure on education by the centre and states put together, around 30 per cent of the expenditures has been incurred on secondary education consistently over a long period of time, except in the late 1990s (see Annexure Figure A1). The trend clearly indicates the stagnant level of resources allocated over a long period and a decline in resource allocation towards secondary education in recent years.

Further, looking at the distribution of expenditure on secondary education by the central government or Government of India (GOI), major share of the expenditure is incurred on the Navodaya and Kendriya Vidyalayas. A very little share of total expenditure on secondary education flows towards secondary schools at the state level through centrally sponsored schemes (see Figure 5.4).

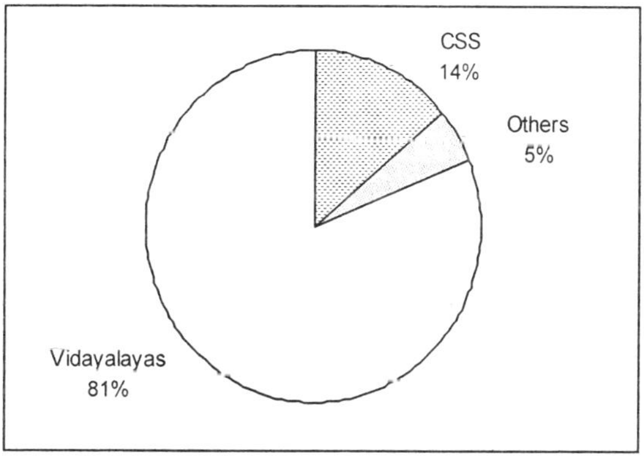

Figure 5.4: Distribution of Expenditure on Secondary Education by the GOI in 2004-05 (B)

Note: Vidyalayas includes Navodaya and Kendriya Vidyalayas; CSS includes other centrally sponsored schemes such as Vocational Education, Computer Education, IEDC, Education Technology, Promotion of Science Lab, Environmental Education, Population Education Project, Open School Programme, Strengthening Cultural Values, etc.

Source: Based on Analysis of Budgeted Expenditure on Education, 2002-03 to 2004-05.

These financial flows are important as they are earmarked for a number of quality improvement programmes in secondary schools at the state level.

As discussed earlier in the context of total expenditures on education, share of secondary education expenditure in GDP reflects the relative priority given to education in the economy. Share of secondary education in GDP has marginally risen from less than 0.5 per cent in 1951-52 to around 1.03 per cent during 1980s, which marginally improved till 2000-01. Indeed, it has declined thereafter till 2004-05(B). Share of education expenditure in the total government revenue expenditure indicates the commitment of the government in financing secondary education. Between 1951-52 and 1970-71, the share almost doubled from 1.5 per cent to little higher than 3 per cent. But thereafter, the share almost stagnated and marginally declined till 1990-91. Even though it improved in 2000-01, there is not much to rejoice at 2004-05 with a decline in the share (see Figure 5.5).

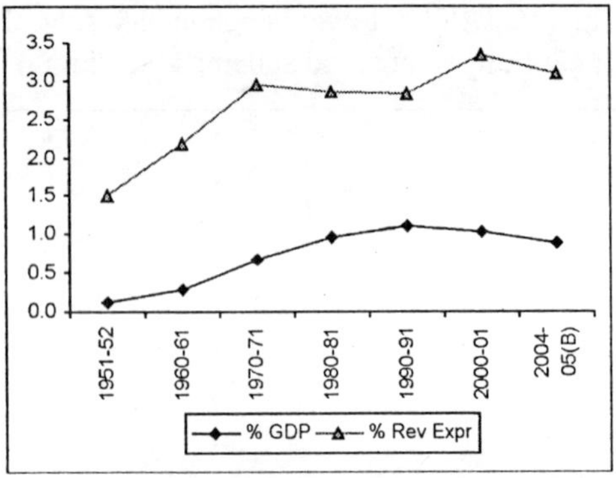

Figure 5.5: Share of Expenditure on Secondary Education in GDP and Revenue Expenditure

Source: Based on Analysis of Budgeted Expenditure, various issues.

Looking at the similar shares of expenditure on secondary education at the sample states bring out interesting similar situations in Kerala and Maharashtra towards higher share of State Domestic Product and also state revenue expenditures/budgets (see Table 5.4).

Table 5.4: Share of GDP and Revenue Expenditure in Secondary Education in Sample States

	Andhra Pradesh		*Kerala*		*Maharashtra*		*Uttar Pradesh*	
	% SDP	*% Rev exp*	*% SDP*	*% Rev exp*	*% SDP*	*% Rev exp*	*% SDP*	*% Rev exp*
1985-86	1.13	5.44	2.12	9.53	1.22	7.19	1.19	7.92
1995-96	0.80	5.06	1.82	8.70	1.04	8.24	1.23	6.20
2004-05(B)	0.68	4.06	1.27	6.75	1.09	7.56	0.84	4.60

Source: Based on Analysis of Budgeted Expenditure, various issues.

Andhra Pradesh and Uttar Pradesh even though had, similar shares, but declined since then in Andhra Pradesh while fluctuated in Uttar Pradesh in terms of share of SDP. But in terms of share of state budgets, both the states show a continuous decline. Indeed, this decline in the public investment on secondary education gets reflected in the fast and rapid expansion of private schools and their enrolment especially in these two educationally backward states.

Yet, another important dimension is to look at whether the increase in budget expenditures is in real terms or not. It is because the current (nominal) expenditures include inflationary effects. Besides, the time series data is dynamic in nature. The budget expenditure on secondary education has increased by twenty times from ₹ 12250 millions in 1981-82 to ₹ 249900 millions in 2004-05 (BE) at current prices in India (see Figure 5.6). The need to adjust the public expenditure at current pries for inflation has been well recognized. The budget expenditure on secondary education at current prices was converted into 1993-94 prices using gross domestic product deflators.

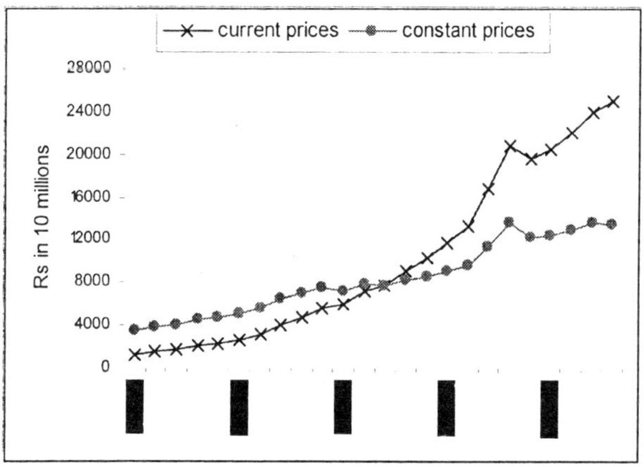

Figure 5.6: Secondary Education Expenditure in Current and Constant Prices

Source: Based on Analysis of Budgeted Expenditure, various issues.

Secondary education expenditure at current prices in 1980s grew at the rate of 18 per cent per annum, which declined to 12 per cent in the 1990s. While, in real prices, the rate of growth in the 1980s was 5.3 per cent and in the 1990s it was a mere 6 per cent.

Similarly, expenditure on secondary education at current and constant prices in sample states indicates that the growth of expenditures is minimal in real prices (See Annexure Figures A2 to A5). The budget expenditure on education has increased by five times from ₹ 2790 million in 1990-91 to ₹ 13850 million in 2004-05 (BE) at current prices in Andhra Pradesh. A similar five-time increase can be found in the other two sample states of Kerala and Maharashtra, but the expenditure on secondary education increased only three times in Uttar Pradesh. In constant prices, the budget expenditure on secondary education in all the three sample states except Uttar Pradesh (1.2 times) increased just by two-times during the same period. The trend of growth rate for the period 1990-91 to 2004-05 (BE) is little less than the national average of 6 per cent in Andhra Pradesh and Kerala (5 per cent) while higher than the national average in an economically advanced state of Maharashtra (7.8 per cent). A very small 2.05 per cent of trend growth rate is found in the economically backward state of Uttar Pradesh.

Plan and Non-Plan Expenditure on Secondary Education

Share of plan expenditure accounts for developmental activity, viz., building schools, acquiring additional classrooms, infrastructure, etc. Plan expenditure accounts for addition or creation of something new. Plan expenditure is generally incurred in the future development of education, including a marginal expansion of the system. They include activities such as construction of new buildings, recruitment of new teachers, facilities for new enrolment, expenditures on innovations, etc. All expenditures on developmental schemes, either existing or new, are categorized as 'plan' expenditure. Non-plan expenditure, on the other hand, is meant for maintenance of the existing infrastructure. All existing and continuing schemes for maintenance of on-going activities in a sector are categorized as 'Non-plan'.

The declining plan expenditure, therefore, means declining effort for creation or addition of new educational facilities and the swelling non-plan expenditure denotes increasing burden of maintenance expenditure on the shoulder of the state government. However, a major share of the expenditure is taken away for the non-plan activities, i.e. salary and other expenditures, as education is predominantly a labour-intensive sector, especially at the elementary level. Share of plan expenditures has improved during the 1990s. This may be on account of a number of centrally sponsored schemes introduced during the middle of 1980s in secondary education.

The plan and non-plan composition of expenditure on

secondary education in all the sample states indicates that expenditure on secondary education is essentially used for maintenance of the existing system. The plan expenditure has been very negligible. However, the plan share was the highest in India ranging between 4 and 12 per cent during 1980-81 and 2004-05 (see Table 5.5).

Table 5.5: Share of Plan and Non-plan Expenditure on Secondary Education in Sample States (in %)

	Andhra Pradesh		Kerala		Maharashtra		Uttar Pradesh		India	
	Plan	Non-plan	Plan	Non-plan	Plan	Non-plan	Plan	Non-plan	Plan	Non-plan
1980-81	1.0	99.0	5.6	94.4	3.4	96.6	2.1	97.9	4.4	95.6
1985-86	5.8	94.3	1.8	98.2	3.1	96.9	0.3	99.7	4.3	95.7
1990-91	2.8	97.2	1.3	98.7	1.9	98.1	2.9	97.1	8.8	91.2
1995-06	7.6	92.4	2.8	97.2	6.6	93.4	6.1	93.9	11.8	88.2
2000-01	2.5	97.5	2.4	97.6	2.5	97.5	3.2	96.8	9.9	90.1
2004-05(B)	2.5	97.5	1.8	98.2	0.9	99.1	2.8	97.2	8.3	91.7

Source: Analysis of Budgeted Expenditure on Education, various years.

All sample states spent the lowest plan share of 1 to 6 per cent. However, there has been a lot of fluctuation between different points of time as can be noticed from Table 5.5. However, a little higher level of share of plan expenditures on secondary education can be found in Andhra Pradesh and Maharashtra ranging between 1 and 7 per cent.

Inter-functional Allocation

Yet another important aspect of allocation of resources is the inter-functional allocation in secondary expenditures. It reveals that around 58 per cent of the expenditures has been allocated to private aided schools and another 34 per cent to government and local body schools (see Table 5.6). Private aided schools receive almost half of the total expenditure on secondary education. These privately managed but publicly funded private-aided schools occupy a dominant share of public finances of the secondary education[3]. Hence, limited resources remain for any quality improvement in terms of teacher training or access or equity related interventions.

Table 5.6: Distribution of Public Expenditure on Secondary Education in Sample States in 2002-03

Items	*A.P.*	*Kerala*	*Maharashtra*	*U.P.*	*India*
Assist. to Govt and LB Schools	70.68	33.05	6.37	8.8	33.76
Assist. to PA Schools	17.82	56.91	92.5	85.41	58.54
Others	11.5	10.04	1.13	5.79	7.7
Total	100	100	100	100	100

Source: Analysis of Budgeted Expenditure on Education, 2002-03 To 2004-05.

Inter-functional allocation suggests three different patterns. One type of states like Maharashtra and Uttar Pradesh, where private aided schools get more than 85 of the expenditure on secondary education, while in Kerala, the private aided schools get more than half of the total expenditure on secondary education. Unlike these three sample states, in Andhra Pradesh, government schools get more than 70 per cent of the total expenditure on secondary education. Within secondary education expenditures, the assistance to private aided schools in the form of grants-in-aid occupied more than 80 per cent in Maharashtra and Uttar Pradesh and above 50 per cent in Kerala. Hence, it is equally important to examine the policy and practice of the provision of grant-in-aid across the sample states in detail, which assume significance in the growth and development of secondary education.

Distribution of expenditures on secondary education by items at the institutional level across government and private aided schools in one of the sample states, that is, Kerala suggests that more than 90 per cent of the expenditure goes for salary of the teachers (see Table 5.7).

Table 5.7: Distribution of Expenditure at the Institutional Level in Kerala in 2001-02 (in %)

	Schools	*Salary*	*Maintenance*	*Scholarship*	*Library*	*Lab*	*Sports*	*Teaching Aids*	*Other*
Government	Cotton	95.97	Nil	3.03	Nil	0.35	Nil	Nil	0.43
	Peroorkada	94.88	Nil	1.85	Nil	3.17	Nil	Nil	0.43
	Tholikkodu	96.74	Nil	2.45	Nil	0.62	Nil	Nil	1.7
Private	Pattom	97.42	2.08	NA	0.52	0.13	NA	NA	3.18
	Kaniyapuram	91.43	0.09	8.14	Nil	Nil	Nil	Nil	7.25
	Anad	95.60	0.19	3.44	0.07	0.49	0.06	0.01	0.05

Source: Based on the information from Kerala case studies.

The quality components like library, teaching aid etc. get either meagre or no resources at all. It is the same story on student welfare activities like sports, scholarships, etc. Indeed, this is the same picture even at the national and state levels as well. The impact of economic reforms on education indicates that the major proportion of total government expenditures on education at any level is on salaries. Since it is not possible to cut down the expenditures on these during the periods of expenditure compressions, the axe falls on materials and equipment, student welfare activities and on capital formation. These measures have adverse impact on the quality and equity of services rendered in government delivery systems.

Sources of Income

So far, the expenditure on education in its various aspects and dimensions has been examined. It is equally important to look at the other side of the coin, that is from where the resources come. The sources of income are classified into government funds, non-government resources consisting of fee and other income. Government sources of income include funds from the central as well as state governments and the local bodies; fees include tuition fees, hostel fees and other fees paid by students. Other income includes income from endowment and other sources. The contribution of government to high school education had increased from 1980s to the beginning of 1990s (see Table 5.8).

Table 5.8: Relative Share of Sources of Income in Secondary Education in India (in %)

	Secondary Schools			*Higher Secondary Schools*		
	Govt	*Fees*	*Others*	*Govt*	*Fees*	*Others*
1981-82	93	6.73	0.40	84	13.92	2.41
1985-86	92	5.91	2.24	84	14.15	2.26
1990-91	94	5.69	2.22	88	10.12	1.82
1992-93	97	2.91	1.02	85	12.91	1.72
1993-94	94	3.94	2.23	82	16.00	1.73
1994-95	95	4.81	1.38	85	13.83	1.61

Note: Income here refers to recurring income.
Source: Education in India, Vol. II(s), (various issues)

Conversely, the share of fee income has declined from 7 to 3 per cent in total income. Contributions from endowment and other sources of income remained stagnant. In higher secondary education, reliance on government funds increased in late 1980s and marginally declined in the beginning of 1990s. It may be noted that the share of fee income is higher by little more than two-fold than high school level. For instance, in 1994-95, the latest year for which such information is available, the increase in fee income in higher secondary schools vis-à-vis high schools is 10 percentage points (see Table 5.8). The share of government contribution decline from high to higher secondary schools while the share of fee income increased in higher secondary schools compared to high schools. Hence, it is worthwhile to look at the fee levels at secondary education in the sample states.

Levels of Fee in Secondary Schools in the Sample States

Three facts stand out with regard to the fee structure in secondary education at the national level and across various states including the sample states:

Fee rates have been prescribed by the state governments is applicable to both government and private aided schools. Schools can charge, for instance, development fees etc, other than tuition fee.

Primary education has been fully fee-free in Kerala since 1954-55, while upper primary education became tuition fee-free in 1955-56. In 1960-61, the state government abolished tuition fees in standard VIII and later on from 1969-70 onwards, fees were abolished in lower secondary covering classes IX and X. Other fees, referred as special fee at upper primary and lower secondary levels are minimal both in government and private aided schools (see Table 5.9).

It may be noted that for about three decades, the state government did not make any attempt to hike fees. However, since 2002-03, the fee rates have been revised from ₹ 7.50 to 12.50 at upper primary level and from ₹ 10 to ₹ 25 at lower secondary level. Further, the Kerala government declared, in 1991-92, that higher secondary education is free and hence, in Kerala education is free upto higher secondary level, though at the higher secondary level, the state of Kerala charged fees totaling to ₹ 160 per annum during 1990-91,

Table 5.9: Particulars of Fees in School Education in Kerala (per annum in ₹)

Particulars	V-VII	VIII-X	XI-XII
	2002-03	2002-03	1998
Tuition fee	Nil	Nil@	Nil
Games Fee	2.00	3.00	25
Library Fee	2.00	6.50	10
Lab Fee	1.50	6.00	25$
Audio Visual Unit Fee	0.40	2.00	10
Stationery	1.30	4.00	10
Festival Activities	--	--	20
Extra-curricular*	2.80	3.50	--
Others #			60
Total	10.00	25.00	160

Note: Apart from tuition fee, all other fees are called special fees;

* Includes activities such as Excursion, Scouting, Junior Red Cross, Youth Festival, Physical Education activities, etc.

$ For Physics, Chemistry, Botany and Zoology separately;

includes Application Fee, Admission Fee, Calendar Fee, Medical Inspection Fee, Association Fee, Magazine fees.

Source: KER, (2003); Nair, (2002); Government of Kerala (2000), Directorate of Higher Secondary Education, Trivandrum, Kerala

including tuition fee of ₹ 124. However, with revision of fees since 1991-92, no tuition fee is charged at higher secondary level. But, looking at the fee rates as in Table 5.9, the abolition of tuition fee is compensated with a rise in special fees (consisting of other fees). The student has to pay the same amount of fee as earlier in the name of tuition and other fees and since 1998 in the name of other fees.

While in Maharashtra, the fee rates at secondary schools are minimal in both government and private aided schools, the standard rate of tuition fee in primary schools ranges from ₹ 2 to ₹ 5 for standards I to VII. Admission fee is equal to one month's tuition fee and term fee is also equivalent to one month's tuition fee for each term. It is to be noted that the Constitutional Directive is free and compulsory elementary education for children in the age group 6 to 14. However, for secondary schools, tuition fee ranges between ₹ 5 and ₹ 10 for standards V to X in Greater Mumbai but in other parts of the state it is fixed at ₹ 5. In higher secondary schools, tuition fee is ₹ 16 to ₹ 18 per month. In large municipal corporation areas and Grater Mumbai, it ranges from ₹ 18 to ₹ 20 and ₹ 20 to ₹ 22 per month respectively. Entrance fee and term fee is equal to a month's tuition fee. Laboratory fee is ₹ 35 per annum (NCERT, 1999).

Fee structure differs at various stages of school education in Uttar Pradesh, though nominally. The amount of money charged as fees varies from ₹ 51 to ₹ 71 annually at different levels of secondary education in Uttar Pradesh (see Table 5.10).

Table 5.10: Rates of Fee in Uttar Pradesh (in ₹)

	Secondary	*Higher Secondary*
Library Fee	8	8
Lab Fee	18	36
Games Fee	4	6
Student welfare fund	1	1
Other dev. Fund	20	20
Total	51	71

Source: Sixth All India Education Survey, NCERT, New Delhi.

As is clearly evidenced, at secondary level, fees are nominal, while at higher secondary level the fees are relatively higher across the sample states both in government and private aided schools.

GRANTS-IN-AID TO SECONDARY SCHOOLS: POLICY AND PRACTICE

The policy and practice of grants-in-aid have been in existence since Lord Ripon's period. The same system of grants-in-aid continued even after independence for the spread of education through private institutions. Prior to 1947, philanthropic individuals, institutions and trusts established schools with the main objective of providing education. Expenditure on the construction of buildings, payment of salaries and provision of other infrastructural facilities in the schools was taken care of by the private sector. Educational institutions were paid some token amount by the government for meeting the incidental expenditure.

As illustrated, private participation in providing secondary education has been strong in India since the British era. The basic principle involved in grants-in-aid is to stimulate local effort and cooperation in secondary education. Over the years, state governments increased the quantum of grants and financed almost all the expenditures of the private aided schools. As a result, private aided management manages large number of institutions, their enrolments and the interests of their serving teachers in the secondary education system. In other words, the system of grants-in-aid contributed to the growth of large number of private aided secondary schools in India.

And also, they occupy a predominant share in the total government expenditure on secondary education. Almost half of the government resources are enjoyed by private management schools, which has been consistent during 1990s and also in the new millennium (see Table 5.11).

Table 5.11: Percent of Schools and Resources Allocated by Type of Management in India

	Schools		*Resources Allocated*	
	*Govt**	*Pvt Aided*	*Govt**	*Pvt Aided*
1990-91	44.05	43.63	40.4	51.7
1991-92	43.51	43.37	40.3	51.8
1992-93	43.82	41.77	39.5	52.03
1993-94	47.03	37.8	41.31	51.1
1994-95	45.32	37.84	40.19	51.29
1995-96	45.02	36.62	40.48	50.56
1996-97	45.70	36.19	42.16	48.75
2001-02	42.45	33.99	41.13	50.88
2003-04®	39.33	28.67	43.60	48.59

Source: Education in India, Vol. I(S); Selected Educational Statistics, 2003-04; Analysis of Budgeted Expenditure on Education, (various issues).

The share of private aided secondary institutions has however been declining since the 1990s. The growth of government schools remained stagnant in the last decades, while the local body schools have declined. There is a drastic decline of the share of private aided schools from 43 per cent to a 29 per cent share and also share of government schools as well has been on the decline. This clearly indicates that the share of private unaided schools has been gradually rising since the middle of 1980s. The private unaided sector has emerged as an alternative to the government and government funded private aided secondary education. Despite their declining share, private aided institutions got around

49 per cent of the total resources allocated for secondary education even in 2003-04. The heterogeneity and diversity of India can be visible only when we examine the grants-in-aid system in India focusing on the major states.

In many states like Gujarat, West Bengal, Uttar Pradesh and Maharashtra, 90 per cent of the total secondary schools are under the private aided management (see Annexure Table A3). However, the resources allocated to these schools do not seem to be based on the extent of private aided schools or enrolment therein in Uttar Pradesh, West Bengal and Maharashtra, especially during 1990s. On the contrary, in Gujarat and Kerala, allocation seems to be on the basis of share of private aided schools or their enrolment. It may be noted that in many states, per cent of enrolment in private aided schools are higher than per cent of private aided schools. Though it is quite contradictory to observe the declining share of private aided schools and their enrolment in the total schools, their share in total secondary education expenditures has remained stagnant with marginal fluctuations. Often, the principles of grants-in-aid policy did not always correspond to the amount of grants actually given in practice. The grants-in-aid system is indeed not based on any objective criterion.

Grants-in-Aid Policy and Practice in Sample States

The grants-in-aid system needs to be examined separately with a focus on sample states because this has been dominant in three out of four sample states. Almost the entire secondary education system is managed by the private aided sector in Maharashtra and Uttar Pradesh. In Kerala, more than 45 per cent of the schools and their enrolment are managed by the private aided sector (see Table 5.12 and Annexure Table A3). It is unique to note that in Kerala, the proportion of allocation to private aided secondary institutions and the proportion of enrolment therein are almost similar, indicating a somewhat fairly equal distribution of allocation either in terms of institutions or enrolment, except in 2003-04.

It is because sanctioning of grants-in-aid has been restricted since the middle of 1980s across all the sample states. For instance, the Government of Kerala, since 1957 i.e., with Kerala Education Act, has consistently followed a policy of almost equal share of government

Table 5.12: Government Assistance Vs. Share of Private Aided Secondary Schools and their Enrolment in Sample States

States	*Govt. Asst. to PA as a % of total expr on sec edn.*	*% of PA schools*	*% of PA Enrolment*	*Govt. Asst. to PA as a % of total expr on sec edn.*	*% of PA schools*	*% of PA Enrolment*	*Govt. Asst. to PA as a % of total expr on sec edn.*	*% of PA schools*
	1989-90	*1986**	*1986**	*1993-94*	*1993***	*1993***	*2003-04®*	*2003-04$*
Andhra Pr.	22.2	11.9	11.5	18.1	11.5	18.2	16.4	8.0
Kerala	51.5	55.7	57.1	50.6	53.8	54.7	52.3	46.4
Mahrashtra	87.9	63.8	77.8	89.0	62.1	80.0	91.5	68.6
Uttar Pradesh	82.0	74.9	83.3	80.6	64.9	77.8	85.7	35.6
India	49.2	44.8	52.8	51.0	37.8	46.5	48.6	28.7

* NCERT (1992);
** NCERT (1999);
$ NCERT (2002).

Note: PA indicates private aided schools. R refers to revised estimates.
Source: Analysis of Budgeted Expenditure on Education;

and private aided schools. Further, since the Fourth five-year plan (middle of 1960s), opening new schools has been restricted and hence new schools have rarely been added to the list of private aided schools. Fair distribution of grants could be on account of these two important policy factors of the Government of Kerala. The system of grants-in-aid followed after 1957 has been based on certain financial guarantee and certain other important criteria as per the Kerala Education Act, 1958, such as Financial Guarantee (Rule 7). No school, which has not been included in the development plan of the Educational Authority, if any shall be opened (KER, 2003, p.88).

As per the grants-in-aid policy, which is practiced now, the Government of Kerala sanctions 100 per cent grant for the year in which the school is recognized. The government pays the salary of teachers and non-teaching staff in the aided schools. Scale of pay of the teachers is similar to that in government schools. In addition, government provides a maintenance grant to the aided schools on the basis of their enrolment. Currently it is ₹ 5 per pupil per annum[4] in the lower secondary school, which forms a mere 1 per cent in the total grants, the major chunk of grant-in-aid is paid for teacher salaries. The mere 1 per cent of the total grant-in-aid to private schools, i.e., the maintenance grant is to take care of a long list of maintenance activities (see the Report on Secondary Education in Kerala).

There is also take over of management of schools whenever it appears to the government that the managers of any aided school have neglected to perform any of the duties imposed or under this Act. It becomes necessary to take over management of the school by the government for a period five years in public interest. As is evident, no resources had been left for quality improvement. Resources allocated for maintenance were infinitesimal and the quality of maintaining the existing infrastructure also remained unsatisfactory. In addition, teachers were appointed on temporary basis even in lower secondary schools in recent years.

The grants-in-aid Policy in Maharashtra in the beginning of 1980s, i.e., in the middle of Fifth five year plan itself was to restrict opening of new secondary schools only in places where it is not possible to absorb the available students in the existing schools (Government of Maharashtra, p. 132, Annual Plan: 1982-83). Later, during the 6th five-year plan (1985-90), few private institutions were allowed to start secondary schools on no grant-in-aid basis (Government of Maharashtra, p. 165, Draft, Annual Plan: 1987-

88). In addition, *ad-hoc* grants were sanctioned with a view to overcome financial difficulties, faced by unaided schools in the initial years of their establishment (and until such time that they become eligible for grant). This *ad hoc* grant shall be given to girls' schools and schools in tribal sub-plan area for a period of five years or until such time all these schools become eligible for grant-in-aid, whichever period is less. Over a period of time, these *ad-hoc* grants got regularized. Many schools, initially started with no grant-in-aid basis, were later provided with *ad-hoc* grants. It may be noted that the expansion is still taking place in the private-aided schools, though at a highly restricted level in Maharashtra. It is true that expansion in secondary education is more in the case of private-aided schools and enrolment.

Even though, only a marginal share of schools and enrolment are managed by the private aided sector in Andhra Pradesh, the dynamics of their operation in getting the grants, especially in teacher recruitment is vocal. Indeed, the state governments have been finding it as a stupendous task to monitor them. However, in order to wind up the litigation, the State Government promulgated an ordinance regulating grant-in-aid, which was subsequently passed into an Act giving statutory status to the earlier orders. Since 1985 Government of Andhra Pradesh has been very cautious in admitting any new school/section into the grant-in-aid. As a part of this, the government constituted a Committee, after which, no new school/class/section has been admitted into the grants-in-aid.

The policy of grants-in-aid in Uttar Pradesh is not much different from other states, which has also restricted the sanction of new private aided schools in the list since 1986. Indeed, private unaided sector was encouraged to meet the emerging demand for secondary education as a policy of the state. Uttar Pradesh was showing a higher preference towards private unaided sector in the last few years, although the state government has covered large number of schools under grant-in aid system till early part of the current decade. It may be on account of the fact that politicisation of secondary education has been remarkable than any other levels of education in the state. It is because under article 171 (iii)(c) of the Constitution of India, secondary teachers have been given a reserved representation in the Upper House (Legislative Council) of the state Legislature. Indeed, there is a nexus among politics, education finance (grants) and teachers in Uttar Pradesh.

Grants-in-Aid Formula

A standard or specific formula based on any objective criterion does not exist to provide grants-in-aid in any of the sample states. Salary payments of teachers are fully taken care of by the state governments and a meagre amount is provided for maintenance. For instance, the Government of Maharashtra claims that grant-in-aid is paid on the basis of approved formula. The approved formula is nothing but an annual increment of the share of getting grants and eventually granting 100 per cent grant. The amount of grants and the share of grants have been revised during various five years as reported in Table 5.13. However, schools in tribal areas and girls' schools would be eligible for 100 per cent grant-in aid only from the 4th year of their recognition under the grant-in-aid list during tenth plan (2002-2007).

Table 5.13: Rates and Share of Grants Paid during the Recent Five-Year Plans for New Private aided Secondary Schools

Share of grant	*Year on which eligible for grant (during 8th and 9th plans)*	*8th plan 1992-97 ₹ in millions*	*9th plan 97-2002* ₹ in lakhs*	*Year on which eligible for grant Since 2000*	*Share of grant*	*10th plan* 2002-2007 ₹ in lakhs*
100 % grant	from 7th year	0.35	0.48	from 9th year	100 % grant	0.80
75% grant	from the 6th year	0.22	0.36	from the 8th year	80% grant	0.64
50 % grant	from the 5th year	0.17	0.24	from the 7th year	60 % grant	0.48
25 % grant	from the 4th year	0.09	0.12	from the 6th year	40 % grant	0.32
No grant	First three years			From 5th year	20% grant	0.16
				First four years	No grant	

* Amounts are only approximate.
Source: various plan documents, Government of Maharashtra.

Private unaided schools (recognized) are growing rapidly, on the one hand, while the government schools, (which already occupy a minimal share) have been declining, on the other side. Share of private aided schools as well has been declining not only in Maharashtra but also in many other states. Still, the highest share of resources flowing to the declining share of secondary schools indicates dominance of the private aided schools in getting the resources even now. Indeed, there is a vocal nexus between education, politics, finance and private managers, not only in Maharashtra but in other sample states as well.

Since sanctioning of grants-in-aid is not based on any objective criterion, the grants-in-aid formula needs to be revised. In order to improve the quality of government funded secondary education system, grant-in-aid incentive may be provided on the basis of the performance in the board examinations, on the per cent of first class divisions, etc. Grant-in-aid could be given according to a graded scale so that poorer and more backward areas get it at higher rates than schools in other areas, which would ensure regional balance within the state. Grant-in-aid system needs to be modified which is to relate grants to various school performance indicators such as percentage of total expenses spent on non-salary costs (to encourage quality improvements), percentage of total funds raised from non-fee sources such as parental donations (to encourage equitable resource-generation), percentage of parents who are satisfied with the school (to encourage accountability), and average number of students per class (to encourage cost-consciousness), etc.

Impact of Restrictions on Private Aided Schools

It is evident that all the state governments (the sample states specifically) have restricted, perhaps almost stopped, to include the number of new secondary schools (private unaided) to bring them into the list of private aided schools since the middle of 1980s. However, they have expanded the system under the clause-sanctioning of new secondary divisions and teachers to make room for expansion in the existing institutions for instance in Kerala and Maharashtra-which has resulted in the construction of new buildings, the space for which otherwise would have been available for children to play or for other common activities of the school. This also resulted in congested and crowded classrooms, which would seriously hamper the quality of secondary education.

State governments neither seriously attempt to improve the quality of secondary schools, both under government and private aided managements, nor restrict the growth of rapidly coming up of private unaided schools. This automatically denies an equal access for quality secondary education for the students coming from low-income families, deprived sections-women and minorities, and for children in rural and remote areas. This has resulted in a dual system-one, the private unaided for those who can afford and another, the resource-starved institutions managed by government, local bodies and private aided schools serving for the unaffordable, wherein both the quantity and quality of the system has been deteriorating. Indeed, this is what has been observed from our case studies. This has also resulted in a parallel system with a mushrooming of coaching/tuition centres to supplement the government or government—funded secondary education. This has widened the inequities existing in the system, especially at secondary and higher levels of education, which are the terminal states for majority of the students.

Declining budgetary resources for education per se and secondary education in particular has seriously resulted in the growth and quality of the secondary education system. This has been evidenced in the analysis of Public-Private dichotomy and also on the Internal Efficiency of Secondary Education. The decision of many state governments not to allow new schools/or under no grants possible does affect equity at least for a couple of reasons. The recent additional demand for secondary education obviously comes from those who have entered the education system at a later stage–probably the first generation learners and also the most deprived sections of the society. Even the regions where such expanding demand exists also correspond to backward areas (see the Chapter on Educational Expansion: Access and Coverage). Therefore, the resource constraint directly impinges on the deprived and backward.

Government not allowing any new schools into the list of private aided would affect the access for the low-income students. Government needs to strengthen the infrastructure and quality of the existing government and private aided schools to meet the emerging demand. The emerging trend shows the changing social composition of students. Majority of the students attending are from the economically and socially deprived sections of the society.

UNIT COST ANALYSIS

So far, we have examined the pattern and interesting trends and issues that emerged from financing education, financing secondary education with a detailed analysis on the grants-in-aid policy and practice in the sample states. It is also equally important to examine whether the change in policy on financing has impacted on the expenditures per student. In this regard, this section attempts to examine unit cost in secondary education and also elementary education at the national and state levels focusing on sample states. Further, it also attempts to examine the nominal and effective unit costs in addition to unit cost by managements of schools.

Unit Cost on Secondary Education

Unit cost or per student expenditure on education[5] is an important efficiency indicator as it relates the input with an output. Per student expenditure on elementary education was ₹ 131 in 1980-81, it increased by 16 times to ₹ 2224 at 2003-04 in current prices (see Table 5.14).

Table 5.14: Unit Cost on Secondary and Elementary Education in India at Current and Constant Prices

(in ₹)

	Per student Expr on Elementary Education		*Per student Expenditure on Secondary Education*	
	Current Prices	*Constant Prices*	*Current Prices*	*Constant Prices*
1980-81	131	366	447	1250
1985-86	262	540	1073	2210
1990-91	496	674	2249	3054
1995-96	987	826	4491	3757
2000-01	2274	1431	3355	2112
2003-04®	2224	1263	3604	2046

Note: ® refers to revised budget estimates

Source: Based on Analysis of Budgeted Expenditure on Education and Selected Educational Statistics, National Account Statistics, Central Statistical Organisation, (various issues)

The increase was only by 3.4 times in real prices. Per student public expenditure on secondary education in 1980-81 was ₹ 447, which increased to ₹ 3604 in 2003-04, registering a trend growth rate of 9.5 per cent per annum. But the per student public expenditure on secondary education in terms of real prices indicate a growth rate of less than 2 per cent.

Unit Cost: Inter-state Variation

Unit cost on elementary and secondary education at selected points of time during 1990s for major states indicates a wide range of per student government expenditures both at elementary and secondary levels of education. At the national level, the per student expenditure on elementary education has increased to 3.1 times, while in secondary education the rise is only 2.3 times. It is interesting to note that the per student expenditure on elementary education increased across all states from 1998-99 to 2000-01, except in Uttar Pradesh. While at the same time, it is discouraging to note that during the same period in almost all states, the per student expenditure on secondary education declined, except in Tamil Nadu (see Annexure Table A4). This clearly indicates that the resources have been diverted from secondary to elementary level of education across the country.

Unit Cost in Sample States

The per student budget elementary expenditures at current prices in Andhra Pradesh have increased by four times between 1990-91 to 2003-04, but in real terms, the increase is not even 2 times (1.5 times). While the trends in the per student budget secondary expenditures in current prices in Andhra Pradesh have increased by mere 2.3 times, but in real terms, the increase is not even one time (0.95 times) (see Table 5.15 and Annexure Table A5).

In Kerala, the per student budget expenditures on elementary education has increased from ₹ 1231 in 1990-91 to ₹ 7385 in 2003-04 with rise at current prices of 6 times. While in real terms, even in Kerala it had drastically come down to 2.2 times. Per student budget expenditure on secondary education rose from ₹ 832 to ₹ 1178 during the same period. The increase in per student budget expenditure on secondary education was 4.6 times and in real price not even two times (see Annexure Table A6). However, the trends in per student budget expenditure on secondary education in Kerala were better than Andhra Pradesh. In an economically better off state, Maharashtra, in current prices in per student elementary expenditures raised from ₹ 670 to ₹ 2982 during the same period. The increase was about 4.5 times at current prices, which was just 1.7 times in real prices (see Annexure Table A7). The per student budget expenditure on secondary education was ₹ 1084 in 1990-91 and rose to ₹ 3727 in

Table 5.15: Per Student Expenditures on Elementary and Secondary Education at Current and constant prices in Sample States in 1990-91 and 2003-04

(in ₹)

	Per student Expr on Elementary Education		*Per student Expenditure on Secondary Education.*	
	Current Prices	*Constant Prices*	*Current Prices*	*Constant Prices*
		Andhra Pradesh		
1990-91	582	823	978	1384
2003 04®	2240	1246	2274	1265
		Kerala		
1990-91	1231	1741	832	1178
2003-04®	7385	3863	3846	2012
		Maharashtra		
1990-91	670	949	1084	1533
2003-04®	2981	1702	3727	2127
		Uttar Pradesh		
1990-91	729	986	1290	1744
2003-04®	1281	725	2325	1315

Note: R refers to revised budget estimates.

Source: Based on Analysis of Budgeted Expenditure on Education and Selected Educational Statistics, National Accounts Statistics, Central Statistical Organisation (various issues).

2003-04. The increase in nominal prices was 3.4 times and in real prices was as low as 1.4 times. In an economically and educationally backward state of Uttar Pradesh, per student budget expenditure on elementary education grew from ₹ 729 to ₹ 1281 in 2003-04. Even in nominal prices, the rise was not even two times and obviously in real prices, the increase was marginal (see Annexure Table A8). The trends in per student budget expenditure on secondary education were still worse in the state with ₹ 1290 in 1990-91 that rose to ₹ 2325 in 2003-04.

Except Uttar Pradesh, other sample states show better trends in terms of per student expenditure on elementary education at least in nominal prices. Another important aspect to be noted across the sample states and over a period of around 15 years show that per student budget expenditures both on elementary and secondary education fluctuate across states (see Annexure Tables A5 to A8). Except, Kerala, the per student public investment on secondary education has not improved much. This clearly indicates that the focus and priority is towards elementary education.

Unit cost at the institutional level is almost at the same level as at the national average (see Tables 5.14 and 5.15). However, unit costs at the institutional level vary by management. It is found to be very low in private unaided schools, at ₹ 820 as against ₹ 9400, the highest expenditure in residential schools. Unit cost of a student is found to be low in government schools at ₹ 3995 as against the aided schools, which is ₹ 4041 (see Table 5.16).

Table 5.16: Per Student Expenditures at the Institutional Level in Andhra Pradesh

Govt.	*Aided*	*Unaided*	*Residential*	*Total*
3955	4041	820	9400	3125

Source: Based on the information from Andhra Pradesh case study.

Though per student cost or normal unit cost is widely recognized as an efficiency indicator, in developing countries like India, there is a wider gap between enrolment and successful number of students. The difference between or the ratio of unit cost per enrolled student and unit cost per examination appeared student indicates the inefficiency of resource-use on account of drop-outs in the secondary education system. This ratio reflects internal efficiency of the system partly as it considers only the drop-out, which was around 7 per cent during 1980s but declined to around 5 per cent in 1990s (see Table 5.17). Though it indicates that there has been some improvement in reducing the gap between enrolled students and students appearing for examinations, there is still much to be desired.

The effective unit cost or the cost per successful student will be an important efficiency indicator for manpower planning, which also relates cost with performance. Ratio of unit cost per examination appeared student and effective unit cost indicates the lack of internal efficiency in the secondary education system on account of failures. This ratio has been around 2 in many years during 1980s as well as 1990s. However, in the last two years, the ratio tended to decline. The ratio of effective unit cost to normal unit cost indicates the extent

Table 5.17: Normal and Effective Unit Cost on Secondary Education in India

	Per student cost (in Rs.)			*Ratio of Appeared to Normal*	*Ratio of Effective to Appeared*	*Ratio of Normal to Effective*
	Normal	*Appeared*	*Effective*			
1980-81	421	3199	6599	7.60	2.06	15.69
1982-83	542	3038	5925	5.60	1.95	10.93
1986-87	956	5977	11894	6.25	1.99	12.45
1990-91	1323	6333	11362	4.79	1.79	8.59
1995-96	2082	13404	26882	6.44	2.01	12.91
1997-98	2776	13348	25161	4.81	1.89	9.06

Source: Calculated based on analysis of Budgeted Expenditure, Selected Educational Statistics, Results of High School and Higher Secondary Examinations, MHRD, Department of Education, Planning, Monitoring and Statistical Division, New Delhi, various issues.

of ineffectiveness on account of both drop-outs and failure in the system, ranging from 8 to 15. The larger the gap, the higher is the inefficiency in the system. Comparing the values of these three ratios, most of the problem lies with the largest gap between the enrolled and the students appeared for examinations.

Even in sample states, that too an educationally advanced state of Kerala as well presents a similar trend (see Table 5.18). Even though gross enrolment ratio, using the projected school going age-group population, stood at 94.51 per cent for the high school age-group in Kerala in 2001, failure and drop-out in the secondary stage rose a serious problem in this educationally advanced state and across states as well.

For instance, in Kerala, this ratio of effective unit cost to normal unit cost has been around 4 in many years from the beginning to the middle of 1990s which increased to 6.8 in the later part of 1990s, while in Uttar Pradesh in a most recent year, the ratio was 3.5. This also indicates the unsatisfactory quality of secondary education in the state to a greater extent. In Kerala, unlike the primary stage, the secondary stage has serious drop-out problems. Schools make use of the provision to detain 20 per cent of the children, in an effort to maintain or improve performance. The pity is that failed students are not retained in the same schools. They either join other schools or

Table 5.18: Normal Vs. Effective Per Student Secondary Expenditure in Kerala and Uttar Pradesh

	Normal P/S Sec. expr	Effective P/S Sec. expr	Ratio of Effective/Normal P/S Sec. expr
		Kerala	
1999-00	4443	30267	6.81
		Uttar Pradesh	
2003-04	2325	8322	3.58

Source: Based on Selected Educational Statistics, Analysis of Budgeted Expenditure on Education, MHRD and Directorate of Public Instruction, Tirvandrum, Kerala.

drop-out of the school system altogether. Some of the students do appear for the SSLC examination as private candidates[7] (see the chapter on Internal Efficiency of Secondary Education). The analysis reveals that there is a considerable scope for effective utilization of resources.

Unit Cost by Type of Management

Unit cost per student and unit cost per school of government expenditure by type of management of schools indicate the extent of iniquitous allocation between these two types of schools and enrolment therein. This inequity is rather limited between students enrolled either in government and private aided schools, and is nil between schools managed by government and private-aided bodies in Kerala (see Table 5.19).

In Maharashtra, this inequity has of late widened to 3.5 times between students enrolled in government and private aided schools, while their ratio has been 3.3 times higher between schools managed by government and private-aided bodies (see Table 5.21).

Household Expenditure on Secondary Education

So far unit costs on the public domain have been examined. The social or total cost of education consists of two domains–the public and the household. Household expenditure is incurred on various items in order to acquire education by the children but spent by their family. Hence, it is essential to look at the other domain of expenditures incurred by the households. The expenditure incurred

Table 5.19: Per Student Government Expenditures on Education by Management of Schools in Sample States

	*Per student cost **			*Ratio of PA/G*	*Per institution cost (in 000s)***			*Ratio of PA/G*
	Govt.	*PA*	*All$*		*Govt.*	*PA*	*All$*	
				Kerala				
1990-91	919	1418	1555	1.54	789	870	940	1.10
1995-96	1839	2905	3164	1.58	1766	1952	2100	1.11
1999-00	3385	4859	5543	1.44	2800	2789	3083	1.00
				Maharashtra				
1990-91	836	1353	1308	1.62	584	944	913	1.62
1995-96	2242	4249	4028	1.90	1243	2104	2025	1.69
1999-00	2838	10244	9229	3.61	1490	4974	4523	3.34

* corresponds to enrolment in high schools alone;
** corresponds to institutions in both high and higher secondary schools;
All$ excludes private unaided schools and enrolment therein.
Source: Based on Economic Review, Government of Kerala and Analysis of Budgeted Expenditure on Education, MHRD; Based on Education at a Glance, Performance Budget, School Education Department, Government of Maharashtra, (various issues).

by the individual is of two types, direct and indirect cost. Indirect cost or invisible cost is the opportunity cost of the child attending school, which is incurred by the student and his/her family implicitly. Direct cost includes expenditure on admission fee, tuition fees, books, stationery, examination fee, boarding and lodging for hostel students, etc. This is the household expenditure on education or out-of-pocket expenditure on education. In addition to the per student budget expenditure on secondary education, the individual student spent is ₹ 1236 on an average to acquire secondary education. Per student household expenditure on secondary education varies across region–the lowest ₹ 1072 was in rural areas in government schools and the highest expenditure ₹ 4073 was found in urban areas and by type of management private unaided schools (see Table 5.20).

The components of household expenditure include a number of items such as direct cost (tuition fees, examination fee and other kinds of fees) and out-of-pocket expenditures (books, stationery, uniform, transport, coaching and other expenditures). Direct cost or fees alone constitute 24 per cent of the total household expenditure on secondary

Table 5.20: Per Student Househohold Expenditure on Secondary Education

Type of Institution	*Rural*	*Urban*	*All*
Government	1072	1609	1236
Local body	1034	1809	1349
Private Aided	1331	2455	1861
Pvt. unaided	1848	4073	3061

Source: NSSO (1998).

education, the second largest share of expenditure, the first highest share being expenditure on stationery and books (See Figure 5.7).

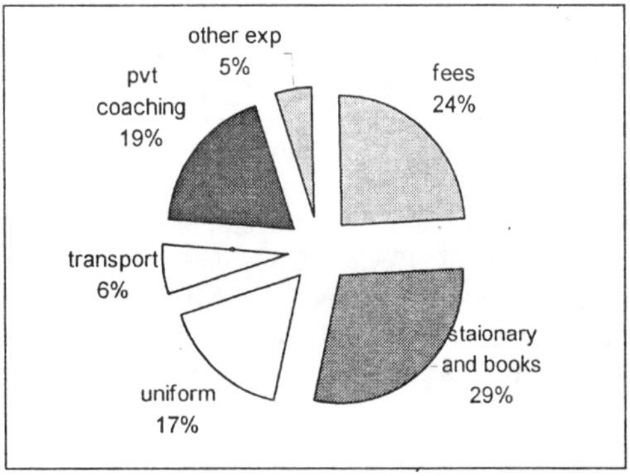

Figure 5.7: Household Expenditure on Secondary Education by Components (in %)

Source: NSSO (1998).

Private coaching also occupies a higher share in household expenditure on secondary education, which is indicative of the unsatisfactory quality of secondary education. Indeed, private coaching/tuition is a parallel system which provides supplementary support to students and parents as in many developing countries including India.

SUMMARY

Trends in inter-sectoral allocation and in intra-sectoral allocation indicate that the allocations remained stagnant in secondary education. Within the education sector, the resource allocation certainly is in favour of elementary education. Trends in intra-sectoral allocation in five year plans indicate that from the first to fifth five-year plans, secondary education received less than 20 per cent share in the total education expenditures. Only in the sixth plan, the allocation to secondary education improved. But again from the seventh plan onwards, it has been declining and in the ninth plan the share came down to 19 per cent of total education outlay. Trends in expenditures clearly indicate that states' allocation to secondary expenditure is stagnant, while centre's allocation has declined. Centre's allocation mainly goes for the schools managed by the central government.

At the national level and across states, overall budgetary resources for education declined during 1990s, though there have been signs of marginal improvement in the later years. This can be interpreted as the effect of new economic policy being implemented in the country. The new policy aims at reducing the size of public expenditure and relying more on private support. It also tries to enhance the contribution from students. On account of these changes at the macro level.

The system of grants-in-aid contributed to the growth of a large number of private aided secondary schools till early 1980s. But since the middle of 1980s, almost all states including the sample states, stopped adding new schools in the list of private aided schools. Despite this, the resources allocated to these schools do not seem to be based neither on the share of private aided schools nor on the students enrolled therein.

The new economic policy resulting on decline in the public expenditure on secondary education, more specifically in Uttar Pradesh and Andhra Pradesh combined with state policies on 'no-grant-in-aid' resulted in large expansion of the private unaided sector in the country. Emergence of private unaided sector across sample states is prominent in Uttar Pradesh both at the secondary and higher secondary levels and in Andhra Pradesh at higher secondary level.

Even though the Government of India has already thought of planning for universalizing secondary education with a separate sub-committee which looked into various issues and dimensions (including the additional financial requirements) on 'Universalising Secondary Education' by the Central Advisory Board on Education (CABE) (GOI, 2004), yet, another committee was set up to exclusively examine the ways and means of achieving the goal of 6 per cent of GDP to education. The committee also examined the intra-sectoral allocation, which suggested that 1.5 per cent of GDP needs to be allocated for secondary education if 6 per cent goal is realized (GOI, 2005). However, the debates and discussions are yet to be pipelined.

If the government increases the allocation to overall education and also secondary education, the expansion would be taking place in governance of government funded schools as it is happening in educationally advanced and economically better off states of Kerala and Maharashtra. Otherwise, massive expansion of the private unaided sector in secondary and higher secondary education, as happening in Uttar Pradesh and at higher secondary level in Andhra Pradesh, would be the order of the day in other states, irrespective of whether they are economically or educationally developed or not.

NOTES

1. Selected Educational Statistics, 2003-04.
2. Emphasis in Italics is added as the information and analysis correspond to sample states.
3. Hence, it is essential to examine the policy and practice of grants-in-aid to secondary schools. It is discussed in detail later.
4. It was fixed in August 1979 (KER, 2003, p. 399).
5. Includes revenue expenditure only.
6. The information on enrolment includes students enrolled in private unaided schools as well in per cent of appeared and passed students.
7. Based on our interviews and school survey, many schools do retain the students as repeaters in the same school itself.

REFERENCES

Bhushan S. (2003), Report on Grant-in Aid Policies and Practices-Secondary Education in Bihar, submitted to National Institute of Educational Planning and Administration, *mimeo*, New Delhi.

Debi, S. (2005), "Financing Secondary Education in Orissa: Grant-in-Aid Policies and Practices" *Journal of Educational Planning and Administration*, 18(4), pp. 449-472.

Duraisamy P. and M. Duraisamy (2003), "Public Expenditure and Grants-in-Aid for Secondary Education in Tamil Nadu" *Journal of Educational Planning and Administration*, 17(4), pp. 449-480.

George, K.K., G. Zachariah and Ajith Kumar (2003), "Grants-in-Aid Policies and Practices Towards Secondary Education in Kerala" *Journal of Educational Planning and Administration*, 17(2), pp. 199-225.

Gill S.S., S. Singh and J.S. Brar (2005), "Educational Development, Public Expenditure and Financing of Secondary Education in Punjab", *Journal of Educational Planning and Administration*, 19(3), pp. 335-374.

Government of India/MHRD (1986), *National Policy on Education*, Ministry of Education, Government of India, New Delhi.

Government of India (2001), *Approach Paper to the Tenth Five-year Plan: 2002-2007*, Planning Commission, New Delhi.

Government of India (2003), *Tenth Five-Year Plan: 2002-07*, Planning Commission, New Delhi.

Government of India (2004), *Report of the CABE Committee on Universalising Secondary Education,* June 2004. Available at www.education.nic

Government of India (2005), *Report of Committee on National Common Minimum Programmes Commitment of Six Per Cent of GDP to Education,* National Institute of Educational Planning and Administration, New Delhi. Available at www.niepa.org

Government of Kerala, *Selected Educational Statistics,* Education Department, Trivandrum, Kerala, (various years).

Government of Kerala, *Economic Review*, State Planning, Trivandrum, *Kerala, (various years).*

Government of Maharashtra (2002), *Human Development Report, Maharashtra*, Mumbai.

Government of Maharashtra, *Selected Educational Statistics* School Education Department, Mantralaya, Mumbai (various years).

Government of Maharashtra, *Education at a Glance,* School Education Department, Mantralaya, Mumbai, (various years).

Government of Maharashtra, *Performance Budget,* School Education Department, Mantralaya, Mumbai, (various years).

Government of Maharashtra (1992), *Eighth Five Year Plan 1992-97, Maharashtra Part I*, Planning Department, Maharashtra.

Government of Maharashtra (1997), *Ninth Five Year Plan 1997-2002, Maharashtra*, Planning Department, Maharashtra.

Government of Maharashtra (2002), *Tenth Five Year Plan 2002-2007, Maharashtra*, Planning Department, Maharashtra.

Kamdar Sangita (2004), "Grants-in-Aid in Secondary Education: The Case of Maharashtra", *Journal of Educational Planning and Administration*, 18(1), pp. 21-48.

KER (2003), *Kerala Education Act, 1958 and After,* Trivandrum, Kerala.

Kingdon, Geetha and Mohd. Muzammil (2003), *The Political Economy of Education in India: Teacher Politics in Uttar Pradesh*, Oxford University Press, New Delhi.

MHRD (1999), *Annual Financial Statistics of Education Sector: 1997-98*, Government of India, New Delhi.

MHRD, *Results of Higher Secondary Examinations*, Department of Education, Planning, Monitoring and Statistical Division, New Delhi, (various years).

MHRD, *Education in India, Vol.* I (S),(various years).

MHRD, *Analysis of Budgeted Expenditure on Education*, (various years).

Ministry of Finance, *Economic Survey*, 2000-01, 2001-02.

Muzammil, Md. (2003) Report on Grants-in-Aid for School Education in Uttar Pradesh, submitted to National Instittue of Educational Planning and Administration, *mimeo*, New Delhi.

Muzammil, Md. (2004), Report on Secondary Education in Uttar Pradesh, National Institute of Educational Planning and Administration, *mimeo*, New Delhi.

Nair, V.R. (2002), *Handbook on Important Orders on Higher Secondary Education*, Trivandrum, Kerala.

NCERT (1999) *Sixth All India Educational Survey*, NCERT, New Delhi

NSSO (1998), *Attending an Educational Institution in India: Its Level, Nature and Cost*, NSS 52nd Round, July 1995-June 1996, NSSO, Government of India.

Panchamukhi, P.R., S.Debi and V.B. Annigeri (2003), Report on Public Financing of Secondary Education in Karnataka: With Special Reference to Grant-in-aid from the Government, submitted to National Institute of Educational Planning and Administration, *mimeo*, New Delhi.

Qamar Furqan (2003), "An Empirical Analysis of Grants-in-Aid rules, Financing Pattern and Cost Structure in Secondary Schools in Delhi", *Journal of Educational Planning and Administration*, 17(3), pp. 331-67.

Reddy S. and A. Reddy (2003), Report on Financing Secondary Education (A Study with Special Reference to Grants-in-aid Policy of Government of Andhra Pradesh) submitted to National Institute of Educational Planning and Administration, *mimeo*, New Delhi.

Reddy, S. et al. (2004), Report on Secondary Education in Andhra Pradesh, National Institute of Educational Planning and Administration, *mimeo*, New Delhi.

Shah K.R. and S. Agarwal (2003), "Financing of Secondary Education in Gujarat", *Journal of Educational Planning and Administration*, 17(3), pp. 299-330.

Sharma, J.N. (2003) Report on Financing Secondary Education (Grant-in-aid Policies and Practices in the State of Rajasthan) submitted to National Institute of Educational Planning and Administration, *mimeo*, New Delhi.

Annexure

Table A1: Share of Education Expenditures on SDP in Selected States of India

States	1980-81	1985-86	1990-91	1995-96	2000-01	2004-05(B)
Andhra Pradesh	3.98	5.12	3.95	3.30	2.86	3.08
Kerela	6.09	7.13	7.10	6.42	4.11	4.57
Mahrashtra	2.96	3.36	3.50	2.99	4.34	3.00
Uttar Pradesh	2.65	3.44	4.64	4.26	3.71	3.08
Bihar	3.37	4.48	6.02	6.18	0.77	6.64
Gujarat	3.06	4.13	4.35	3.60	3.79	2.50
Haryana	2.65	3.02	3.14	3.15	2.83	2.36
Himachal Pradesh	6.46	6.64	8.12	7.67	6.64	5.64
Karnataka	3.47	4.71	4.27	4.24	3.41	3.63
Madhya Pradesh	3.05	3.97	4.62	4.55	6.86	2.58
Orissa	3.50	3.13	5.49	5.18	4.90	3.69
Punjab	3.50	3.23	3.35	2.07	3.12	3.12
Rajasthan	3.72	4.70	4.87	5.43	4.23	3.89
Tamil Nadu	3.77	4.51	5.21	4.15	3.47	2.97
West Bengal	2.74	3.26	4.74	3.25	10.03	2.74
India	3.09	3.66	4.07	3.60	4.38	3.52

Source: Analysis of Budget Expenditure, various issues.

Table A2: Share of Education Expenditure on Education in Total Budget of Selected States of India

States	*1980-81*	*1985-86*	*1990-91*	*1995-96*	*2000-01*	*2004-05(B)*
Andhra Pradesh	25.09	24.72	22.37	20.79	17.39	18.26
Kerela	34.89	32.06	30.58	30.77	24.17	24.21
Mahrashtra	23.38	19.77	23.21	23.74	27.71	20.89
Uttar Pradesh	21.60	22.90	24.07	21.49	20.72	16.97
Bihar	23.82	26.38	28.06	24.63	25.21	25.52
Gujarat	22.21	25.34	25.75	23.78	18.67	17.62
Haryana	20.04	20.47	19.85	14.47	21.70	16.75
Himachal Pradesh	24.89	19.97	20.96	19.86	20.62	19.58
Karnataka	21.65	22.94	22.10	22.58	21.34	18.88
Madhya Pradesh	21.01	22.85	25.78	24.47	33.73	15.23
Orissa	22.27	19.47	24.24	23.68	21.48	15.12
Punjab	28.36	23.16	22.27	13.07	17.58	14.42
Rajasthan	24.92	23.92	25.58	21.97	22.20	21.60
Tamil Nadu	23.63	25.21	25.54	22.71	22.50	19.97
West Bengal	23.56	25.11	29.10	24.29	63.46	18.73
India	9.27	13.53	10.46	13.34	14.42	12.27

Source: Analysis of Budget Expenditure, various issues.

Table A3: Government Assistance Vs. Share of Private Aided Secondary Schools and their Enrolment in India

States	Govt. Asst. to PA as a % of total expr on sec edn.	% of PA schools	% of PA Enrolment	Govt. Asst. to PA as a % of total expr on sec edn.	% of PA schools	% of PA Enrolment	Govt. Asst. to PA as a % of total expr on sec edn.	% of PA schools
	1989-90	*1986**	*1986**	*1993-94*	*1993***	*1993***	*2003-04®*	*2003-04$*
Andhra Pr.	22.2	11.9	11.5	18.1	11.5	18.2	16.4	8.0
Kerala	51.5	55.7	57.1	50.6	53.8	54.7	52.3	46.4
Mahrashtra	87.9	63.8	77.8	89.0	62.1	80.0	91.5	68.6
Uttar Pr	82.0	74.9	83.3	80.6	64.9	77.8	85.7	35.6
Assam	86.0	27.7	13.3	85.2	11.6	8.1	85.6	12.4
Bihar	5.8	5.2	54.7	5.9	4.7	5.7	0.0	1.4
Gujarat	89.8	90.9	88.4	86.4	88.2	89.1	89.1	71.1
Haryana	3.2	12.6	18.1	6.7	7.7	14.6	5.2	4.1
Himachal Pr.	0.5	7.3	3.9	0.6	5.5	4.2	1.2	2.2
J. & Kashmir	1.5	7.1	7.5	1.4	4.5	4.3	0.6	0.0
Karnataka	14.5	46.3	52.7	15.1	40.7	52.2	10.4	28.4
Madhya Pr.	8.1	12.4	13.8	12.0	7.1	9.8	6.6	3.4
Orissa	65.4	60.0	53.5	70.1	49.6	49.6	6.4	8.7
Punjab	7.3	15.3	20.1	11.0	13.5	20.1	7.4	9.6
Rajasthan	5.0	9.2	20.7	4.5	6.9	10.7	4.0	2.4
Tamil Nadu	33.3	25.6	38.7	34.3	27.2	38.4	35.1	17.3
West Bengal	90.1	97.1	95.3	95.2	75.3	73.6	93.9	94.4
India	49.2	44.8	52.8	51.0	37.8	46.5	48.6	28.7

Note: PA indicates private aided schools.
Source: Analysis of Budgeted Expenditure on Education; *NCERT (1992); **NCERT (1999). $NCERT (2002).

Table A4: Unit Cost on Elementary and Secondary Education across Major States

States	*Unit Cost on Elem Education (in Rs)*				*Unit Cost on Sec. Education (in Rs)*			
	1991-92	*1995-96*	*1998-99*	*2000-01(B)*	*1991-92*	*1995-96*	*1998-99*	*2000-01(B)*
Andhra Pr.	616	969	1457	1997	1092	1284	1635	1149
Kerala	1264	2685	3306	4682	897	1632	1976	3164
Maharashtra	847	1273	1656	2317	1239	1901	2464	1903
Uttar Pr	582	938	1948	1890	1348	1954	3204	1049
Arunchal Pr.	2607	2608	3301	4549	1720	2505	3120	1350
Assam	745	1293	1798	2753	1296	1632	2554	1169
Bihar	791	1214	1355	2330	1417	2164	2542	625
Gujarat	751	1226	2115	2262	2044	3108	5099	1188
Haryana	1141	2181	2369	2165	786	1290	3571	2230
Himachal Pr.	1224	2233	4843	6053	1693	2350	4128	2727
Jammu & K	745	1015	1730	2547	1239	4815	3977	2007
Karnataka	685	1016	1441	1940	1632	2674	3843	1117
Madhya Pr.	560	827	1132	1147	1743	1462	2140	308
Orissa	660	986	1473	1818	1258	1955	2848	636
Punjab	816	311	2307	2845	1832	2561	5130	5504
Rajasthan	819	1310	1738	1875	1828	2618	3861	1055
Tamil Nadu	847	1111	2535	3112	1179	1552	2525	2629
West Bengal	554	587	1110	1303	1445	1824	3120	1768
All India*	760	1198	1925	2409	1473	2084	3125	3411

Source: Based on Analysis of Budget Expenditure on Education and Selected Educational Statistics, (various issues).

Table A5: Unit Cost on Elementary and Secondary Education at Current and Constant Prices in Andhra Pradesh

	Per student Expenditure on Elemetnary Education		*Per student Expenditure on Secondary Education*	
	Current prices	*Constant Prices*	*Current prices*	*Constant Prices*
1990-91	582	823	978	1384
1991-92	616	756	1093	1340
1992-93	719	797	1251	1385
1993-94	859	859	1154	1154
1994-95	991	879	1305	1158
1995-96	969	785	1284	1041
1996-97	1029	786	1393	1064
1997-98	973	690	1335	946
1998-99	1841	1219	2581	1709
1999-00	1376	875	1786	1135
2000-01	1603	990	2043	1261
2001-02	1873	1122	1770	1060
2002-03	2253	1298	4002	2307
2003-04 ®	2240	1246	2274	1265

Source: Based on Analysis of Budgeted Expenditure on Education and Selected Educational Statistics, National Accounts Statistics, Central Statistical Organisation (various issues).

Table A6: Unit Cost on Elementary and Secondary Education at Current and Constant Prices in Kerala

	Per student Expenditure on Elemetnary Education		*Per student Expenditure on Secondary Education*	
	Current prices	*Constant Prices*	*Current prices*	*Constant Prices*
1990-91	1231	1741	832	1178
1991-92	1263	1550	897	1101
1992-93	1361	1507	959	1062
1993-94	1691	1691	1135	1135
1994-95	2172	1942	1381	1235
1995-96	2685	2063	1633	1255
1996-97	2611	1814	1618	1124
1997-98	3482	2236	1961	1260
1998-99	3944	2388	2325	1407
1999-00	3219	1884	4443	2600
2000-01	4309	2351	2770	1511
2001-02	3904	2104	2760	1488
2002-03	8444	4399	4419	2302
2003-04 ®	7385	3863	3846	2012

Source: Based on Analysis of Budgeted Expenditure on Education and Selected Educational Statistics, National Accounts Statistics, Central Statistical Organisation (various issues).

Table A7: Unit Cost on Elementary and Secondary Education at Current and Constant Prices in Maharashtra

	Per student Expenditure on Elemetnary Education		*Per student Expenditure on Secondary Education*	
	Current Prices	*Constant Prices*	*Current Prices*	*Constant Prices*
1990-91	670	949	1084	1533
1991-92	847	1039	1239	1520
1992-93	1652	1830	1354	1499
1993-94	750	750	3338	3338
1994-95	1036	925	1604	1433
1995-96	1273	1045	1901	1561
1996-97	1521	1155	2076	1576
1997-98	1420	1046	1910	1407
1998-99	1565	1109	2132	1511
1999-00	1754	1176	4404	2953
2000-01	3577	2344	3570	2339
2001-02	3499	2153	3390	2086
2002-03	5894	3533	7148	4284
2003-04 ®	2981	1702	3727	2127

Table A8: Unit Cost on Elementary and Secondary Education at Current and Constant Prices in Uttar Pradesh

	Per student Expenditure on Elemetnary Education		*Per student Expenditure on Secondary Education*	
	Current Prices	*Constant Prices*	*Current Prices*	*Constant Prices*
1990-91	729	986	1290	1744
1991-92	582	684	1348	1584
1992-93	568	620	1938	2118
1993-94	572	572	1519	1519
1994-95	825	747	1737	1572
1995-96	938	779	1954	1623
1996-97	1073	821	2151	1645
1997-98	1574	1117	2461	1747
1998-99	1761	1148	2904	1893
1999-00	1620	1037	3028	1938
2000-01	2063	1274	2958	1827
2001-02	2257	1370	2881	1749
2002-03	1538	907	4186	2467
2003-04 ®	1281	725	2325	1315

Source: Based on Analysis of Budgeted Expenditure on Education and Selected Educational Statistics, National Accounts Statistics, Central Statistical Organisation (various issues).

Annexure Figure A1: Share of Secondary Education in Total Education Expenditure (in %)

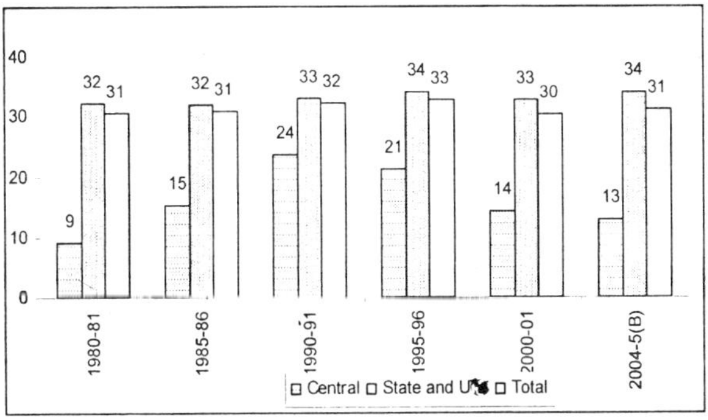

Source: Analysis of Budgeted Expenditure on Education, various issues.

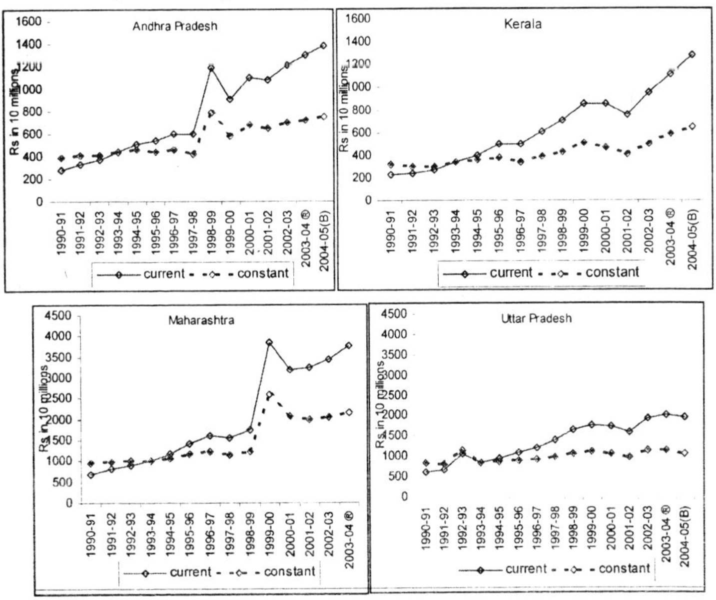

Figures A2-A5: Expenditures on Secondary Education in Current and Constant Prices in Sample States

Source: Based on Analysis of Budgetary Expenditures on Education, National Accounts Statistics, Central Statistical Organisation, various issues.

Index